TRANSMITTING JEWISH HISTORY

THE TAUBER INSTITUTE SERIES
FOR THE STUDY OF EUROPEAN JEWRY

The Tauber Institute Series is dedicated to publishing compelling and innovative approaches to the study of modern European Jewish history, thought, culture, and society. The series features scholarly works related to the Enlightenment, modern Judaism and the struggle for emancipation, the rise of nationalism and the spread of antisemitism, the Holocaust and its aftermath, as well as the contemporary Jewish experience. The series is published under the auspices of the Tauber Institute for the Study of European Jewry—established by a gift to Brandeis University from Dr. Laszlo N. Tauber—and is supported, in part, by the Tauber Foundation and the Valya and Robert Shapiro Endowment.

For the complete list of books that are available in this series, please see www.brandeis.edu/tauber

Yosef Hayim Yerushalmi, in Conversation with Sylvie Anne Goldberg,
Transmitting Jewish History

Cedric Cohen-Skalli
Don Isaac Abravanel: An Intellectual Biography

ChaeRan Y. Freeze
A Jewish Woman of Distinction: The Life and Diaries of Zinaida Poliakova

Chava Turniansky
Glikl: Memoirs 1691–1719

Dan Rabinowitz
The Lost Library: The Legacy of Vilna's Strashun Library in the Aftermath of the Holocaust

Jehuda Reinharz and Yaacov Shavit
The Road to September 1939: Polish Jews, Zionists, and the Yishuv on the Eve of World War II

Adi Gordon
Toward Nationalism's End: An Intellectual Biography of Hans Kohn

Noam Zadoff
Gershom Scholem: From Berlin to Jerusalem and Back

*Monika Schwarz-Friesel and Jehuda Reinharz
Inside the Antisemitic Mind: The Language of Jew-Hatred in Contemporary Germany

Elana Shapira
Style and Seduction: Jewish Patrons, Architecture, and Design in Fin de Siècle Vienna

ChaeRan Y. Freeze, Sylvia Fuks Fried, and Eugene R. Sheppard, editors
The Individual in History: Essays in Honor of Jehuda Reinharz

*A Sarnat Library Book

Transmitting Jewish HISTORY

YOSEF HAYIM YERUSHALMI

In Conversation with SYLVIE ANNE GOLDBERG

Translated by BENJAMIN IVRY

With "Clio and the Jews: Reflections on Jewish Historiography in the Sixteenth Century" and a new foreword by ALEXANDER KAYE

BRANDEIS UNIVERSITY PRESS Waltham, Massachusetts

First edition published in 2012 by Éditions Albin Michel as *Transmettre L'Histoire Juive: Entretiens avec Sylvie Anne Goldberg. Suivi de: Clio et les juifs. Réflexions sur l'historiographie juive au XVIème siècle*
Brandeis University Press edition 2021

Manufactured in the United States of America
Designed by Richard Hendel
Typeset in Quadraat by Integrated Publishing Solutions

"Clio and the Jews: Reflections on Jewish Historiography in the Sixteenth Century" previously appeared in *Proceedings of the American Academy for Jewish Research* 46/47, Jubilee Volume (1928–29/1978–79) [Part 2] (1979–1980): 607–38, and is reprinted with the permission of Derek J. Penslar.

The Institute for Israel and Jewish Studies, Columbia University, funded the translation of this book in memory of Yosef Hayim Yerushalmi, its director for a quarter of a century.

Library of Congress Cataloging-in-Publication Data

Names: Yerushalmi, Yosef Hayim, 1932–2009, author. | Goldberg, Sylvie Anne, author. | Ivry, Benjamin, translator. | Kaye, Alexander, writer of foreword.
Title: Transmitting Jewish history : in conversation with Sylvie Anne Goldberg / Yosef Hayim Yerushalmi ; translated by Benjamin Ivry ; with "Clio and the Jews : reflections on Jewish historiography in the sixteenth century" and a new foreword by Alexander Kaye.
Other titles: Transmettre l'histoire Juive. English. | Clio and the Jews.
Description: Brandeis University Press edition. | Waltham, Massachusetts : Brandeis University Press, 2021. | Series: Tauber Institute series for the study of European Jewry | "First edition published in 2012 by Éditions Albin Michel as Transmettre L'Histoire Juive: Entretiens avec Sylvie Anne Goldberg. Suivi de: Clio et les juifs. Réflexions sur l'historiographie juive au XVIème siècle." | Summary: "This series of interviews brings together exceptional material on Yosef Hayim Yerushalmi's personal and intellectual journey, true reflection on the rupture and transmission, the fabric of history, and of Jewish being in today's world. This work also attests to the astonishing breakthrough of the issues of Jewish history in 'general history.'" — Provided by publisher.
Identifiers: LCCN 2021015522 (print) | LCCN 2021015523 (ebook) | ISBN 9781684580613 (cloth) | ISBN 9781684580637 (ebook)
Subjects: LCSH: Yerushalmi, Yosef Hayim, 1932–2009—Interviews. | Jewish historians—Interviews. | Jews—Historiography. | Judaism—Historiography.
Classification: LCC DS115.9.Y44 A5 2021 (print) | LCC DS115.9.Y44 (ebook) | DDC 909/.049240092—dc23
LC record available at https://lccn.loc.gov/2021015522
LC ebook record available at https://lccn.loc.gov/2021015523

5 4 3 2 1

CONTENTS

FOREWORD TO THE ENGLISH EDITION

Yerushalmi's Last Seminar

ALEXANDER KAYE

The confessional nature of the conversations in this book invites a foreword that goes beyond a conventional account of Yosef Hayim Yerushalmi's scholarship, which the reader may in any case find elsewhere.[1] The remarkable discussions laid out here are intimate exchanges between Yerushalmi and his friend, the French historian Sylvie Anne Goldberg. Those looking for stories—sometimes charming and profound, sometimes absurd or shocking—about the world of elite Jewish scholars will find them here: the tussle between Yerushalmi and his friend Gershom Scholem over who deserved to own which rare book; the debate between Yerushalmi and Derrida about whether the gift of a leather-bound Bible to Freud by his father really did, unconsciously, evoke the foreskin. Even those unfamiliar with Yerushalmi's oeuvre will surely delight in the portrayals of postwar Jewish New York, the drama of Yiddish theater camps, the ferocious politics of the Hebrew University, and the relationships among the founding generation of Jewish studies in the American academy. And even those with no particular interest in Judaism per se will profit from a master historian's musings on the nature and method of historical study. But for all these gems, what elevates these conversations for me is the window they open not just into the mind but into the soul. Many people knew Yerushalmi as a commanding, even imperious personality. Here, we see the vulnerability beneath the armor.

Rereading this book in its new English translation awoke for me memories of Yerushalmi's last graduate seminar in April 2007. The subject of the seminar was the impact of the Spanish expulsion on Jewish history, but Yerushalmi chose to use its last two sessions to talk more generally about history, Judaism, and the search for meaning. With his permission, I made an audio recording of those sessions and revisited them in preparation for writing this foreword. The recordings are redolent with the atmosphere of 513 Fayerweather Hall at Columbia University, a late nineteenth-century building that was august and slightly musty. An imposing brass relief by Boris Schatz, the artist who pioneered Zionist art education in Ottoman

Palestine, hung on the wall. There was always a smell of coffee, brewed by Yerushalmi's assistant Malka Gold in the adjoining room. The conversations are punctured by the sirens of emergency vehicles on Amsterdam Avenue below, and by Yerushalmi's intermittent coughing, which takes on a more ominous undertone in the knowledge that he would die within three years of that seminar.

The very last session opens with the sound of Ophra Yerushalmi, Yosef's wife, making a surprise visit to mark the end of his celebrated career as a university professor. She brings a bottle of wine and some cake. An internationally renowned concert pianist and, later in life, a documentary filmmaker, Ophra was more than a life companion to Yosef; she was also something of a muse. It has been frequently noted that Yerushalmi, a student of poetry before he became a historian, was an unusually lyrical and expressive writer. This makes it even more poignant that writing was very difficult for him. (These pages include more than one reference to his struggles with writer's block.) He once told me that when he was having trouble fashioning a sentence, he would listen to Ophra practicing a phrase at the grand piano just outside his home study. Listening to her playing the phrase over and over, as it gradually grew in fluency and expression, reminded him that he would have many opportunities to refine his prose before it was published, and gave him the courage to set pen to paper.

Yerushalmi reviewed the major scholarly contributions of his great mentor, Salo Baron. Remarkably, he used the final moments of his teaching career to offer his critiques of the master. This testified to his receptivity to new ideas, and to refining old ones, to the very end. It was clear to us all that Yerushalmi revered Baron, as we revered Yerushalmi. Baron was pivotal at key moments in Yerushalmi's career and he spoke in awe of his teacher. When, shortly before my doctoral comprehensive exams, Yerushalmi told me of the exam that Baron had administered for him decades earlier, I could still hear the anxiety in his voice. Yerushalmi considered himself one of Baron's scholarly children, and called his own students Baron's "grandchildren." He once told us that in all of the eighteen volumes of Baron's *Social and Religious History of the Jews*, he had only ever found one mistake. (Baron had written that it was easy to rhyme in medieval Hebrew; his example was that Yehudah Halevi ended every line of his poem "Tsion ha-lo tishali" with the pronominal suffix "*ayikh*."[2] Yerushalmi noted that the lines of the poem in fact end with "*rayikh*," which required substantially more skill from the poet.) And yet, for all the admiration for his teacher, and for all that he followed in his footsteps, Yerushalmi was willing to question some of Baron's most fundamental teachings.

Baron famously fought against the "lachrymose conception of Jewish history," according to which Jewish history is nothing but a series of pogroms, inquisitions, and expulsions. However bad things were for the Jews, Baron had written, they were always better off, at least in Europe, than the serfs who made up the vast majority of the population. In our seminar, Yerushalmi considered whether the Shoah should have prompted Baron to revise his rejection of the lachrymose conception. If one reads the Shoah as, in some respects, a culmination of centuries of Christian anti-Judaism, it makes it harder to downplay the conditions of premodern Jewry. Even when they were relatively secure, Jews still suffered the tentative existence of a people blamed by Christians for deicide and by Muslims for the rejection of the Prophet Muhammad. I wonder now if Yerushalmi's questioning of Baron's most famous assertion was shaped by his own childhood memories of the reports of the Shoah in the New York Yiddish press, which Yerushalmi discusses in these pages: "We were really at the heart of what Baron called the 'lachrymose conception of Jewish history.'" Indeed, even as a young man Yerushalmi's historical imagination raised questions about Baron's analysis. He told us about his experience of a visit to Toledo, Spain, for his doctoral research. He had previously wondered why so many Jews in medieval Spain converted to Christianity, but when he emerged from Toledo's understated historical synagogue to witness the city's imposing Gothic Cathedral soaring over the city, pointedly impressing the message of Christianity's superiority onto the landscape itself, he began to wonder how so many Jews remained Jews.

The faculty of imagination loomed large in Yerushalmi's understanding of history, or, more precisely, of history's limits. Yerushalmi's public persona involved no small dose of bravado. In person, though, he had a tremendous humility not only in his own abilities but in the scope of historical study itself. Reflecting, and implicitly criticizing, the call of the French historian Lucien Febvre for historians to study the "affective life of the past," Yerushalmi acknowledged that no amount of archival research can allow us to feel what people felt. "I cannot begin to describe," he told us, "what I have not experienced." Even his friend Gershom Scholem, who more or less invented the scholarly study of kabbalah, could not experience what it actually feels like for a kabbalist to ascend in meditation to the heavenly throne. It deeply impressed me that Yerushalmi, in some ways the archetype of the historian, was so forthright about the limits of the historical method.

This was not Yerushalmi's only meditation on the limits of history. His conversations with Goldberg make explicit something that is beneath the surface of most of his oeuvre. In his own words, Yerushalmi spent his whole life trying to quench his "existential thirst for the absolute." Hearing this from a scholar of any kind, especially an archival historian, is itself a breath of fresh air. Historians are typically encouraged to keep their own identities out of their research, at least officially. (In this respect, the discipline of history tends to be different from disciplines in which scholars are expected prominently to announce their "positionality.") Of course, historians sometimes acknowledge the personal reasons that motivate them to begin their research, but they rarely talk about history itself as a pursuit of meaning per se. But for Yerushalmi, history was an "existential quest," through which he attempted to understand himself and his own Jewish identity.

This insight should correct some common misreadings of Yerushalmi's most famous work, *Zakhor*. In that book, he distinguishes two ways of approaching the past: history and memory. History, residing in the archive, seeks facts; memory, transmitted through ritual and liturgy, asserts meaning. History emphasizes contingency and human agency; memory reads the past through mythical narratives. Some have read *Zakhor* as condoning one side of this dichotomy and rejecting the other: either approving of the historical method and criticizing religious superstitions, or lamenting the decline of religion in the face of the sterile attacks of modern scholarship. Any close reader of that work knows that these interpretations miss the point. *Zakhor* argues that the modern person embodies both sides of the ledger. Intellectual honesty demands critical appraisal of the past, whereas the human condition requires us to find meaning in our lives. Modern life is tragic to the extent that these two facets of the human experience remain in opposition to each other. The goal, perhaps an unattainable one, is to integrate the two of them.

Nowhere in Yerushalmi's writings does he talk about the desire for that integration as openly and poignantly as he does in the pages of this book. We learn that the study of history became for Yerushalmi a way "to understand the substance of [his] own Jewishness." It was when, as a young man, he moved away from practices such as synagogue attendance and prayer that the desire to understand his own Jewishness became even more pressing. Indeed, Yerushalmi tells us that "had [he] remained religious in this way, [he] probably would never have become a historian." This adds a new, and highly personal, complexion to the statement in *Zakhor* that history is "the faith of fallen Jews." What are we to make, then, of the fact that at the end of his life, Yerushalmi admitted that, in history, "I didn't truly find what I was looking for"? Is this an admission of the failure of his lifelong quest? I don't believe so. For one thing, Yerushalmi found in history a true consolation because it teaches that the future is never determined. This was a profoundly optimistic insight for him: however bad things may seem, history shows us again and again that they can turn around in an instant. More significantly, Yerushalmi never gave up the hope for some kind of integration between modern scholarly skepticism and existential fulfillment. In these pages, Yerushalmi talks about the germ of an idea, that occurred to him in the early 2000s, for an approach to history that affirms the historical "hermeneutic of suspicion" while also taking seriously myths (Yerushalmi never used that word dismissively) that guide people's lives.

Yerushalmi talked more about an integrated "mythistory" in his final graduate seminar. Although he claimed that he was too old to construct a new historical method at that point in his life, he made clear that he was thinking deeply about a historiography that verified the factual record, while also recognizing the importance of myth as a "propelling agent in history," which would allow us to "retell Jewish history in terms of the historical myths in which Jews believed." One of the examples he offered us of this kind of thinking was that of Ahad Ha'am, who had argued a century earlier that the facts of Moses's life (or even the answer to the question of whether he existed at all as a "real" person) matter to Jews far less than the impact of the stories told about him as a mythical character. "Even if you succeeded in demonstrating conclusively that the man Moses never existed," wrote Ahad Ha'am, ". . . you would not thereby detract one jot from the historical reality of the ideal Moses—the Moses who has been our leader not only for forty years in the wilderness of Sinai, but for thousands of years in all the wildernesses in which we have wandered since the Exodus."[3] Another of Yerushalmi's examples was the argument of the Bible scholar Yehezkel Kaufmann that the creation of monotheism was a spontaneous expression of an innate Jewish "genius" for religion. Yerushalmi pointed out that some might interpret this development (as did Kaufmann himself) in non-metaphysical terms, while others might see it as evidence for divine revelation. Either way, the object of study from a "mythistorical" perspective would not be the origins or veracity of a belief, but its effect on those who believed in it. The historian par excellence, Yerushalmi remained, in his own terms, a "*homo religiosus.*" He did not mean by this that he endorsed a traditional—and certainly not an Orthodox—approach to theology. Half-jokingly, he described himself to us as a "heretic," accepting as he did the basic insights of biblical criticism and rejecting literalist readings of the Bible and Talmud. But if he did not satisfy his existential quest in historical research alone, that did not mean that he abandoned it altogether. "Faith and religion, and whatever you want to call it," he told us that day, "are not supposed to make things easy for you . . . so you live with it." And live with it he did.

I visited Yerushalmi in the hospital shortly before his death. On his bedside table was a Hebrew Bible. He told me that he had been reading the book of Job. I don't know for sure which part of that book occupied him, but I imagine it was the final chapters, in which God responds to Job's questions by pointing to the limits of human understanding. "Who is this who darkens counsel, Speaking without knowledge? . . . Where were you when I laid the earth's foundations? Speak if you have understanding."[4] This was the passage that Yerushalmi, in his long-standing seminar "Job and other Arguments with the Lord," taught alongside William Blake's "The Tyger." Like the book of Job, that poem presents the experience of terror and awe at the fierce immediacy of creation, and barrages the reader with a flow of unanswered questions. "What immortal hand or eye / Could frame thy fearful symmetry?" What is the meaning of a world that contains both innocence and experience, the lamb and the tiger? How, we might add, are we to understand the world? As an orderly sequence of events that can be mastered by the skeptical rationalist, the holder of the keys to the archive? Or as an inscrutable jumble of experiences that remain opaque even to the one undergoing them? In different ways, Yerushalmi spent a lifetime attempting to integrate these two truths. The conversations in this book bear witness to his odyssey.

NOTE TO FRENCH EDITION

OPHRA YERUSHALMI

The publication of these conversations gives me the opportunity to pay my respects to readers, the publishers, and Sylvie Anne Goldberg. This book had to wait a long time before it was published; indeed, distrusting posthumous publications, I disapproved of releasing this work that my husband could not review.

Through the years, Yosef and I worked side by side at home; we shared discoveries, experienced moments of uncommon inspiration, and arrived at a perfect mutual understanding of our styles and instincts.

Above all, Yosef Yerushalmi prized spontaneity and imagination, which did not keep him from opting for the rigorous path of scholarship. Since he had planned to write the story of his life, conversations with Sylvie Anne Goldberg, a colleague and friend, seemed like a good way to accomplish this. Sadly, these conversations stretched out over time until a phase when Yosef felt much weakened, and there the project remained.

Nevertheless, as time went by, Pierre Nora convinced me of the usefulness of publishing these conversations. I hope that this volume will offer a new point of view about a historian whom France has always warmly welcomed.

I would like to express my profound gratitude to Hélène Monsacré at Albin Michel Publishers for her understanding and for having completed the difficult task of editing a complex text.

Finally, I thank Sylvie Anne Goldberg for her admiration of, and dedication to, Yosef Yerushalmi.

New York, July 8, 2012

INTRODUCTION

SYLVIE ANNE GOLDBERG

Where Do We Come From? What Are We? Where Are We Going? In the following pages, Yosef Hayim Yerushalmi recounts how the title of Gauguin's famous painting sparked the impetus that led him to dedicate himself to the history of the Jews. Here for the first time, the great American historian who was born in 1932 in the Bronx and died in New York in December 2009, delivers an account of the journey that made him one of the major figures of the academic world at the end of the twentieth century. In the course of these conversations, a singular thread connecting the life of the researcher and his work becomes clearer, a life in which occasional chance and preponderant determination played their parts. Historian of the Marranos, but also a historian of history and memory, Yerushalmi had writing talent that communicated to readers centuries of evolving Jewish life and identity in Europe.

He was a student of Salo Wittmayer Baron, a dominant tutelary figure in Jewish historiography, before succeeding Baron at Columbia University. Yerushalmi benefited from an atypical family and academic education. He had a New York childhood, to be sure, but was steeped in another century and geography. His Russian-born parents were Hebrew and Yiddish speakers, and he attended yeshiva high school. As the 1930s and 1940s advanced, crises occurred and refugees arrived. Poverty reigned at home, but Yerushalmi received a vigorous education from formidable teachers who painstakingly sought to make ends meet by spreading knowledge acquired in Europe's best universities wherever they could.

In 1953, Yerushalmi started an academic course that led him from the Jewish Theological Seminary, where his instructors were great scholars, to Columbia University. With insatiable curiosity, eager to fill what he sensed were gaps in his knowledge, he devoured books, attended all sorts of courses, and started to collect rare volumes. This eagerly initiated itinerary led him to write major works: a biography of Cardoso, who renounced his position as doctor at the court of King Philip IV of Spain to wear a red hat in the ghetto of Venice and end his days with the first name of Isaac as doctor of the poor of Verona; and a Haggadah anthology, whose iconography reveals better than a conventional academic study how the Passover ritual evolves over centuries. Next came *Zakhor: Jewish History and Jewish Mem-*

ory, a concise historiographical text that unexpectedly projected him onto the world stage by opening a continuous dialogue with historians, psychoanalysts, and philosophers that persisted with *Freud's Moses: Judaism Terminable and Interminable*. Beyond these titles, his vast reflection on messianism, the sense of exile, and the Jewish vision of politics prepared new horizons for future generations of researchers.

But his real talent lay elsewhere. Describing some characteristic aspects of Jewish individuality, he outlined evocative features about many forms of contemporary identity. It is tempting to repeat about him his own comment on the eternal dialectic between specific and universal: "Who is more English, and more universal, than Shakespeare? Who is more French, and more universal, than Molière?"

The exchanges presented here are not a biography; they retrace the intellectual itinerary of a person in his century, influences that marked him, readings that shaped him, meetings and friendships that nurtured him, and some missed opportunities. More than a history book, this portrait gallery of Jewish intelligentsia of the past century is also a precious historical document. On the subject of Yerushalmi's exceptional journey, "Clio and the Jews: Reflections on Jewish Historiography in the Sixteenth Century"[1] provides a direct point of entry into his work, and I thank the American Academy for Jewish Research and its president, Todd Endelman, for authorizing its publication.

These conversations in Hebrew, English, and French were the result of several years of discussions, which unfortunately remained unfinished. In a way, they began with an interview about Jewish studies in the United States that took place in Paris in June 1987, when Yerushalmi was teaching at the School for Advanced Studies in the Social Sciences,[2] and were developed over the years and during subsequent meetings. The initial project was associated with the Itineraries of Knowledge collection at Albin Michel Publishers in Paris, directed by Hélène Monsacré. Begun in 2004–2005, on occasion they were interrupted by distance, before being disrupted by illness. Feeling that time was working against him, Yerushalmi considered writing his memoirs himself, and our book advanced no further. Yerushalmi passed away before completing his own project, so these interviews constitute one of the rare accounts given by him of his experiences across the century.[3] Ophra Yerushalmi, his lifelong companion, granted readers the privilege of accessing these conversations that illuminate his entire body of work. We thank her most sincerely.

Paris, July 2012

NOTE TO THE ENGLISH EDITION

It is a tremendous pleasure to express my thanks to those who made it possible for this dialogue to be presented to a new readership: Elisheva Carlebach, the Salo Wittmayer Baron Professor of Jewish History, Culture, and Society at Columbia University, who initiated the project; the Tauber Institute Series for the Study of European Jewry; and Brandeis University Press, in particular Sylvia Fuks Fried. Special thanks to the Institute for Israel and Jewish Studies at Columbia University for funding the translation from the original French edition. My gratitude goes also to Benjamin Ivry, who brilliantly translated these lively discussions into English, and to Alexander Kaye for his sensitive foreword.

My hope is that this volume will touch those who knew Yosef Hayim Yerushalmi and specifically those who are lucky enough to still have to discover his oeuvre.[4]

Sylvie Anne Goldberg
Paris, December 28, 2020

TRANSMITTING JEWISH HISTORY

I

Zakhor, FROM MEMORY TO READING HISTORY

You are one of the few scholars of Jewish history whose international renown transcends the circle of scholars and traditional Jewish Studies readership, insofar as your works have been translated as far away as Japan. In France especially, your Zakhor: Jewish History and Jewish Memory *(1982) struck a responsive chord in terms of problems stemming from Jewish history far beyond the usual limits of the history of the Jewish people. In your opinion, is this phenomenon related in any way to what might be perceived as the specific nature of Jewish history and Judaism?*

Rather than Judaism as history, I always prefer to speak of Jewish history or the history of the Jews. The history of the Jews encompasses, but also surpasses, the history of the Jewish religion. And the Jewish religion must be historicized, because it is only one aspect of Jewish history. If one wants to speak of singularity, it is therefore necessary instead to ask the question at the level of global Jewish history.

When you began to prepare the lectures that would make up Zakhor, *did you have this theme in mind, about the singularity of Jewish history?*

No. I don't believe that *Zakhor* explicitly addresses the theme of the uniqueness of Jewish history at any point. Because no national history is unspecific; each has its own aspect and characterization of historical singularity.

What you suggest might well surprise some of your readers; indeed, among the many responses to your book, readers precisely emphasized the singularity of the history of the Jews.

Why should I be answerable for the way people read my books? During my adult years, I went through a learning process of discovering that people had perceptions of my books that I could not even imagine and that sometimes go completely against my explicitly stated intentions. Therefore, I feel no responsibility for the uses that have been made of *Zakhor*. But

I don't believe that, whether deliberately or not, *Zakhor* emphasizes the theme of a singular character in Jewish history or Judaism.

What struck me most about the reception of this book was that, in a highly mysterious way, it seems to have appeared in a timely manner to address issues of the relationship between history and memory or, to say it more precisely, of historiography and collective memory. Without my knowing it, at the very moment when I was writing *Zakhor*, Pierre Nora had started work on *Realms of Memory*.[1] When *Zakhor* was translated into French two years after its publication in English, I visited Paris and met Pierre Nora for the first time. We were both surprised at the correlation between our two areas of research. It is obviously out of the question to compare my little book to his initiative, which has become an authoritative summation and which at the time had already extended to a second volume. It's true that since the publications of *Zakhor* and *Realms of Memory*, memory has become a kind of industry. For the past few years there has even been a journal called *History & Memory*, edited by Saul Friedländer. I'm a member of the editorial committee, although I don't have much to do with it. I don't even try to follow everything that is published on the subject of memory; there is simply too much. As in other fields, you can only read part of the output. So, I just follow the advice of people who recommend an essential work to me, and that's fine.

Were you surprised by the reception of Zakhor?

Zakhor has been read in every possible way, even the most unpredictable ones. An example, which shows how chance operates, is that the book appeared in English shortly after I moved from Cambridge to New York. One day I bought the *New York Review of Books* and read a positive review in it by Harold Bloom. Meanwhile, in Paris, Éric Vigne, who at the time worked at Éditions La Découverte, read the article, bought the book, read it and decided on his own initiative to translate it. Harold Bloom "made" the book in America, and Éric Vigne "made" it in Europe, first in France, from which it migrated to other countries.

Most reviews were favorable. Obviously there were some exceptions. But even among favorable articles, interpretations of the book differed. The most annoying one, if I may use the term because I avoid complaining about reviews, was where some perceived the book as an attack on modern historiography and sought to view it as a desire to return to ways of premodern thinking. That was absolutely not my intention. To the best of my recollection of what I wrote in a book I haven't opened for years, I never made any such explicit or implicit statement. My intention was simply to expose the problem that uses of memory can pose in the historical field in general, and the field of Jewish history in particular. Fortunately, many historians not working in Jewish history shared the same questions. But I certainly didn't mean to say that the enterprise of modern historiography should be abandoned. I don't know of any other way of practicing history; all we can do is rely on the old methods. This was the first problem that arose with readings of *Zakhor*. One critic of my book, who shall remain nameless, noted in my first lines the assertion that the work would be partly history and partly confession and creed. "Not at all," writes this reviewer: "This book is merely a confession and creed!" What can I say to that? I don't usually respond to criticism. The criticism I took most seriously, especially because it came from my friend Amos Funkenstein,[2] dealt with the first point, of history and memory. I think it was based on a misunderstanding, which I like to believe we resolved since then. The essential argument of his criticism was that there was indeed a Jewish historical consciousness in the Middle Ages and that my book seemed to deny its existence.

Speaking of which, he published a detailed review, which many subsequent critiques were based on.[3] *Did you have a chance to thrash it out in person with him?*

We were only able to discuss it many years later because although we were friends, we seldom met. He was either in Israel or on the West Coast of the United States, while I lived on the East Coast. Sadly, by that time he was already quite ill and would die soon afterwards. I had been invited to Berkeley for a public debate with him, and it was obvious that it would revolve around the issues raised in *Zakhor*. I had other engagements on the West Coast, so I went. We had the dispute in public. Basically, I told him that I did not think that the slightest disagreement existed between us, but that this difference of opinion was due to a subtle misunderstanding. I added that I took responsibility for any reactions that my books provoked, but I had no intention of saying or even insinuating that the Jews had no historical consciousness in the Middle Ages. I simply wanted to insist upon the idea that a clear distinction should be made between historical consciousness and the way it is expressed. My problem was to know—and I believe this is the real question—if there is a historiographical genre or genres, and I feel that the most important Jewish texts of the Middle Ages expressing Jewish historical consciousness are not necessarily texts written in the historiographical genre; for me, this awareness is expressed elsewhere, in exegesis, rabbinical commentaries, the *Halakhah* [religious laws], and so on.

After this public session, we had a moment to chat together. Finally, I think, and I hope it's not an illusion on my part, we understood each other better than the published article reflects. I have nothing against the idea that Jews manifested a historical consciousness; I was just always bothered by current phraseology, according to which Jews have always been outside of history and that only in modern times have they returned to it. To me, that's just nonsense.

In their daily lives, Jews have always lived in history. They have even found themselves situated at the heart and soul of history whenever they were involved in events related to power relationships. So this is not the issue. All Jews who dealt with the powers that be were precisely aware of political situations and configurations. It's less certain that they had exact knowledge of past history. I don't know if they could cite the names of all the kings of France or emperors of the Holy Roman Empire. But that doesn't matter; they certainly had a historical consciousness. And even if you assume that, between the Talmudic and modern eras, several Jewish conceptions of global history developed sequentially, it is absolutely certain that even during the Middle Ages, one of these conceptions indeed prevailed, and far from being static, it should be subject to modification.

Which intellectual figures influenced your journey in career and personal terms, as a mensch [a person of integrity and honor]? I suppose that all such influences are closely intertwined?

I guess they must be. However, my approach to history has been the culmination of an entirely personal progress, and intellectual encounters only occurred after my decision was made. Conjuring up these characters raises the question of where to start. I didn't really read history books seriously until after I received my bachelor's degree. Until then, I mostly read literature, all kinds of literature. My evolution was linked to the question of my own identity. After the bachelor's degree, I immersed myself completely in history, with equal intensity for general history and the history of the Jews, because what I had learned until then in these two fields was not at a high standard. When I began studying at the Jewish Theological Seminary, I devoured as many publications on Jewish history as possible, far more than were necessary for my studies. I literally immersed myself in readings that no one required. Thus I read all the volumes by Heinrich Graetz,[4] everything that existed at the time by Salo W. Baron, including the first edition of the *Social and Religious History of the Jews* in three volumes, but also the first two volumes, which had recently appeared, of what became that work's monumental second edition.[5] I began to read the work of historians of the Jerusalem School,[6] especially Yitzhak Baer.[7] I still have the first edition in Hebrew of Baer's *History of the Jews in Christian Spain*, published in two volumes in 1945. Today it is a rare book, a collector's item.

But my great discovery, and I was not alone in this, was reading the works of Gershom Scholem. I was so excited to read them that I started to read everything he had published in currently available journals. We formed a small group of three or four students who met regularly to discuss Scholem's work. I remember that the text that impressed me the most, far more than *Major Trends in Jewish Mysticism*,[8] was the epochal article "Redemption through Sin" ("Mitzvah haba'ah ba'averah"),[9] about the transgressive theology of Sabbateanism. This essay had an explosive effect on me; it presented a completely new, and frankly revolutionary, approach to Jewish history.

What exactly do you mean by that?

The article made it possible for me to concretely grasp what I had perhaps perceived only intuitively, that for a historian, not for a philosopher but for a historian of the Jews, there can be no fixed essence of Judaism. Or rather, to use Scholem's own words, that the history of Judaism is above all the history of its interpretation. This allowed me to understand that the Sabbateans, even after the conversion of Sabbatai Zevi,[10] and later the Frankists, were neither merely madmen nor purely decadent people. They were simply Jews whose beliefs became possible to reconstitute without endorsement. This allowed me to realize that even the most extreme positions of Frankism could be approached intelligently. Reading this essay, "Redemption through Sin," really introduced me to a whole set of phenomena. The rest of the work was equally magnificent, but this text marked an essential turning point, as far as I'm concerned.

Did any of your teachers influence your career as mentors?

My mentors influenced me in many ways, even if I have never penetrated all their fields of knowledge. My Talmud teacher was Saul Lieberman,[11] who was without a doubt the greatest scholar of the century in the field of Talmud, not only because he knew the Talmud and Midrash inside out, but because he had read absolutely everything written during the period of Late Antiquity, in Latin as well as Greek. He taught what the practice of textual criticism could be. But my great hero was undoubtedly Shalom Spiegel, because with the exception of Scholem, I don't think I have ever encountered any individual in the field of Jewish history who united in one person so much scholarship, imagination, and style. His analysis of the legends of the Binding of Isaac[12] in its original Hebrew version reads like a real adventure story. Their influence was decisive.

In fact, I had the privilege of having the greatest teachers imaginable. For Bible study, I attended the class of Harold Louis Ginsberg;[13] although he wasn't really a great teacher—to understand what he was saying, you had to sit close by and listen attentively—he was, however, an undisputed major biblical scholar. Obviously I am also including Salo W. Baron, but he brought me much more through his writings than his teaching per se, which moreover he did less in lecture classes than seminar meetings. In short, these are the ones who influenced me the most in terms of Jewish history.

In general history, things were entirely different. I started by feeling that I had such huge gaps that two different simultaneous approaches were needed, sometimes completely random ones. I recall I tried to read every volume of the *Cambridge Medieval History* as well as the *Cambridge Modern History*. But as I like to say, a committee can never write a symphony. A bit later, I read other things about the Renaissance and Reformation, and so on. Academically, when I was admitted to Columbia University to prepare for my master's degree and then the doctorate, I also benefited from studying with great teachers. I discovered the Renaissance with Paul Oskar Kristeller.[14] He was supreme in the field, fascinated by the manuscripts that he unearthed, and he found new ones all the time.

Among these great teachers, was there one you particularly identified with?

Not among my general history teachers, at any rate. The intellectual figures of my personal pantheon are among the authors I've read. The first person who made me want to be a historian in his image—and I'm not saying that I would have managed it—was Johan Huizinga, one of the greatest Dutch historians of the twentieth century. Interestingly, he started his career in a completely different field than history, by studying Sanskrit.

He became a historian not only of the Netherlands, but more generally of what is called in contemporary Anglo-Saxon terminology Late Medieval, or Early Modern, Europe, choose the term you prefer. We are still faced with these pesky problems of definitions; the meaning of terms varies from one linguistic area to another.

Johan Huizinga wrote many books. I still consider one in particular to be a pure masterpiece, just as I consider Jacob Burckhardt's *Civilization of the Renaissance in Italy* to be a masterpiece,[15] even if today he is widely ignored. Still, reading Burckhardt is something!

Returning to Huizinga's book, I discovered it in historiography class, the only one that was required for doctoral students at Columbia, where the assignments consisted mainly of reading. So we read the great historians, about whom we had to write a mini-essay. Huizinga had written a book originally published in German under the title *Herbst das Mittelalters*. It was first poorly translated into English as *The Waning of the Middle Ages*, when it should have been called *The Autumn of the Middle Ages*.[16] This book, about the Netherlands and Northern Europe, takes Van Eyck's paintings as a starting point. I thought then, and I still think, that it's difficult to clearly categorize the genre of history that Huizinga writes. It's cultural history, although today this term has a completely different meaning than in his time, but also a form of history seeking to render the spirit of a specific age in a given place. A sort of story that excludes everything based upon written or material documents, which leaves room for the imagination. I remember that my mini-essay (which received a low grade because my teacher did not like Huizinga) commented on a brief passage in which Huizinga describes nocturnal silence in a fifteenth-century northern European city. He evokes this silence in an almost palpable way. One of the passages that stayed with me said, more or less, wherever people were, they could hear the clatter of horseshoes on the pavement as a solitary cavalryman crossed the city. I felt that this way of writing history was sublime, absolutely sublime. Huizinga was really an inspiration to me, although I don't think I tried to do the same.

Another figure who left a lasting impression on me, and whom I have not tried to imitate, is Ernst Kantorowicz. Two of his books struck me in particular: *The King's Two Bodies* and *Frederick the Second*, works in which he made use of interpretations, historical deviations that I would never have dared use. I no longer recall how accurate he was. All I know is that as a historian, he was willing to take more risks than anyone else.[17]

From what you say, one might assume there is a relationship between intellectual approaches that influenced you and the work of the Annales school?[18]

I only discovered the Annales school belatedly. I don't even remember the year when I finally read Fernand Braudel's *The Mediterranean*.[19] As soon as I read it, I immediately understood that it was a great book. And yet, with all due apologies, and despite all the admiration I have for this accomplishment, something was missing from its pages. While reading two massive volumes about the Mediterranean at the time of Philip II of Spain, I never really smelled any hint of the sea. Perhaps I expected something impossible, something like Huizinga's night scene. But I sorely missed any perceptible closeness to the sea.

There is nothing wrong with all that [Braudel] wrote about each event that happened on the shores of the Mediterranean; his research and archival work are all genuinely brilliant. But this came relatively late in my journey, like the rest of the Annales school. For me, the figure of Lucien Febvre was dominant. I admired him intensely, and still do.

What interested you about Febvre's work?

His work on Rabelais[20] was, and will definitely remain, a great book. I have cited him, particularly where he said, "I believe that we should undertake a series of works which we all lack, and as long as we lack them, no history is possible. We have no history of love. We have no history of death. We have no history of mercy, nor any history of cruelty. We have no history of pleasure."[21] That sort of history of emotions and that approach impressed me considerably. Yes, Lucien Febvre ranks among my heroes. But I discovered authors such as Georges Duby belatedly. For me, Duby is a great historian, but I was already educated by the time I read him. And of course there were historians from Spain who really excited me.

Which ones in particular?

For example, Américo Castro. Although, technically speaking, one could argue about whether he truly writes in the historical genre, for me he is still an authentic historian, despite the fact that I don't agree with everything he wrote. Far from it! In *España en su historia*[22] and in its later revision, *La realidad histórica de España* (1954), his chapter on the Jews is brilliant, although I believe that what he wrote about the relationship of the Jews to "purity of blood" and the Inquisition is completely wrong. But still, it's absolutely brilliant.

When you say it's wrong, what are you referring to?

I don't think that Spanish Jews developed a doctrine of purity comparable to the idea of *limpieza del sangre*, or the Spaniard's purity of blood. The latter has other origins, far from simply reflecting a Jewish notion of blood purity. And the same is true for the Inquisition.[23] I don't think he is right, even if his chapter on the Jews remains a beacon, as does his entire conception of the interplay among religions, which has lost none of its relevance. I don't want to go into detail here, but the major controversies between Américo Castro and his disciples and followers of Claudio Sánchez-Albornoz[24] prove this. For Castro, Visigothic Spain is not really Spain yet, while Sánchez-Albornoz thinks it already is. Castro believes that it is not really Spain because for him, authentic Spain cannot exist without interrelationships that develop between the three religions in the Iberian Peninsula. Therefore, he feels that one cannot really speak of Spain before the Muslim conquest. But all this brings us into an overly specialized discussion.

The other great Spanish historian who influenced me a lot is French, Marcel Bataillon. His great book, originally titled *Erasme et l'Espagne*,[25] but the final edition of which, *Erasmo y España*, is in Spanish, taught me a lot, especially about the New Christians and the relationship between history and literature on the Iberian Peninsula. I realize that I have not drawn up a full list of all those I have admired, but that is more or less how things went, with these readings accompanying me, rather than educating me. I would like to add that despite all the historians whom I read, who influenced me, or whom I admired, even including my teachers, I never developed a consistent method. I don't really use any method per se.

What do you mean?

I didn't allot myself a strict, rigorous system of rules to be applied systematically, which historical analysis should be subject to. I have no "method," except in the limited sense that I still believe that what is called a "philological-historical approach" or even "critical approach" may lead to close approximations of the truth. Even if we can always object that we inevitably remain in the realm of probability rather than certainty, I am nonetheless convinced that this approach can lead as close as possible to the truth. Apart from this point, I don't really have a method in the sense of social science or anthropology, although I also read this literature.

Whether you admit it or not is relatively unimportant.
It seems rather odd to claim to eschew any method.

Of course, I employ different methods developed in the humanities. But for each subject I touched upon, and as you know, I touched upon a lot of them, I felt that I needed to design a specific method.

If I had just focused on the plight of the Marranos and Sephardic Jews, perhaps I could have developed this field of study far beyond what other scholars have done. Of course, since it is impossible to read everything that is written, my judgment may be biased. Each theme where the groundwork has been done poses new problems for me, calling for the use of specific approaches, which are not always thought out or even consciously declared. I believe I seek an intangible aspect that I always hope to find in my students, which often happens, thank God. I'm convinced that there is a kind of historical instinct that has nothing to do with intelligence or professional work, but is in the nature of intuition. All my students know the expression, because often I use it, that there is an olfactory nerve that can be described by the French expression, "avoir du flair" [having flair]. Just follow it and employ anything that may seem useful!

I was fortunate in having been hired quickly as a professor at Harvard, without worrying about my work or teaching constantly being evaluated by a committee. This allowed me to feel immensely free in my research and to do what I wanted.

2

CHOOSING HISTORY

What made you decide to become a historian of the Jews?

My reading led me to it. At the time, the best place in New York to study Judaism with a critical approach was the Jewish Theological Seminary, located near Columbia University. In 1953 when I got there, it was really a great institution. In theory, this institution was intended to train rabbis of the Conservative movement,[1] in other words "moderate" rabbis who were neither thoroughly Reform nor absolutely Orthodox. But I knew from one or two of my friends who were studying there, that it was mainly interesting as the greatest concentration of Jewish scholars in all fields outside of Israel. The only important people missing at that time were Salo Wittmayer Baron, who taught at Columbia, and Harry Austryn Wolfson, who taught at Harvard. It was a situation that you wouldn't find anywhere today.

I might add that my *sekhel* or "commonsense" told me that all Bible stories and Talmud *aggadot*[2] cannot be taken literally, or even allegorically. I felt that I lacked basic elements for understanding these texts. As mentioned, I was fortunate to study Talmud with Saul Lieberman and Bible with Harold Louis Ginsberg, among those who deciphered Ugaritic texts[3] in the late 1930s. I studied history with Abraham Halkin,[4] as well as with Salo Wittmayer Baron, who was a visiting professor when I was a student at the Jewish Theological Seminary.

Did you have any personal interaction with these teachers, or did you just attend their lectures?

Each seminary professor knew that classes contained some students who planned to become rabbis, while others would turn to research. I must say that although it was probably unfair, they always preferred those destined for research. Did I therefore get to know my teachers on a personal basis? You must remember that the 1950s were different from the current academic world, especially in terms of student-teacher interaction.

One of my teachers was of decisive importance, although in his lifetime he scarcely published anything; only now, many years after his death, has a disciple finally published one of his manuscripts. This was Shalom Spiegel, who taught medieval Hebrew literature and poetry. To me, he was a polymath, *homo universalis*. I venerated him. Yet, during my years of study, I never knew exactly whether he liked me or not. Only during graduation ceremony did I realize that he had awarded me first prize in his subject.

Nor did I know what Lieberman thought of me; he too was an extraordinary teacher with frequent mood swings. One day, when we had to prepare an assignment in class, I sat by an open window—it was almost summer—and looked outside, hoping that he would ask me to read and comment on a text starting from the beginning of the text, because I hadn't had the time to prepare texts from the conclusion. Suddenly, in his Lithuanian accent, he shouted: "Hey, Yerushalmi! You think I don't realize that you're looking out the window so that I should call on you right away? No way, you'll be the last!" At the Talmud final exam—all exams were oral and individual, and Lieberman scheduled them for between 11 p.m. and midnight—my heart was racing as I took the elevator up to his office. After giving me the exam, he asked, "Okay, now what do you want to do?" I replied that I wanted to study for a doctorate under the supervision of Salo Wittmayer Baron at Columbia University. "Good," he replied directly.

I added: "But I won't be able to begin next year because it's too late to apply for a scholarship." He reassured me: "Don't worry, I'll get you a scholarship from the American Academy for Jewish Research." And that's what he did. Or at least I thought that's what he did. He set only one condition, that I continue to attend his course the following year and, obviously, I agreed.

Only decades later, when I myself became a member of the Academy, did I discover that it did not give out scholarships. Lieberman himself had paid out of his own pocket so I could continue my studies! I learned that he did many such things for different people. So when you ask what my interactions were with teachers, it's difficult to answer. The only sure thing is that I never called any of my teachers by their first names, neither during my studies nor afterwards. I never called Baron "Salo." It was another world with different, more formal ways. Even today, I forbid my students—even doctoral students—to call me by my first name. To them I am always "Professor Yerushalmi." As soon as students receive the doctorate, I become Yosef, because then we are colleagues instead of teacher and student. This became a kind of ritual and I love rituals.

Going from the Jewish Theological Seminary to Columbia, under the direction of Baron, did you remain in a Jewish Studies course, in the narrow sense of the term?

Not at all! At Columbia, I only took two Jewish Studies courses, one with Baron and the other with Zvi Ankori.[5] All the other courses dealt either with general history or subjects that interested me. So I had the pleasure of studying Renaissance philosophy with Paul Oskar Kristeller, as already mentioned, and Renaissance history with Garrett Mattingly.[6] All these professors were prominent authorities. I would attend their lectures as an auditor, since the university's greatest courses were only available for a few years, which is not much if one thinks of all the riches to be gleaned from them. I attended university in America much longer than the time required to complete my studies.

You had the privilege of studying under the direction of Salo Wittmayer Baron, a preeminent authority on Jewish historiography. What was your encounter with him like?

I met Salo Wittmayer Baron when I was studying at the Jewish Theological Seminary. But when I got to Columbia, I didn't sign up for his lecture class because I had heard many of his lectures at the Jewish Theological Seminary and read his writings before. At Columbia, the most important thing was to attend his seminar, which was really special; it never focused on a specific subject. Each year, he simply gathered all his students in the master's and doctoral courses—when I say all, it was at most a dozen students—and we always met in his apartment, quite close to the university. Mrs. Baron served us tea and sweet cakes as we sat around a large table, each working on a different subject. For example, when I was preparing my master's degree, my subject was the Papal inquisition. I don't know, let's say another student might have been working on the history of fourth-century Palestine. In short, there was no common subject. We all gave presentations about the state of our work-in-progress.

Then Baron invited us to comment on these presentations, and finally he added his own analysis. At that time, he really conveyed the quintessence of his teaching. Having the opportunity to hear Baron's comments was an incomparable lesson.

As for his work, it speaks for itself. The second edition of his great history was a Faustian endeavour. I think he only stopped working after the death of his wife, his sole assistant. She was always immersed with him in the subject at hand. One day, when sixteen volumes of his vast work had already been published, I asked him lightheartedly: "How many volumes do you think you will produce?" Smilingly, he replied, "Thirty. All I know is that I signed my part of the contract, but I don't know if the good Lord signed his." Having the privilege of being a Baron student was very meaningful for me, because he was the last historian, now and in the future in all likelihood, to master Jewish history in its entirety. Indeed, the final volume of his work deals with China and Ethiopia. Remarkably, he never imposed anything upon his students, no subject or method.

This encounter with Baron played a determinant role in what I became. Apart from his extraordinary learning, which he communicated in class, he also allowed his students to be fulfilled by remaining true to themselves as he helped them to achieve their own findings.

Among the ten students in the seminar, have others apart from yourself achieved careers or publications?

One of the group became a professor. Above all, I was preceded by Gerson Cohen, who was older than me and whom Baron had identified as an heir apparent. Later, Cohen left Columbia to become chancellor of the Jewish Theological Seminary.[7]

One story might give an idea of the kind of person that Baron was. A young student at the seminary was writing a master's thesis on Ephraim Deinard (1846–1930). Deinard was a great Zionist who lived in Newark, New Jersey; he also wrote essays, especially against Hasidim, and, as a remarkable bibliophile, founded major public libraries. At the end of his life, Deinard settled in New Orleans with a library of ten thousand rare books in Hebrew that Harvard bought when he died. They formed the nucleus of the great Harvard Library Judaica Collection. And I, with the chutzpah of youth, I called out to the student who was working on this subject, "Come on, why are you working on the history of American Judaism? Is the history of American Judaism so essential when compared to that of Europe or Asia, or even Africa? And apart from that, why is Deinard so interesting? How important can his story be?" At the end of the seminar, Baron asked me to stay after the others had left his apartment. He was visibly upset and said to me, without losing his temper:

"Yerushalmi, how can you say such things? You are talking about the largest Jewish community in the world!" Of course he was right.

Today, studies of American Judaism are plentiful and in any major bookstore in the United States, a section is devoted to this theme. But let's return to when you enrolled at Columbia with the help of Professor Lieberman. How did that work out?

Very simply, I qualified for my master's degree. Today, the master's dissertation is not much, because the master's degree is equally worthless. But in those days, the dissertation was a real thesis, certainly shorter than a doctoral thesis, but nonetheless a text of some hundred pages of original research. During this time of my life, I was particularly interested in the history of the Jews of the South of France. In my reading, I discovered the medieval Inquisition, including the Episcopal Inquisition and later the Papal Inquisition after the Albigensian Crusade. The Inquisition fascinated me, and I wrote a dissertation on *The Inquisition and the Jews of France in the 13th and 14th Centuries*.[8] This interest in the Papal Inquisition gradually led me to study the Spanish and Portuguese Inquisitions. It wasn't really new to me, but I continued to read and proceed with this line of study. From there, I wound up with the extremely complex subject of Marranos.

Do you remember exactly when, and under what circumstances, you first learned about the Marranos?

This may surprise you. I discovered the Marranos around the age of eleven. My parents, who always pushed me to study, kept giving me books in any language, even in Yiddish. I still recall that there was a collection of little books in Yiddish for ten- or twelve-year-old readers, called *Kinderbibliothek* (children's library). Most of the books were biographies of great figures in Jewish history, and my parents gave me one about Don Isaac Abravanel.[9]

I no longer recall who wrote it, although I can visualize the format of these books perfectly. Through the figure of Abravanel, we naturally saw his era go by with Marranos, the Inquisition, and all the rest. The book included reproductions of woodcuts as full-page illustrations; among them is one that I have never forgotten. It shows a seder held among the Marranos of Seville, and we see that they are all together in a cellar. A seder table is set absolutely as it should be, the whole family is united, and all the dishes as well as ritual objects placed on the table are totally identifiable. The grandfather is standing. The engraving shows the moment when the door is flung open by Inquisitors who are there to arrest them all. This illustration impressed me a lot. In a way, this image precisely illustrates for Jews the conventional social imaginary of marranism. It means that marranism is just another form of normative Judaism, with the difference being that our seder is celebrated in broad daylight and theirs is held in a cellar. Later in my critical studies, I broke away from this view, but it was my first contact with the Marranos. Then Cecil Roth's book[10] made me rediscover them. But I went straight from the Papal Inquisition to the Spanish and Portuguese Inquisitions. The way I chose my own doctoral thesis subject is a topic for a new chapter.

How did you see the future?

When I was a doctoral student at Columbia, it was impossible for me to predict whether I could find any job anywhere after I received the diploma. At that time, only two university chairs in Jewish Studies existed in the United States, and they were at elite institutions. It should be remembered that the project by the members of the Wissenschaft des Judentums[11] started almost at the beginning of the nineteenth century, to promote the founding of chairs in Jewish history at universities in Germany of the time. But this dream never came true in Germany or anywhere else in Europe. It became a reality for the first time in the United States, at Harvard in 1925. It was not a chair in history, but in Jewish literature and philosophy, because it had been created specifically for Harry Austryn Wolfson, the towering historian of philosophy. Therefore, Harvard had Harry Wolfson, who enjoyed international renown for his work on the Jewish philosophy of Philo of Alexandria and Hasdai Crescas,[12] as well as his volume on the philosophy of the Church Fathers.[13] Just as Saul Lieberman had read everything that had been written in Greek and Latin, Wolfson had read all the philosophical literature written in Greek and Latin as well as Hebrew and Arabic. He knew more languages than Étienne Gilson![14] The second chair was established in 1930 for Baron at Columbia. This was the situation. Two giants occupied the two existing chairs, and I was perfectly aware of this. I'll come back to that, but it's pretty amazing to think that I had the good luck to teach at these two universities. All I knew was that I had to finish my research, someday.

Why did you finally choose history?

My choice to study history is linked to a specific event. I don't recall how old I was, perhaps twenty. I went to the Museum of Fine Arts in Boston, and saw one of Gauguin's most famous paintings, an incredible long canvas done during his stay in Tahiti. The painting impressed me less than its title: *Where Do We Come From? What Are We? Where Are We Going?* I had studied Jewish texts throughout my childhood, in a traditional way, without any introspection, and I realized that all this knowledge did not enable me to answer the question asked directly by Gauguin's painting. That's why I hoped that practicing history would allow me to answer the first two components, if not the third. Knowing where we come from and what we are: that is, what I am now, and what forces, events, and developments brought me to what I am. In my view, this is the sole possible legitimization of the historical quest, in addition to that given by one of my teachers. When asked why we should study history, he replied: "Because it's interesting!" Certainly, but that is not enough.

Does the final part of the question, "where are we going," have religious overtones?

Yes, as soon as we start to talk or write about that, we stop being historians.

3
BACK TO CHILDHOOD

Before the "epiphany" in the form of Gauguin's painting, did you see any early signs of a historical vocation?

I have no precise memories from my early childhood, but I was sure that the world was wide open. I think when I was four or five, I dreamed of being a baseball player, but that is irrelevant. When I was a teenager, I knew that I didn't want to be a doctor, without being able to explain why. I really liked mathematics and I was even pretty good at it. But I had a friend in class whose math skills far surpassed mine. Which basically meant that the only future I could see in mathematics was to teach at a high school or third-rate college. And that didn't suit my ambitions. A bit by default, I decided to become a lawyer. And it became an obsession, although I couldn't really analyze why.

What did lawyers signify for you? Did you see them as defenders of causes?

Yes, my image of lawyers were people who defend the poor, underdogs, widows and orphans. Also those who plead grandiloquently in a courtroom. I had another motivation; I was sixteen when the State of Israel was proclaimed. I thought that someday, I might work at the Israeli Ministry of Foreign Affairs. But that did not amount to a project or decision, it was just a vague idea. Anyway, at the end of high school, I applied to three highly prestigious law schools and was accepted to all three. I believe it was in April of my senior year of high school. After receiving three letters of admission, I had some reservations. Did I really want to be a lawyer? I had asked friends of my parents who were attorneys, and they explained that the main part of the job was not about making fine courtroom speeches, but mostly spent in libraries immersed in dull research about case law. That wasn't quite what I had imagined. At the same time, I was experiencing some different growing pains about my Jewish identity. To make this identity crisis comprehensible, my social background must be described.

In short, I realized at university that my vaguely defined Jewishness, which I nevertheless felt deeply, had never been a personal choice. Jewishness was first given to me by my parents, and next by the education I had received. I received an intense Jewish education starting at the age of eight. When I was ten, I was already studying the Talmud. The yeshivot where I studied, especially the Rabbi Israel Salanter Yeshiva,[1] were considered to be "modern" yeshivot, the likes of which I believe no longer exist. What did modern mean at the time? There were no girls in class, all the boys wore kippot, and the language of instruction was Hebrew. Even the Talmud was not translated into Yiddish, but studied in Hebrew. We also studied the Bible, commentaries, modern Hebrew literature, and even a little history.

And at home?

Home was entirely different. My parents were both Russian. My mother was sixteen years old when she travelled with her mother to join the rest of the family in the United States. She wanted to study, but her family decided that she had to learn a "real" trade and do something useful. So she was sent out to learn dressmaking. She became a wonderful seamstress, but her studies ended there. I think that was the biggest disappointment of her life. My father is another story. He and one of his brothers were raised in a Zionist family in the small town of Goloskov, Ukraine.[2] Because my grandfather was wealthy, my father was sent to Odessa to study as a teenager.

Was this the era when most great turn-of-the-century Russian Jewish thinkers were in Odessa?

He probably met them there. The start of the twentieth century was a golden age of Hebrew literature and development of Zionism in Odessa. After studying at the Odessa Gymnasium, my father went to university. About a year later, the 1917 Revolution broke out. I only know that during the civil war that followed the Revolution, my father and one of his brothers escaped from Russia after trying a variety of routes. They managed to take a boat to a port somewhere in the Black Sea, and left for Palestine.

That's how they landed in Jaffa around 1920. Both were *halutsim* (pioneers). My father worked at all kinds of jobs. He even lived on a kibbutz, Givat HaShlosha, I think.[3] In 1923, his brother—an uncle I never knew, like the rest of my father's family, by the way—returned to Russia to bring my grandfather to Palestine. Neither of them returned.

1923 was a dark year that saw the beginning of Soviet anti-Zionist persecution. My family was lucky not to be killed; but most of them—it was a very large family—were exiled to Siberia. I believe that my uncle was sent to Irkutsk and my father remained alone in Palestine. I have pictures of him from when he was in Palestine. I know they are of my father, but I don't recognize him. It's him, the man in a crimson shirt, armed on horseback, but that isn't my father. Because the man I knew couldn't do that kind of thing. In 1928, he became very ill with malaria. I think one of his friends wrote to him from the United States to offer him medical treatment with the plan that he would return to Palestine when he was better. He went and stayed in America for the next fifty years. He was no longer physically able to work; he had no money or profession. He made a big mistake. He should have enrolled in an American university and continued his studies. Instead, he spent most of his time attending Zionist conferences. The only job he ever did was teaching Hebrew to children.

Did he receive a Jewish education in a yeshiva?

I'm not sure. I know he attended a *heder*,[4] but in Odessa that could mean either going to Hebrew school or taking private lessons. I don't think he went to yeshiva. My grandfather was what is known today as Orthodox, but I don't think he would have used that term. When he left Russia, my father was neither Orthodox nor religious in the usual sense of the terms. The best example I can give of my father's attitude to Jewish tradition is that he always went to synagogue during holidays, but not on Shabbat. On Friday evenings, my mother lit candles, my father recited kiddush before dinner, and after meals, he always smoked a cigarette as part of the "pleasure" of Shabbat. For my part, I never saw any contradiction there.[5] The Bronx where we lived, which is different today, was a Jewish quarter, but not particularly Orthodox. There were Orthodox Jews, but also Zionists, Bundists,[6] and even Communists. The neighborhood lingua franca was Yiddish, so my two mother tongues were Yiddish and Hebrew.

You spoke Hebrew with your father and Yiddish with your mother?

Yes. And all three of us spoke together in Yiddish, because my mother didn't speak Hebrew, although she knew many songs in the language. My parents gave me the opportunity to practice two languages, but they could have given me a third, Russian. All their friends said that my father and mother spoke and wrote Russian masterfully. But they kept Russian as a secret language. I heard them singing many Russian songs. For a long time, I blamed them for playing a trick on me, because I could've also known Russian, which I was very keen about. Maybe one day I will start to study it.

Yet generally speaking, the secret language of parents can be learned quickly by children who want to know what they are saying.

Well, I couldn't do it. Nevertheless, I feel that even today, a considerable part of my inner self is Russian. I have strong affinities with Russian literature, although I only know it in English translation, which isn't the same thing, I realize.

Anyway, Russian or not, until the age of five I hardly spoke English either. There was no need for it at home or in the neighborhood. So in 1937, when I was sent to public school at age five, I still couldn't speak English.

I recall that as soon as the fall term began in September, we started to rehearse a Christmas play. I knew the story of Saint Nicholas, and I wanted to play that part. But the teacher said, "No, no! You can't, you don't speak English." So I cried a lot and told everything to my parents, who immediately hired a teacher to come to our home and tutor me. He was an Englishman. This is undoubtedly why when I speak English today, people have trouble placing my accent. Not genuinely British or American, it sounds New York without being New York . . . It's . . . it's my accent!

What language do you think in when you are alone?

All three. I switch interchangeably from one language to another. When I'm alone, I never translate my thoughts. I do translate when dealing with French, German, and Spanish, but in terms of thinking, Yiddish, Hebrew, and English are my three native languages.

Regardless of the intent of what you are expressing?

True, it can fluctuate sometimes, depending upon the intention, and that's something of a strange phenomenon. I think I have feelings that I can only express in Yiddish, while other feelings I can only say in Hebrew. But it always depends upon the thought and context. My wife is Israeli and when I met her, naturally we spoke Hebrew. But today we unwittingly speak Hebrew and English interchangeably and simultaneously.

Let's return to 1937. You enter kindergarten, you study English at school, and you want to play the role of Saint Nicholas while living as a Jew in a Jewish neighborhood. At the time, were Saint Nicholas and Chanukah the same thing for you?

No, there's a big difference. But you can't live in New York as if in a walled ghetto. We sometimes went to Manhattan to shop and walk around. In New

York, it is difficult to escape Christmas, but I never felt directly involved with the Yuletide holiday. There was no possible competition between Chanukah and Christmas. Chanukah is Chanukah. Chanukah is *our* festival. I never wondered why or how others differed from us, or about the real origins of Christmas. I'm not even sure if I knew the name of Jesus at that age. Anyway, I studied at this school for three years until the day my father took me aside, saying:

"Look, Yosele, we've decided to send you to a different school, a yeshiva. Mornings, all the subjects will be in Hebrew, and afternoons you'll study the same things as in public school."

Then he added something that I find intriguing and significant in retrospect. He said, "I'm sending you to a yeshiva because I believe that only this kind of school can give you the Hebrew and Jewish education that I want for you. But I want you to know that in this school you'll be taught to do things that I don't do and not to do things that I do. And I hope it won't lessen your esteem for me. As for you, you're free to do whatever you want."

And that is how it was. In any case, I never had any conflicts with my father.

As a teenager, I spent some time in the Zionist youth movements Habonim[7] and Hashomer Hatzair.[8] To tell the truth, I changed membership mainly according to where girls belonged whom I was in love with, or I thought I was in love with. I wound up joining Bnei Akiva, where I felt completely at home.[9] They professed a religious Zionism, and the movement was led by remarkable men devoid of fanaticism. They were completely open-minded. Bnei Akiva still exists today, but I'm not sure that it corresponds to the organization of my young years. And that's the whole story. My father wasn't religious in the conventional sense of the term, but he was no atheist, either.

And your mother?

My mother was probably a little more religious than he, but her case is also impossible to define simply. Clearly she wasn't Orthodox. Of course, we kept kosher and meat especially was always kosher, but my mother didn't go so far as to use separate dishes for meat and dairy. The Passover Seder was the big family celebration. My father taught me the *nusach* or cantillation for chanting ritual readings, which can never be learned from a book. The cantillation bequeathed by my father remains part of me.

Is this why you focused on Pesach Haggadot[10] *in a book that was published, somewhat incongruously, right after your major work on Isaac Cardoso?*[11]

In fact, the former book is dedicated in Hebrew to the memory of my mother. Although I associate Pesach with my father because of the transmission of the *nusach*, the festival was mainly due to my mother's effort. She organized everything and like all Jewish women of her generation, almost never sat down at the table. She was in the kitchen all the time. By the way, when my parents came to the first seder that my wife and I organized in our own house and saw me carving the turkey in the kitchen, she almost blew a fuse. She informed me in Yiddish, "Excuse me? You're in the kitchen? Slicing the turkey? In my house, men don't belong in the kitchen!"

How did the project to publish Haggadah and History *originate?*

At the time, as editorial committee director for the Jewish Publication Society (JPS), I had to suggest ideas for publications. Facsimile editions of illuminated Haggadah manuscripts had already appeared, but these were sort of coffee-table books that readers might leaf through once in a while. I thought that a pictorial story of printed Haggadot was really missing, so I developed a project accordingly. JPS and its editors thought that was a good idea and said, "Do it!" I considered that after the Cardoso book, this was just what I needed. I set aside manuscripts, limiting myself to Haggadot produced from when the printing press was invented until today. That's how I became a self-taught Haggadah specialist. I think that apart from Avraham Yaari[12] and Cecil Roth, I am currently the one who has looked at the most Haggadot in the world, at least those published through the 1970s. I had access to two splendid collections at Harvard and the Jewish Theological Seminary, thanks to librarians at both places.

4
THE PATH TO CARDOSO

Apart from school and yeshiva, what was the Jewish environment of your childhood and adolescence like?

My parents always thought it was necessary for my health to spend summers out of the city. At the time, there were many Jewish vacation camps, and each Jewish ideological current had its own vacation camp in the countryside. The socialist Arbeter-ring (Workmens' Circle) supervised *Kinder Ring* (Children's Circle); Poale Zion (Workers of Zion) had a *Kinderwelt* (Children's World), while the Communists supervised *Kinderland* (Children's Country); and there were *massaot* (backcountry excursions). I went to most of these camps, but especially *Kinderwelt*, where the official language was Yiddish. All the ceremonies and public gatherings were conducted in Yiddish, even though most of the children did not speak the language.

Camps for adults were always located near the youth camps. In summertime, actors from New York's Yiddish [Art] Theatre took advantage of their off-season to present weekly classics of the Jewish theater.

It was a much more austere theater than today's dances and musicals. When the troupe came, serious performances were also given in the youth camp, led by one of the New York actors. It turns out that my Yiddish was perfect and I apparently showed some dramatic talent, so that starting when I was eight years old, the camp arranged with my parents that I could attend camp for free if I acted in the weekly plays.

It was hardly what you'd call amusing. I especially remember one year when the theater for adults staged Goldfaden's *Shulamith*.[1] I acted and sang in the play. In a traumatic scene set in a tent, Shulamith sings, expressing the extent of her feelings for her lover. The lover, in this case, was me. At one point, she sang, "I'm sick, I need a doctor!" And I was supposed to emerge from behind the tent flaps, shouting, "I'm a doctor!" But my vaguely biblical costume included a long sword. You see, at the key moment I stumbled over the sword while screaming, "I am the doctor!" and did a pratfall in front of the hysterically laughing audience.

What was your greatest success in the summer theater?

There weren't really any significant ones, except at the end when I was thirteen or fourteen. In the adult camp, the troupe performed *the* great classic of the Yiddish theater, S. Ansky's *The Dybbuk*.[2] They needed a young actor to play the main role of Khanan, and naturally they called on me.[3]

Did the role of Khanan particularly influence you? Did you identify with him?

It made a big impression on me, for unexpected reasons. In fact, it was a genuine ordeal. Leah was played by an actress about thirty-five years old and I was just fourteen. I later learned that Maurice Schwartz, director of the Kuntz (art) Theatre, was in the audience that evening.[4] He walked up to my parents and said:

"Next year we bring *Di mishpokhe Karnovski (The Family Carnovsky)*[5] to New York by Israel Joshua Singer, the brother of the other Singer. The role of Benjamin in this play is terrific, and I would like to cast your son."

My parents did the right thing in such cases, they let me decide. And I immediately refused. During all the summers spent acting, although I was certainly pleased by all the applause, I had suffered so much that I eventually came to hate the work, especially after what happened with *Shulamith*. Having had the opportunity to observe the New York actors backstage in their makeup with their petty rivalries, envies, and jealousies, I was convinced that I didn't wish to enter that world. So ended my theatrical career.

How did your teenage years conclude?

I returned to Yeshiva High School in the 1940s. The 1930s had been painful for all Americans and over a decade later, effects of the Great Depression were still felt. The 1930s were years of economic crisis for everyone, but things were even worse for my father as a schoolmaster. Although my parents were quite poor, as an only child I never lacked for anything. My father also had his pride. I can still see the day when a social worker visited our home and started asking questions. My father lost his temper and kicked her out of the apartment, telling her he didn't need any help. He finally found a job, but in Philadelphia. My mother did not want to move because that would have meant a change of school and environment for me. So for two years, he worked in Philadelphia each week and returned home weekends. Then he finally found another job in Chattanooga, Tennessee.

Why was a Hebrew teacher needed in Chattanooga?

There was a Jewish community! All over the South are exceptionally fine Jewish communities. So for a whole year, apart from school vacations, I didn't see my father. Things got better in the 1940s, when he started working for the United Jewish Appeal.[6] Then he stopped teaching in small schools and worked to raise funds for Israel Bonds, debt securities issued by the Zionist movement.

At the time, in New York as elsewhere in America, underpaid public school teachers earned extra money by teaching afternoons at Yeshiva High School. So I was lucky to receive a wonderful secular education from the best teachers from the most reputable high schools who came to the yeshiva to make ends meet.

I was in my final year of high school. Since I had decided not to be a lawyer, I had to choose an alternative. It may have been a bit naive on my part, even at that age, but I couldn't be satisfied with being a product of other people. I wanted to, how shall I say, be my own person. And being my own person meant having the ability to choose. I hadn't chosen Judaism or Jewishness. So I decided that the only pathway was to understand what Judaism, which I had studied continuously since the age of eight, could be.

The only way to pursue this investigation was to study Judaism and Jewish history critically, which I had not done before. There was no critical tradition in the curriculum that I followed, and among the wonderful teachers that I had, few had this sensibility. In middle school, for a class on the Book of Daniel, I went to the New York Public Library to find books of commentary. I recall that one of them was part of the International Critical Commentary series. What it claimed was incredible, so I went to see my middle school teacher and asked if the Book of Daniel really comprised at least two different works, and wasn't from the time of Persian rule but rather the Hellenistic era. He replied, "Don't worry. That's what non-Jews say." I never forgot that response. Many years later, I learned that this teacher was a great specialist in Arab literature who had edited Maimonides's *Treatise on Resurrection*.[7] But obviously we didn't talk about this kind of thing at yeshiva, even a modern one. I never forgot that response, which I accepted at the time, although it wasn't convincing. That's why later on, I decided to study more critically.

Isn't it odd that you never focused any research on your own Ashkenazi heritage?

That's a good question, but I have no justification. I was fascinated by the Sephardic phenomenon, the Inquisition and the Marranos. Besides, I didn't speak the language.

But Yiddish was your mother tongue and you couldn't speak Spanish either, at first.

Yiddish did not suffice! And of course, we didn't speak Spanish at home. I studied French in high school, and Spanish and German in university. In German, I'm really self-taught. The transition from Yiddish to German is quite easy, so I only needed a grammar book. I got to Portuguese through Spanish, although I don't always understand the spoken language because its pronunciation is unlike Spanish. I studied Latin at school, and Aramaic through the Talmud. In fact, the only language I conspicuously lack is Russian. I'm afraid it's probably too late.

Why did you to choose Isaac Cardoso as a thesis subject?

I was already broadly interested in the Inquisition and the Marranos, but I found Cardoso indirectly and perhaps a bit surprisingly. At the time, I was already a book lover. When I was young, rare books of Judaica cost little, which allowed me to assemble a fine library. I was particularly interested in Judaica printed in Spanish and Portuguese. I regularly received catalogs from an Oxford bookseller, Rosenthal, who always listed rare books.[8] One day I noted that he was selling a copy of *Las Excelencias de los Hebreos* by a certain Isaac Cardoso. Although the book cost too much for me, it piqued my interest. I looked up Cardoso in a Jewish encyclopedia with a slightly longer biography than the catalog, but was uncertain about his birthplace. Was he born in Portugal or Spain? We just knew that he was a doctor in Spain before reaching the Venetian Ghetto, and then moving on to Verona, where he writes in Spanish *La Excelencias*, a masterpiece of Jewish apologetics. No matter how much I looked, I couldn't find out anything else about him.

A month after this excitement, I went as usual to Ideal Bookshop near Columbia University, which had some old books, and even a few rare ones. That day, in a corner, I saw a pile of dusty books, all of them Judaica in Spanish. And among them is *Las Excelencias de los Hebreos*. The prices ranged from ten to twelve dollars; but when I asked the bookseller about *Las Excelencias*, he said, "This seems to be a special book. The price is fifty dollars." At the time, I didn't have that much. I told this story to some friends of my parents, and they gave me the fifty dollars. That is how I made contact with *Las Excelencias*.

Cardoso's name probably fascinated me so much because I already knew that Abraham Cardoso had been a major figure in the Sabbatean movement.

Gershom Scholem's great book on Sabbatai Zevi wouldn't be published until 1967. When you started your doctorate, what did you know about the Sabbatean movement and its importance to Jewish history?

Monographs already existed, especially the essay "Redemption through Sin" (Mitzvah ha-ba'ah ba'averah), published in 1937.[9]

Scholem's landmark article correctly suggests that there was a strong element of Marranism in Sabbateanism, and that this allowed him to retain many followers despite Sabbatai Zevi's apostasy. Marranos in bygone times, who had learned to lead two different lives simultaneously, Jewish inside and Christian outside, could conceive of a Messiah who externally became Muslim while continuing internally and mystically to achieve a redemptive mission.

Suddenly, I discover that Isaac Cardoso, the brother of Abraham, despite being a former Marrano, was staunchly anti-Sabbatean. I saw that this was a genuine empirical case of two brothers, Marranos, one of whom remains an ardent devotee of Sabbatai Zevi even after the latter's apostasy, while his sibling is an opponent. Obviously I had to present my project in Baron's seminar. Meanwhile, I discovered that the Oxford Libraries owned two letters from Abraham Cardoso to his brother Isaac, but without any replies. Yet as always, I was anxious about presenting this subject to Baron, fearing that he would consider the documentation too flimsy and doubt my ability to find more. I was so frightened that I asked Baron for permission to bring my wife along to the tutorial. When I presented the items in my possession, he gave me the green light. So I carried on. In my third year of doctoral studies, I no longer had any courses or exams, I was married and had obtained a scholarship. So nothing prevented me from following Cardoso's geographic path as far as possible.

Did any details of the journey shed light on your approach as a historian? Starting in New York with the few sources you had access to, how did you unravel the trail?

Cardoso was thought to be a native of Celorico da Beira, Portugal. So when I landed in Lisbon, I immediately went to the National Archive of Torre do Tombo, the Portuguese national archive. There I learned that all Portuguese parish archives have just started to be centralized in Lisbon. In this special Arquivo dos Registos Paroquiais,[10] I found the registers for Celorico da Beira. Just a few months later, *Los Judíos en la Edad Moderna y Contemporánea*, an interesting, although highly prejudiced, three-volume study was published. Its author, the Spanish anthropologist Julio Caro Baroja, agreed that Cardoso was born in Portugal, but in Trancoso.[11] Having already planned my research in Spain, I had no time to delve into the Trancoso archives. Fortunately, the Portuguese, who are highly considerate, did the research for me, but found nothing there about Cardoso. Yet several mentions of Fernando Cardoso were found in the Celorico archives.[12] Admittedly, this is a common Portuguese family name. I checked the phone book in my Lisbon hotel as soon as I arrived, and found ten whole pages with listings for Cardosos.

Interestingly, before going to Spain, I did a little tourism in Portugal, which has some wonderful cities such as Coimbra, where the oldest Portuguese university is located, with a magnificent library. Next I had to go to Salamanca. I took a train and when crossing the border in Ciudad Rodrigo, we had to change trains because the rail width differs between countries. So I was now seated in a Spanish train. As I felt a bit hungry, I went to the dining car and sat at a table facing Franco's portrait. I brazenly changed places to sit at the other side of the table, but on the opposite wall was a portrait of Franco too. So I ate with Franco, who was impossible to escape. All this happened in 1961.

When I arrived in Salamanca, I went to the tourist office to find a hotel. The only one within my budget was the Hotel Generalísimo Franco. Since I wrote to my wife and parents, I went to buy stamps at the post office, where the choice of image was either Franco's head or a crucified Jesus. I opted for the latter. Returning to the hotel, I encountered a noisy crowd gleefully invading the streets. Suspecting a local holiday and seeing that the afternoon was just starting, I joined the mob that led me to the Plaza Mayor in Salamanca. Spanish people are justifiably proud of this main square, perhaps the most beautiful one in the country, where Salamanca Cathedral is located. Today it is already crowded. Suddenly, the imposing cathedral doors open. How could I have guessed? On this day Corpus

Christi was celebrated with the adoration of the Blessed Sacrament. The doors opened, allowing the archbishop of Salamanca to emerge, bearing a cup containing the Host, surrounded by his retinue according to an elaborate ritual.

Suddenly the whole crowd fell to their knees, except me. I remained standing while everyone else had their faces to the ground. As a little Jew who came to Spain looking for the Inquisition, I wondered what they were going to do to me. They did nothing, but what an experience.

The next day, I go to the university, the oldest and most beautiful in Spain where the trivium was taught.[13] Latin, Greek, and Hebrew were studied here. In the archives, I met a priest who helped in my research. Together we found a Fernando Cardoso. Perhaps he is "my" Fernando Cardoso? Sadly, there's no information about the seventeenth century.

From Salamanca, I left for Madrid, where a lot of work awaited me. In a chapter of *Las Excelencias*, Cardoso attacks an anti-Semite whom he met in this city. Along those lines, it should be pointed out that autobiographies by Marranos are rare. Any details they might have given would probably endanger their families or associates in Spain. Cardoso is an exception. So he writes that in Madrid, he knew a mayor named Don Juan de Quiñones and the latter had written in a book that all Jewish men have tails and menstruate once monthly according to some sources, or once annually on Good Friday, according to others. He adds that this debate remains to be settled by scientists. In the Lisbon library I had already located many of his books, but not this one. But in Madrid, I happened upon a manuscript signed by him. I understood its significance at once, and felt like I was on the right track. I started to read it, telling myself, "Well, that's the one Cardoso mentioned!"

In Madrid, I mostly worked on an Inquisition trial that had intrigued me in Caro Baroja's work, although it was unconnected to Cardoso. Even then, I was already sure that the latter had never been arrested by the Inquisition.

When I was leaving Madrid, a new development occurs. On the title page of one of Cardoso's printed works, a Latin treatise on medicine, I found the inscription: "Fernando Cardoso, formerly a professor in Pinciano." Pintia was the Latin name of Valladolid, a city north of Madrid. It is already quite hot in early summer, and I was getting weary of my research leading to nothing or almost nothing, which is usual in archival work. I really wondered if I should go to Valladolid. I told myself that if I don't, remorse and guilt will await me upon my return to New York. So I bought a second-class train ticket, with third class probably being reserved for goats since their odor can be perceived for the whole trip. Wasting no time after getting to Valladolid, I went to the university, where the provincial and university archives are kept.

How were you received in the archives? Did you mention that you were working on a Marrano, a Jew, or did you just give his name without further details about the subject of your research?

I just said, "I'm looking for information about a man, a certain Fernando Cardoso, who taught here in the first half of the seventeenth century. Maybe you have something about him?" Maybe? In less than ten minutes, the archivist returned with two boxes that contain his entire career in Valladolid, including how he got his chair after a time-honored debate between candidates, the debate subject and contents, everything was there! So I made microfilms, microfilms, and more microfilms.

From Spain, I went to Venice. Indeed, the Inquisition was also rampant in Venice, obviously much less harshly than in Spain. Cecil Roth, who was familiar with the Venetian archives, had advised me well. On-site, I found no Fernando Cardoso file, although other files speak of him incidentally, describing him as "previously Christian in Spain." But he was never indicted in Venice or in Verona.[14] Cardoso obviously had contacts in the higher echelons of power. Finally, from Venice I went to Verona, where I found a copy of his *Philosophia Libera*, a large folio containing Cardoso's only handwritten inscription.

No Inquisition records, even indirect ones, exist about Cardoso?

No, although there is a bit of information in other files. In the preface to my book, I wrote that scholars deplore this state of affairs, because an inquisitorial file would have been a mine of information. But how can we blame him for fortuitously escaping their clutches, just because we want to know more about him?

That said, apart from my teachers, I think studying comparative literature helped me make the best use of sources by and about Cardoso, although those studies were not done using contemporary approaches. I don't think this sort of thing can really be taught. It's like being a historian. A historian cannot be manufactured within a university. I am not the first to say this. In the nineteenth century, in his first lecture as rector of the University of Berlin, the great German historian Theodor Mommsen expressed the same idea.

5

THE MELODY OF HISTORY

If we cannot learn to be historians, there must be a sufficiently profound urge in the future historian to direct an entire lifetime. As a young researcher, the journey that took you from one city archive to another implies that you were fully absorbed by this quest as an intense part of your life. How did this appetite or urge for, or delight in, making history begin?

Proof of being fully committed to research is when it starts promptly, with a fixed and precise aim, and this is necessarily compelling. However, I cannot say the same about my entire career as a historian. It hasn't always been at the center of my life. History isn't the only passion of my life. I have a wide variety of interests, which is indeed one of my problems, even in terms of what I read. If I read more history books, would I be a better historian? Who knows? I do certainly read!

You say that your study of literature was decisive to doing historical research. Yet especially in terms of research in America, aren't these two separate fields? Literature is connected to texts, and history to contexts. How can the two be coordinated?

I understand and accept the distinction you're making. But remember that unlike yourself, I am too old to belong to the generation of deconstruction and postmodernism. In the field of literary criticism, I belong to the generation of what was called New Criticism, which is nothing new today. New Criticism focused on a rigorous reading of texts, but at least with my teachers, without forgetting historical contexts or completely detaching from textual context. When I say that literary studies were a major input, I mean that they taught me to heed brief notes and grammatical forms that can illuminate an entire text. In this way, the most illuminating parallel conceivable is of biblical exegesis by commentators from all eras. However, philosophical and linguistic methods are radically different from exegetical ones. If I could start over again today, I would seriously study linguistics and even philosophy. I acutely regret these deficiencies.

In the 1990s, when your Freud[1] *appeared, you simultaneously published an article on the relationship of historians to archives.*[2] *You admitted that your recent work would have been much the same had you not consulted any archive. How do you explain the difference in approach between* Cardoso *and* Freud*?*

An apparent contradiction might be seen between the archival excitement that obsessed me when I worked on Cardoso and its near-total absence during my research on Freud. But it should not be inferred that I discounted the importance of archives in the latter project. After all, the publication of introductory manuscripts is based on sections of the Freud archives available to the public. I asked a different question in the article, part of a series of lectures given in London dealing with archival matters. My position was as follows: unlike Cardoso, whose works have never been analyzed, except perhaps *Las Excelencias*, we read and reread Freud in dozens of languages. Freud's letters have been published and there is a vast literature about him. As a result, I felt that Freud's archives could no longer offer major revelations to improve our understanding of his work. Admittedly, somewhere in those archives may be information that throws specific light on the personal relationship between Freud and his sister-in-law. Some speculate that they slept together, based on the fact that Freud spent holidays with his sister-in-law, rather than with his wife. First of all, this detail does not interest me in any way. Next, even if this infidelity were proven, I don't see how it would change our view of Freud or his importance. We could deduce that he had weaknesses like everyone else, but that has nothing to do with his teachings. In my opinion, it is much more vital to seriously revise translations of Freud.

That's part of your stringent approach to texts.

I am increasingly convinced that many things can be called a text. I'm not the first to say that generally speaking, history itself is a text. Léon Bloy, among others, said that, and Borges also presents the past as a text.[3]

Let's return to Cardoso. Based on archival sources, you write the text that is your Cardoso*. In retrospect, how do you see its development from raw document to text?*

First of all, I wish to point out that long ago, I gave up reading everything written about the Marranos since my *Cardoso*. Today it is a real industry with everyone participating, Spanish and Jewish researchers alike as well as those interested directly or indirectly in religious phenomena. At the risk of appearing horribly conceited, I must say that until now, I have only found bibliographical details requiring me to significantly update the book's contents. Others may disagree.

Yet despite what you say, didn't you make him an archetype?

I don't believe so. In my view, the book closest to mine is Yosef Kaplan's *From Christianity to Judaism*,[4] which he was already working on when I published mine. There are many parallels between our books. But Orobio de Castro is not Cardoso, and Cardoso is not Orobio de Castro. They are two different cases. But you were saying that archival materials, on the one hand, can be distinguished from historical "rewriting" that I performed on these materials, on the other. In other words, to use contemporary terminology, I "constructed" the figure of Cardoso or, to go to the other extreme of so-called postmodernism, I "invented" Cardoso. This is a fundamental question, and I don't know how to address it. Whole libraries would be required to deal with the problem of the relationship of fact to its "invention," in all the polysemy of the term. I imagine Hayden White,[5] whom I know through his works rather than personally, telling me: "Archives, archives, that's fine and dandy! The fact remains that you *invented* your Cardoso." By speaking this way, he would reveal how our viewpoints are opposed. He would say, "Your Cardoso is a novel" or at best, qualify that by adding, "A historical novel."

I must say that I feel increasingly outnumbered among historians, and not just Jewish ones. Perhaps I'm already a fossil, but I still want an irreconcilable difference to exist between history, even historical invention, and the novel, even a historical novel. The difference is simply the status of the novelist. Novelists can also draw upon archives. When Tolstoy wrote *War and Peace*, his friends in St. Petersburg provided him with archival information. But without implied criticism, all the world's Tolstoys lack any duty to provide evidence to construct their compositions. The difference between them and historians is therefore due to the question of historical criticism.

Let's take an example. I passionately love *Amadeus*, the play and film. I've always been a fervent admirer of Mozart and his music. Well, I completely disagree with critics who quibble that such and such a detail of the film isn't truly "historical." Certainly, we have no evidence of whether Salieri killed Mozart. Still, for me, this work presents admirable metaphors for genius and mediocrity. Add music, and they become even more so. In other words, I don't expect from the playwright Peter Shaffer what I would expect from a historical biography of Mozart.

There's another difference between history as a scientific discipline and historical novels. Many contemporary historians, not necessarily those of the previous generation, distinguish between the historian's narrative stemming from historical fact—and facts are facts—and what falls under narrative style. This despite the fact that the very definition of a "fact" might be endlessly debated. I was also criticized over the issue of literary style in history. My friend Derrida[6] wrote that in the last chapter of my *Freud*, when I suddenly change the narrative style to address a monologue to the founder of psychoanalysis, I depart from historical approach. I admit I was a bit surprised that this sort of critique came from Derrida.

Yet the dialogue form is often used in philosophy, particularly to teach students to philosophize and argue with a text. This connects your desire to gain more philosophical grounding with textual concerns.

Certainly. But a "Monologue with Freud" still isn't a dialogue.

During a discussion with Derrida, I replied that only a historian could write such a monologue. I don't think my argument convinced him. But I would like to point out something. There is a small, exceedingly clever book by Carlo Ginzburg, *History, Rhetoric, and Proof*,[7] published in the Jerusalem Lecture Series. In my view, this concise work makes a remarkable contribution by insisting that so-called rhetoric cannot be divided from evidence. Rhetoric is part of the proof, which is to say that the way in which history is written is already part of putting forth the proof. That's all.

In short, history is written through rhetoric and literary talent. Can anyone be a good historian without knowing how to write and express oneself suitably?

Historians in all fields have written poorly, yet made significant progress in historiography, if we agree that historiography is progressing. It matters little whether they lacked ability or if writing well was the least of their concerns. I'm trying to recall a specific example, but for the moment, I have none. In any case, I often read history books from which I learn a lot, but the reading process turns out to be grueling or tedious. Still, I had a teacher who always said, "There's no such thing as a bad book. Something can be learned from every book."

6

FROM *Zakhor* TO *Freud*

Let's return to the question of historical consciousness. You maintain that such a consciousness has certainly always existed. Nevertheless, your book Zakhor *has often been used to refute, or at least set aside, the idea of historical consciousness in Jewish experience. I don't know how* Zakhor *was received in the United States, but that's clearly how it was read in France.*

If anyone went as far as to interpret my book as rejecting the idea that historical consciousness exists, my view—but why should an author have a viewpoint?—would be that the book has been read sideways. On the other hand, if we read it as questioning the absolute value of modern historical consciousness, then we are closer to my intent. But, as mentioned earlier, I'm not responsible for the way my books are read. These things happen. One or two years after the French edition of *Zakhor* was published, a publishing house—I don't remember its name, but it was notorious for publishing works of Holocaust denial—released a book, not by Faurisson[1] but another notorious character whose name I forget. My publisher, La Découverte, sent me a photocopy of its back cover bearing a single quote, from *Zakhor*, of course taken completely out of context. In this quote, I mentioned one of those things that keep worrying me, namely that despite immense and relentless efforts made by historians, their works don't have the impact that they could, or should, have. About the Holocaust, I wrote: "I have no doubt that its image is being shaped, not at the historian's anvil, but in the novelist's crucible."[2] It was a flowery metaphor used to say that Elie Wiesel[3] influenced Holocaust representation more than any historian who helped build the enormous corpus that now exists. This quote extracted from *Zakhor* was used by the publisher of Holocaust denial material to legitimize itself. Shortly before this incident, someone else—again, by no accident, I've forgotten his name—published a review of *Zakhor* in *L'Arche*, claiming that I had written an extremely dangerous book that would provide weapons for Holocaust deniers. Maybe someone in the Holocaust-denying publishing house read the review and got the brilliant idea of extracting the quote from it.

Perhaps because *L'Arche* is a Jewish community monthly, for the first and only time I thought that this review called for a response. But the response could not come from me. So I phoned Elie Wiesel. I've known him since the days when he was correspondent for the big Israeli daily *Yedioth Ahronoth*,[4] long before he became the major figure known to all today. My wife and I were perhaps the first people to have read *La Nuit*, even before it was translated into French.[5] So I went to show him the article, and he agreed to write a reply denouncing the nonsensical accusation. This reply was published, although the editorial staff of *L'Arche* chose to accompany it with other reactions for the sake of balance. But the main thing is that Elie Wiesel's reply was published.

Later, an editor at La Découverte, not Éric Vigne, asked me if we should consider suing the Holocaust-denying publisher. Remember that according to French law, there is no need to ask for a publisher's permission to accurately quote under ten lines that are correctly credited. None of these conditions were violated, but at the time I was so unnerved by this morally unacceptable use of my name that I wanted to find a way to punish these people. So I contacted a friend, a prominent Philadelphia lawyer who later became president of the American Bar Association. After I told him the whole story, he said, "Here in the United States, it would be risky to prosecute."

I replied: "But aren't there special laws to defend people against this kind of action?" He responded, "Yes, but . . . " Here is the example he cited: "Let's imagine you are at a train station and someone who wants to harm you arranges for a woman who looks like a prostitute to stand near you while he takes photos of you. You don't know this woman, but to all appearances you are in some kind of relationship with her. Unknowingly, you've been trapped." Then the discussion became more academic. Anyway, if we started a lawsuit in France, even if we won, the publisher would gain more in notoriety than he would lose financially. So we took no action. I'm only mentioning this to give an example of the variety of reception that a book can elicit and the diversity of readers it encounters.

Whenever I write a book, I receive moving letters, sometimes from strangers, convincing me that the project was worthwhile. Some are from readers more attentive than even the most sympathetic professional critics. In *Zakhor*, I evoked the image of a sea battle with buffeting by the waves and no idea where you'll land. I have only one thing to add on the subject of *Zakhor*'s reception: I am in no way responsible for it!

Over twenty years later, if you could redo the book, would you write it the same way?

Obviously, no one can rewrite the same book twenty-five years later, because no one stays the same over twenty-five years. But if the question is whether I would revise *Zakhor*'s main thesis, my answer would be no, absolutely not. On the other hand, would I do things a little differently? Certainly. I would further clarify the distinction between historiography and historical consciousness. I would also examine the notion of collective memory a bit more. Finally, cultural memory wasn't even on our horizon of questioning in the 1980s when I wrote *Zakhor*, but we would have to address it along the lines of Jan Assmann,[6] for example. What I wouldn't do, but someone will have to do someday, is completely reoccupy the *Zakhor* worksite. After all, *Zakhor* is only the text of four lectures. There's little room for questions as vast and complex as history and memory. If anyone embarked on a project to write a fuller and more detailed history of Jewish collective memory and historiography, that would be a big publication. But I'm quite sure that for my part, I won't embark on this project. Clearly it's not in my nature to stick to one subject for long.

Mention of Jan Assmann, author of Moses the Egyptian, *leads us to your* Freud's Moses. *How did this project become imperative?*

I started taking an interest in psychoanalysis at age eighteen. At the time, I had a close friend in analysis, whom I envied although I had only read scant amounts of Freud. I felt that at an age when you really get to know yourself, the kind of knowledge provided by psychoanalysis opens tremendous perspectives. As for myself, I've been analyzed twice. Do people admit such things, even though there's nothing to be ashamed of? But it must be said that neither of these two experiences was conclusive. The first time, I couldn't afford the fees of New York psychoanalysts, so a psychiatrist friend told me: "New York Psychoanalytic Society & Institute organizes training sessions, and they are looking for guinea pigs. If one is accepted, one gets to see a trainee psychoanalyst and each consultation costs two dollars an hour." Needless to say, the value of things does not depend on their price, but in this case, they really were what might be called two-dollar sessions. Even so, I spent four years with an analyst intern, just before I went to Harvard.

My second experience took place in Israel during a sabbatical year. One of our friends told me about a Jungian psychoanalyst who shared a practice in Haifa. I started seeing her during the summer and after we moved to Jerusalem, I drove to Haifa once weekly. It didn't bother me to leave Jerusalem periodically. I deeply love the city of Jerusalem, but must escape it because I feel the weight of too much history there, unlike Haifa which is relatively devoid of historical burdens. At the time, roads were safer, there was a sea view, and on certain days Haifa suddenly appeared on the Carmel hills through the mist. These weekly sessions were an interesting experience. The psychoanalyst,[7] an old Jewish lady who had lived in Switzerland for a long time, was no ordinary Jungian. She was part of the "apostolic succession" trained by Jung himself, who even wrote a preface for one of her books. She and her husband, also a Jungian analyst, were long-time Los Angeles residents before they made *aliyah*.[8]

I discovered something that sounds like a joke, that in Freudian therapy, patients have Freudian dreams, and in Jungian therapy, patients have Jungian dreams. This absolutely happened to me and that year, I really had Jungian dreams! Had I stayed in Israel beyond the sabbatical year, I would certainly have continued to see her. She was a wonderful old lady and very, very serious. One day she said to me, "We are going to ask the *I Ching*."[9] Jung was fascinated by this ancient Chinese manual's different hexagrams and combinations. You can consult it by tossing coins. Imagine the scene: sitting on the floor of her house, she and I are tossing coins and watching the *I Ching* structures fall into place. In the middle of all this, a thought crosses my mind: "What are you doing, sitting on the floor of a Haifa apartment and throwing coins in the air with an old lady?"

What I mostly discovered that year was that finally, underlying theory is relatively unimportant. What really matters is the analyst's personality, or to put it in Freudian terms, whether transference occurs. With the first analyst, I don't think it ever happened. Maybe countertransference worked, but certainly not transference!

So these psychoanalytic experiences formed the background of my research. Then things happened exactly as I describe them in the book's prologue. In 1981, a year after I returned to New York from Cambridge, I receive a phone call from someone who tells me that for the past few months, a group of thirteen psychoanalysts has been meeting monthly to discuss a specific issue related to applied psychoanalysis: does psychoanalysis have anything important to say about anti-Semitism? I was intrigued by the way the question was put. At this point in their research, the thirteen psychoanalysts had decided to call upon a historian likely to prevent them from scattering in all directions, so they invited me to join them. I must admit that I was a bit frightened at the idea of being the only layman amidst all these big names in New York psychiatry. But my fears were unfounded. They genuinely welcomed me to their regular meetings. I also worried that they might be dogmatic, having already arrived at certainties. I discovered that they were very open and after ten years of monthly meetings, I still think they are. This fascinating experience led to the publication of a book that offered no final conclusions.[10] Toward the beginning of this adventure, to be better informed for our conversations, I decided to read all of Freud, which I'd never done before. So I read everything Freud had published, first in English translation, then about half of his work again in German, which isn't always the same thing. I was mostly struck by the fact that the only "Jewish" book by Freud is *Moses and Monotheism*, apart from his book on humor, *Jokes and Their Relation to the Unconscious*.[11]

When I first read *Moses and Monotheism*, I must have been twenty years old. It angered me so much that I threw it across the room. Not this time, however. By then I had already confirmed my interest in Jewish historiography and I took up this work with the idea that the psychoanalytic history of the Jews according to Freud also belonged to Jewish historiography, and therefore had to be relevant to research on anti-Semitism. For this rereading, I began by doing historical work. I went to the library to read books on Freud and his *Moses* book. The almost unanimous verdict of all these studies, including Marthe Robert's,[12] was that by identifying Moses as an Egyptian, Freud bid farewell to Judaism, the Jewish people, Jewish identity, and so on. And I thought from the start that this was wrong, just plain wrong. To be sure of it, I only had to reread the book, but to prove it I needed more evidence. So I began to read Freud's newly published letters and everything else available on the subject. It became increasingly clear to me that they were all wrong.

A simple rereading of the text was enough for you to be sure that everyone else was wrong about Freud's rapport with his Jewishness?

Absolutely, and I think authors like Paul Ricoeur and especially Marthe Robert, an intelligent woman who writes fascinating things, didn't understand anything about Freud. To sum it up in one sentence, Freud addressed a long letter to Oscar Pfister, a Swiss disciple and Christian pastor, asking: Why did psychoanalysis have to be discovered by a godless Jew? As a good theologian, the pastor replied that Freud wasn't really "ungodly." The phrase

Freud used was "*ein ganz Gottloser Jude*," a completely godless Jew. My attention was riveted to why Pfister only noted the term "godless" and relatively ignored the other term, Jew? My book deals with the second term. Freud writes, "I am a Jew without God." Admittedly, he was an atheist, I never question that. But he was, and considered himself to be, Jewish. His only major problem since the beginning was to prevent psychoanalysis from being considered as a Jewish science. Because science must be universal. This is the crux of the story; everything else is just commentary.

How was your book received in the United States?

The reviews I saw were very kind. I particularly recall two, from shortly after publication, in the Sunday *New York Times Book Review* and the *New York Times* daily book review. But while reading them, I felt that the essence of my book had been misunderstood. I phoned my agent, Georges Borchardt,[13] to tell him: "I read those two reviews. They are both favorable, even very favorable, but I feel frustrated because they didn't understand what I had written." Borchardt replied, "Two reviews in the *New York Times*, and you want to be understood too? Greedy!" So there was no cause to complain.

In France too there were reviews, but I didn't read them all. There was a particularly negative one written by a woman whose name I choose to forget, as usual. She attacked a passage in which I suggest that Freud probably knew Hebrew, because of the dedication written by his father[14] and he had to know Yiddish. I provided some evidence. First, Theodor Reik,[15] who regularly visited Freud at his parents' home where he lived until he was twenty-nine, recounts in his memoirs[16] that Freud's mother spoke only Yiddish. So how could Freud, who always heard his mother speak Yiddish and lived in the family home until the age of twenty-nine, have avoided speaking Yiddish? Then, reading Freud's letters, I found thirteen instances of Yiddish words or phrases. French critics charged that it was ridiculous to claim that Freud spoke Yiddish based on thirteen quotes in Yiddish, half of which were in common usage in Vienna and Europe at the time, which I had indeed pointed out in my book.

But an important fact which I had not emphasized was that all these usages occur in letters to a single correspondent, his closest friend before the "discovery" of psychoanalysis, Wilhelm Fliess,[17] with whom he would quarrel later. Their friendship was so intimate that it was only natural that Freud included these sentences or allusions. Other than that, I don't recall having read other reviews in French.

As you just mentioned, the problem is that Freud wanted psychoanalysis to be recorded in the universal domain of science rather than considered a Jewish science. You returned it to the Jewish pathway, at least for readers who never considered this aspect. Isn't that a discrepancy, or even a stalemate?

I am convinced, and believe it can be easily proved, that Freud had only contempt for Christianity, or more exactly that he despised all religions, but probably Judaism less than the others. His relationship to the religion of his fathers is analogous to a joke I include in the book:[18]

"West End Avenue. An upper-middle-class Jewish couple. The father, liberal, intense, a vociferously militant atheist. Wanting a superior education for their son, the parents enrolled him at Trinity School, which, whatever its denominational origins, is now secular, open to all. One day, after about a month, the boy comes home and says, casually, 'By the way, Dad, do you know what Trinity means? It means the Father, the Son, and the Holy Ghost.' Whereupon, barely controlling himself, the father seizes the boy by the shoulders and declares, 'Danny, I'm going to tell you something now and I want you never to forget it. There is only one God—and we do not believe in him!'"

Okay, that's a good example. However, isn't there an obvious difference between being Jewish by subscribing to a religious tradition or because tradition defines one as such, and being Jewish from the sole point of view of identity?

I do talk about this in the book and Freud wrestled with this question. I want things to be clear, because this kind of important point is difficult to make in general conversation. The fact that I tried to penetrate Freud's ideas on a whole range of subjects, including Judaism, religion, Jewish history, and anti-Semitism, doesn't mean in any way that I share a single one of his ideas. That is fundamental, otherwise I would be too far gone! I think his introduction from the 1930s to the Hebrew translation of *Totem and Taboo*[19] contains the most explicit statement of his thought. In this text, he says how happy the publication of his book in Hebrew makes him, and he addresses the question of his Jewishness. He writes this, more or less: "I'm not a Jew in the national sense, I'm not a Jew in the religious sense, and yet there is a kind of vague current in me that tells me I am a Jew. Perhaps one day science will manage to unravel the question of understanding my Jewishness." He defines his Judaism by default, *via negationis:*[20] I'm not Jewish in this or that way, but I am Jewish! What can I add to what he says? This type of paradoxical statement is frequently found in Freud.

In 1938 in Paris, at the last prewar European Congress of the International Psychoanalytical Association, Freud entrusted Anna[21] to read an excerpt from *Moses and Monotheism*, and not randomly, specifying one about Rabbi Yohanan ben Zakkai.[22]

We understand that he is likening Vienna to Jerusalem, and Freud is Rabbi Yohanan ben Zakkai. If he is forced to flee, the way his predecessor had to abandon Jerusalem, it isn't the end of the story. Something can be built from that point onward. This was Freud's message of hope. Was it a Jewish hope? In any case, the context of Europe in 1938 led him to believe it for Jews and psychoanalysis.

7
DERRIDA

Did your interactions with Jacques Derrida begin with his writing about your Freud?[1]

Indeed, that added depth to our interactions, but I had already read his book before we met. I have a fairly large collection of his works because at one time, I received every book he published at Galilée,[2] and he published a lot. I must confess that to this day, I still don't fully understand them. I think that part of the problem I have, not just with Derrida but many modern French thinkers—Lacan isn't a good example—is that I lack solid philosophical training from the French perspective. So certain developments in philosophy, linguistics, and psychoanalysis written in French, a language whose clarity I have always noted, seem opaque to me.

Here's a story about Lacan: In the early 1980s, shortly after *Zakhor* was published in French, I was invited for the first time to lecture in France as part of an annual, solemnly titled Colloquium of Jewish French-speaking Intellectuals.[3] The meeting's theme was obviously about memory, which is why they invited me.[4] During a break, a nice young woman whom I didn't know approached me and asked offhandedly: "Mr. Yerushalmi, do you know Lacan?" I had decided once and for all that with questions of this kind, I would no longer beat around the bush. So I admit, "Yes, I've read him, but I didn't understand anything." She looked at me with an air of pity and commiseration, put her hand on my shoulder, and said to me unforgettably, "Well sir, that's because you *read* him!"

It took me a while to figure out what she meant. Reading Lacan isn't enough. If you hadn't the privilege of attending his seminars, you couldn't understand him.

As for Derrida, certain things elude me in his texts, but I understand others and even find them essential. But we had never met before a certain conference in England in 1994. Things took an incongruous turn. My lecture was ready and I was in London, but the day before the proceedings began, I took to my bed with the flu. So I gave my text to an English psychoanalyst who read it for me while I was shut up in my room. At the end of the day—we were all staying at the same hotel and people came and went—someone said to me, "You know, Derrida spoke today and mentioned you at great length." I was astonished. And everyone I spoke to later assured me that he did so in positive terms and I should feel honored that Derrida had spent so much time talking about me, or more precisely about my *Freud's Moses*, during his long lecture. Yet I left London without meeting Derrida.[5] A bit later, he sent me his book *Archive Fever*. Finally I was able to read what he had said and discovered that in fact, a significant part of his book was devoted to my *Freud*. I read it carefully with moments of great exaltation, because Derrida was a truly original spirit. Of course, I would never have thought, as Derrida had, to compare my way of speaking to Freud at the end of the monologue with the way Hamlet speaks with his father's ghost. And this comparison turned out to be invaluable to me. So I wrote him a letter of praise, in which, naturally, I called him "my ideal reader." That's how it all started, through the intermediary of these two books.

After this exchange, when Derrida visited the United States—which he did often because he was better received there than in France, or at least his success was more lasting there—we finally met. I no longer recall if we had dinner or a coffee together, but we had a long conversation. For the occasion, I twice reread the passages about my book on Freud and discovered that he had written things that I just couldn't accept. Especially the claim that in the last chapter, I stopped being a researcher and historian. Of course, all readers have the right to their own opinions, but as I said, I was surprised that this sort of criticism came from Derrida. In my naivete, in this last chapter I chose to adopt a style as a rhetorical strategy and nothing more. But who knows? Since we are sometimes oblivious to our deepest intentions, someone else may reveal them to us. What bothered me more was his interpretation of a text I had quoted in my *Freud*, the dedication in Hebrew that Jacob Freud wrote in the Philippson Bible[6] that he gave to his son for his thirty-fifth birthday.

This text, taken up by Derrida in *Archive Fever*, is difficult for the uninitiated reader to understand because of its Talmudic style. That is, it consists of a real mosaic of biblical quotations that take on new meaning when juxtaposed. Jacob Freud's inscription begins: "Be-sheva be-yemei shenei hayeikha," a biblical expression that literally means "On the seventh of the days of the years of your life," or "at the age of seven years." Jacob Freud was telling his son: "At the age of seven, we started studying the Bible together, and that permitted you to find a framework for marvelous things."

The father's message essentially says: "You have abandoned this Bible, but today I am giving it back to you." The obvious question is, why write a dedication in Hebrew for someone who doesn't read the language? But Derrida didn't ask that. He preferred to interpret it as a lengthy allusion to circumcision. In fact, in his dedication, Jacob Freud points out that he has united the Philippson Bible's two volumes with a leather binding, using the Hebrew word *'or* (skin). Derrida preferred not to think of leather, but rather a different skin, foreskin, connecting it to the mention of the "seventh day" at the start of the dedication. So when we met, we basically talked about this. I told him that I knew that there were different ways of interpreting a text, that I knew all these debates, and that I even knew a few things about deconstruction, but with the best will in the world, it was necessary to admit that the seventh day of a life could not refer to circumcision. Seven is clearly written and not eight, and circumcision is done on the eighth day after birth, not the seventh. Had Jacob Freud consciously or unconsciously wished to refer to circumcision, he would never have made this mistake. He would have written eight and not seven, that's all. Arguing otherwise was like cauterizing a wooden leg.

Was this an obstacle between you?

I was attracted to something about this man's personality, conduct, and manner of speech, and from that day on, we became friends. I would not go so far as to say that I entered the circle of his closest friends, and although I don't know any details, his relationship with Levinas[7] was probably more intimate. After all, we were usually separated by an ocean. However, we stayed in touch and we saw each other from time to time in New York.[8] But we only met publicly on one rather odd occasion, during an evening hosted by a philosophy professor at The New School for Social Research. That evening, a public debate was to take place between Jacques Derrida, Richard Bernstein,[9] and me. I don't recall if Freud had been mentioned as the debate's subject, but the fact remains that I hadn't really written a text for the occasion. I just jotted down a few quotes intended for use and I didn't do very well, because I got stuck reading the quotes.

At one point, I said about a Derridean idea:

"To paraphrase Mark Twain, all the reports that the author no longer exists are greatly exaggerated." It was clumsy of me, and in his speech Derrida quite rightly replied, "I never claimed that the author doesn't exist." This was the only public encounter I had with Derrida.

In *Pirkei Avot*,[10] there is a saying (5:17) that accurately sums up how I consider our friendship and interaction: "Kol mahloket shehi le-shem shamayim sofah lehitkayem" ("Every dispute that is for the sake of Heaven [or truth], will in the end endure; but one that is not for the sake of Heaven, will not endure.")

I really feel that we weren't opponents, but something went beyond us both. The philosopher criticized certain issues in my book, particularly my indictment of what I call Freud's psychological Lamarckism, or the idea that acquired elements stemming from individual life experience may be inherited by descendants. In my view, Freud got caught in this trap as he did with his theory of the murder of the primitive father and his hypothesis about the murder of Moses in the desert.

I never wrote about Derrida. I never answered him in writing, but I know what I saw in him. He was frightfully impressive. It's purely subjective, but I really felt that this man was living an authentic philosophical life. I believe that he was one of the rare philosophers I met who was palpably imbued with philosophy to his fingertips and for whom philosophical problems were really his problems. And he had a charismatic personality, what more can I say? When he visited Columbia University one year after September 11, 2001, he spoke to a vast audience with complete spontaneity, without any text. At certain moments, it was clear that each attendee was utterly moved by this man.

Among his books, the one I prefer is *Adieu to Emmanuel Levinas*, neither a philosophical nor a deconstructionist text.[11] But were I to wonder what he saw in me, any answer might be difficult. In fact, I wonder why he had these interactions with me. This man, who could converse with important people around the world, took the time to write to me and visit me during his visits to New York. This isn't false modesty. Derrida knew everyone and everyone knew Derrida in Europe and in America alike. So why talk to me? I have my theory about this; his need to visit me was directly linked to the question of his Jewish identity. I think that for him, it was a real problem that remained unresolved. I think—again, I don't know details of his rapport with Levinas and I don't even know what Levinas might have said about this—that for him, I represented a Jewish intellectual who knew a lot of Jewish history and who certainly had all kinds of Jewish problems, but not about basic identity. An individual who, although I didn't understand his complete works, was intellectually equipped to converse with him.

Sometimes we spoke about his Jewishness. One day, I returned to our dispute about circumcision, because he had published *Circonfession*[12] and told me that he hadn't circumcised his own son. I said:

"I don't know much about your life, but I do know the few things that you mentioned about your experience in Algeria. I can understand that at thirteen, when your parents forced you to take bar mitzvah preparation courses and you had to phonetically memorize Hebrew that made no sense, it was just a tedious duty. I can easily understand that you hated the whole thing, which didn't make Judaism dear to your heart. I can understand that when the Vichy regime was installed in Algeria and you were expelled from school, it left a deep scar. But why worry about circumcision? Who remembers his own circumcision? No one ever said to me, 'My circumcision was an unforgettably grisly experience!'" I don't recall his reply, but it wasn't really convincing.

In his last book, *Learning to Live Finally*,[13] which you just gave me, I discovered another aspect of his paradoxical relationship to Jewishness. To the question, "You say you don't like to say 'we'" (in reference to the expression "we Jews"), Derrida agrees that generally he does not like to say "we," although he sometimes uses this pronoun. Then he adds, speaking about Jewishness, that Israel no longer represents Judaism, the diaspora, or original Zionist movements today, because they were manifold: "Well, in spite of all that and so many other problems I have with my 'Jewishness,' I will never deny it. I will always say, in certain situations, 'we Jews.'"[14] By the way, I only read this yesterday, and I don't know exactly if he's referring to the State of Israel or the Israeli government. Of course, I would prefer if he was referring to the government.

In this context, I'm not sure he makes any distinction.

Nor do I, but no matter. In any case, he goes further than Freud, who despite claiming in the introduction to *Totem and Taboo* not to be Jewish by nationality, approved the colonization and reconstruction of *Eretz Yisrael*,[15] starting in the 1930s. Yet Derrida also defines matters *via negationis* when he states, "I am not a Jew like this or that, but all the same, I'm Jewish." Which I don't believe he needed to do. The fact that people will always remind him of it has nothing to do with the issue. I believe that a person of that stature can make his own decisions, whatever reactions they may elicit. If an American Jewish writer tells me, "I'm not a Jewish writer," all right, I accept it, why not?

Anyway, those were our interactions. Then he became ill, and I knew it was serious. Pancreatic cancer. I spoke to him on the phone one summer, and he told me that his medical treatment was difficult. He must have endured terrible suffering. Maybe his death was a relief. In any case, I regret that I couldn't say a real goodbye.

Among your Columbia University colleagues,
have you had the opportunity to meet Edward Said?

Barely. You could say that I met him "technically," but I never spoke to him. When I arrived at Columbia in 1980, he was already the Parr Professor of English and Comparative Literature. Full of goodwill, I tried to contact him three times. The first time, I invited him to a conference on messianism; he didn't come. The second time, I invited him to a biennial conference cycle; he didn't come to that either. The third time, I tried a strategy. Back then, no one at Columbia taught modern Hebrew literature. Arabic literature studies were mainly limited to the medieval era. So I suggested that we two combine efforts to establish posts of modern Arabic and modern Hebrew literatures. He didn't reply, so I gave up. On the other hand, my wife Ophra who is a pianist spoke with him now and then, when they crossed paths at the campus market. He probably knew she was a musician, and he was too, in some ways, so they had common ground.

I've read some of his books, including, of course, *Orientalism.*[16] Although today this book has reached near-iconic status, I still think it is full of errors. Moreover, he is deeply unfair in dealing with an area he partly created—Western research on Islam and the Middle East—when he deliberately ignores all authors who do not conform to his theory on colonialism and postcolonialism. To take just one example, he doesn't say a word about the nineteenth-century Jewish orientalists Abraham Geiger,[17] Carl Paul Caspari,[18] and above all Ignaz Goldziher,[19] rightly considered as one of the founders of modern Islamic studies, but whom Said, as I recall, doesn't even mention. Of course, Goldziher never wrote about colonization, inferiority, or anything like that. There were also non-Jewish Arabs who fully identified with their subject. First of all, Louis Massignon, the French Arabist who wrote *The Passion of Al-Hallaj.*[20] Massignon's stature was such that I believe he was the only European allowed to speak and preach at Cairo's Al-Azhar Mosque. True, he did not convert to Islam, but neither did many others. That is my primary reproach for Said.

There is a second one, too. Unlike him, as director of the Center for Israel and Jewish Studies, I've always been careful not to politicize things, to ensure that the university doesn't become yet another battlefield. I kept quiet, even when Said did things I deeply disapproved of, that shocked me. I especially remember that after the assassination of Sadat,[22] Said was interviewed by one of the major television channels. The reporter asked him, "What do you think about the fact that Sadat was murdered?" He replied succinctly, "I think he deserved it!" A real provocation. I always thought that Said's refusal to meet me was tied to the fact that I ran the Center for Israel and Jewish Studies. If its name had only been Center for Jewish Studies, I believe he would have agreed to speak with me.

The story has an epilogue. *Freud and the Non-European*, his final book or rather lecture, genuinely shocked me.[22] Based mostly on *Moses and Monotheism*, Said addresses Israelis but also Jews in general to tell them that Freud was really a great man. How so? Because Freud renounced Moses's Jewish identity and called him an Egyptian. Said takes up a notion developed by Isaac Deutscher, an old Trotskyist, in *The Non-Jewish Jew*.[23] For Said, Freud identified as a non-Jewish Jew. But, he continues, Israelis (and, in fact, all Jews, since Deutscher's argument that he cites addresses all Jews) cannot. The rest of his text is written in an incredibly arrogant tone. By the way, he mentions my book and misspells my first name as Josef, giving it a slight Central European air. He compliments me by claiming that mine is likely the most sophisticated attempt to analyze Freud's Jewish identity, before concluding that if non-Jewish Jews can exist, what about non-Palestinian Palestinians? Has this anything to do with the response to my *Freud*? At least it can be said that he read it.

8

NEW YORK: 1939–1945

What memories do you have of the Second World War, when you were still quite young?

I wasn't that young. Some children are more childish than others. I was thirteen when the war ended. And by 1943, my parents had heard what was happening from the circles they frequented, and they told me promptly. The information filtered informally but quickly, right down to our camps, by which I mean summer camps. I recall that in one, an offshoot of the Yiddishist Sholem Aleichem group rather than a politically oriented camp, on Tisha B'Av[1] the director read a list of extermination camps: Auschwitz, Majdanek, and so on. These things were known at home. We were made aware of the Warsaw Ghetto Uprising, and we talked a lot about it. I don't know by what specific channel the information reached my parents, but my father belonged to several Jewish organizations. Hitler's horror was ubiquitous. I remember that one day before the United States entered the war, I was with my mother on Manhattan's Upper East Side and we passed by the district of Yorkville, then mainly a German neighborhood. We heard a distant brass band at what seemed to be a demonstration. Suddenly men appear, parading in black shirts; I don't recall if they were wearing swastikas. I can still see my mother's fear when she saw this procession. She pushed me into the subway, and we went home. After we got back, I asked who those people were. She replied that they were Nazis, and explained who they were and what Hitler was doing to the Jews. In the 1930s, long before the ashes of destruction, I remember attending a gigantic meeting with my parents organized by the American Jewish Congress to call for a boycott of German products.[2] Rabbi Stephen Wise, the Reform rabbi and Zionist leader, spoke. This happened long before the concentration camps opened. Everyone was talking about the events in Germany. We knew what was going on.

At the time, there were four or five Yiddish daily newspapers in New York, including *Forverts* [The forward], *Morgen Freiheit* [Morning freedom] *Der Tog* [The day] and the *Morgn Zshurnal* [Morning journal]. In one of them, a daily illustrated section appeared, headlined *Haynt in der yiddisher geshikhte* [Today in Jewish history]. This section only presented tragic events that happened to the Jews, a pogrom here, a pogrom there, and so on. It was absolutely terrifying. We were really at the heart of what Baron called the "lachrymose conception of Jewish history," as a series of sufferings and persecutions. A member of my family, perhaps an uncle, had the habit of cutting out the newspaper headlines and pasting them into a notebook. The notebook was sent to my parents, who gave it to me. I was seven or eight years old at the time. This shows that early on, we were well informed and discussed the subject frequently.

Immediately after the war, when refugees started to arrive, my mother became involved in welcoming them. One of the closest places to our home was an orphanage in the Bronx, where teenaged orphans were lodged. My mother prepared packages for them and I accompanied her to distribute them. I never spoke to any of them; they seemed strange. Then, little by little, I started to meet survivors. I can't say anything about my own family's fate. My mother's side had already left Europe; as for my father's, I still have no idea what happened to them. Were they captured during the Nazi advance on the Russian front? To this day, I have no idea. But as for the rest, we knew what was going on.

In a sense, you didn't have to discover the destruction of European Jews, since you always knew, growing up with this knowledge.

Yes and no. In 1954, the first book I read about the Holocaust had just been translated into English. It was Léon Poliakov's excellent *Harvest of Hate*.[3] I met Poliakov once and only briefly, sorry to say; he was an interesting man.

Is there a relationship between the destruction of European Jews and your choice to work with Jewish history?

Absolutely none. I know it may sound odd, but the answer is no. Perhaps because I never thought of becoming a Holocaust historian, not even as a possibility.

Why not?

Probably for several reasons. One was that I felt the need to delve much further into the past than the contemporary destruction of the Jews. Even to understand that phenomenon, we needed to go back further. For example, I give an annual course on anti-Judaism and anti-Semitism from a historical perspective, to understand modern anti-Semitism.

I don't know what would've happened had my parents been survivors. I can't even imagine. But as we've already said, although I'm the son of Russian Jews, as an academic I didn't choose to study European Judaism. Until now, the Holocaust has challenged me with problems it poses for everyone and myself as an individual. Above all, the Holocaust forces me to ask the fundamental question at the heart of *Zakhor*: what do we remember and what do we forget? This question is already posed in Nietzsche's *Untimely Meditations*.[4] After *Zakhor* was translated into French, a conference was held at Royaumont[5] entitled *Uses of Forgetting*,[6] a very French title, incidentally; to resolve memory, we start by forgetting. On this occasion, I raised the problem of memory of the Holocaust, without formulating any genuine solution.

I'm not sure how, and to what extent, we must remember the Holocaust. I do know that hyperemphasis on the Holocaust has always made me uncomfortable. First of all, for the surreptitious distortion it inflicts on Jewish history; secondly, for the consequences it has on American Jewish identity, which today, as far as I can see, is based on two elements, neither of which deriving from indigenous creativity: the Holocaust and Israel, with particular emphasis on the former. That's it, the entire content of that identity. I've never given a course devoted specifically to the Holocaust, but always approached it in an annual course on modern Jewish history. I refuse to teach the way the Jews died to students who have no idea about the way they lived, even without going far back in time.

9

WHO MAKES HISTORY? QUESTIONS OF INTERPRETATION

Your personal commitment is tangible in your teaching and research. Is there a Yerushalmi historical method?

I've already mentioned that my Jewishness was the decisive reason why I devoted myself to Jewish history. It wasn't the only reason, but it's central, and this existential quest continues with me today. When I'm asked why I chose Jewish history and I answer this way, I almost always hear the same response: "So how can your research be objective?"

Because you identify as a Jew in history?

As a Jew, of course, but especially as a historian who studies history for highly personal reasons. My answer is that I don't think this poses a fundamental problem. I have had students of all origins. I've directed as many theses for non-Jewish students as for Jewish students. I've supervised theses in Germany as well as one for a young non-Jewish Polish woman. I continue to state that my Jewish identity isn't an epistemological obstacle. Imagine two historians, one French and the other Polish, who plan to write about Napoleon. Both obviously seek a certain degree of objectivity. Why wouldn't that be the case for a Jewish historian, even an exceedingly Jewish one, who researches Jewish history?

Especially since, in my view, neither history nor literature are written with a universal intent. We can sometimes attain the universal, but only through what is specific. So, to use an example that is dear to me, who is more English and more universal than Shakespeare? Who is more French and more universal than Molière? In my opinion, the problem of objectivity is inherent in the concept of historical work. I believe that historical work permanently oscillates between the capacity to identify with one's subject and the faculty of keeping it at a distance, so that one may reidentify with it and keep it at a distance in a perpetual pendulum movement.

Would you say that you wanted to produce a specific work as a historian of the Jews?

In any case, I never dreamt of being a second Baron, any more than I dreamt of writing even a single volume on Jewish history as a whole. The education my parents gave me bestowed the confidence, or perhaps daring, to take up a theme and follow its progress through each historical period. For example, that's what I did with *Zakhor*; because in my case, the theme initiates the subject. If the subject grips me, I will seek its manifestation in all periods of history. Sometimes I can't find what I'm looking for, especially since I don't know some languages. I read Latin, but not Greek, which can be an obstacle in studying certain epochs.

To return to the example of the Marranos, would you say that the marranist phenomenon can be seen in every era?

In theory, absolutely. In practice, this represents archival work across every era and country, and a single human lifetime wouldn't suffice. I met an Israeli academic, Nadia Zeldes, who researched in the Sicilian archives, which have always fascinated me. She wrote a beautiful book, *The Former Jews of this Kingdom*,[1] dealing with Jews who converted after the expulsion of 1492 from Spain; indeed, Sicily was Spanish at the time. Converts already existed then, so there were Marranos and, naturally, an Inquisition. I went to Palermo just to see those archives, but could never have produced the work she's done.

Can't the Marrano experience of concealing religious beliefs or identity be found among Jews of any era in Christian and Islamic nations?

During the Arab conquests, Jews weren't forced to convert. Many centuries later, under the Safavids, there are Marranos in Persia, especially in Mashhad and Isfahan. In short, for me, all this has no importance. I don't want to, nor do I do like to, consider Marranos except in the strict sense of the term, meaning those of the Iberian Peninsula and Sicily, for example. Certainly, many phenomenological parallels exist between marranism in Spain and Portugal and other historical Jewish experiences. That's what I tried to show in an essay on the relationship between anti-Semitism in medieval Spain and Portugal and nineteenth-century Germany.[2] But these parallels only become relevant after the difference between assimilation processes in the medieval and modern eras is truly understood.

In the Middle Ages, conversion was the sole means of entering non-

Jewish society. Strikingly, the massive entry of Jews into non-Jewish society as Christians or Germans, rather than Jews, is initially successful from the point of view of non-Jewish society, but then the movement suddenly reverses. Which implies a shift in hatred from a religious basis to a racial one. Being racist doesn't necessarily mean using the modern word or concept of race. Whenever we say that a group or people whom we hate has unchangeable qualities, we are being racist without using the word race.

Although the word "race" itself is already present in Spain, the development of racist thinking is one of the main components of the debate during the French Revolution about granting full citizenship to Jews. Those in favor shared one thing in common with those who were against: neither loved Jews as they defined them.

Nor did Jews love themselves under the conditions of the time, at least some Jews . . .

Admittedly, this was true for some trailblazers, particularly the *Maskilim*.[3] In any case, the essential difference between advocates and opponents of emancipation was that the former thought that if Jews were given citizenship status, their particularism would vanish by itself, while opponents claimed that since the Jewish character was unchangeable, this status wouldn't change anything. I summed up the problem in the form of a question in seminars I taught in Paris over twenty years ago: Did the Jews create their own history, or did history create the Jews? If history made the Jews, then altering history means changing the Jews.

In reality, the choice is obviously not as clear cut as this cursory choice would suggest. I personally believe, although I can't prove it, that for the most part, Jews made their history, but that doesn't mean that they haven't been deeply affected by non-Jewish history. For example, the aforementioned Muslim conquest greatly affected the history and social status of the Jews.

It conspicuously influenced their social condition and religious world.

Absolutely. And now we can say that Ashkenazi Jews weren't cut off from their environment either, although we tend to see Ashkenazi Judaism as more on the fringes of medieval Christian society than Sephardic Judaism during the same era. Baron had a fine formula to illustrate this truth, evoking the idea bolstered by nineteenth-century historians that external relations are decisive in national histories. He argued that anti-Semitism is one aspect of external relations for Jewish people. It's a splendid classification for anti-Semitism, removing the emotional and mythical aura usually surrounding it.

Indeed, it's downplayed. The longstanding, well-established problem is that if we disregard tragic events in Jewish history, such as the Babylonian captivity; persecutions by Antiochus; the destruction of the Temple; Almohad fanaticism; the Crusades; the Inquisition; and the Expulsion, we're faced with an almost total lack of events, or at least lengthy epochs when nothing appears to happen. These voids may translate to times of interdependence without ill will, but sources are lacking to prove that all goes well. Isn't that why the Jewish history we hear appears to be mostly forged from these bad interactions?

I'm not sure we can say that about the range of sources available on Jewish history.

The problem remains of how sources are used. A number of them are still untapped, because they haven't been perceived, conceived, or identified as potential sources. This is the case with rabbinical literature, especially responsa,[4] as well as commercial sources about markets and trade fairs. The latter non-Jewish sources are found in registers maintained in small villages. Now teams of German researchers are practicing regional history, which involves studying medieval archives of small villages. From these sources, they make fascinating discoveries about the early Middle Ages, always considered as an era for which documentation was scarce. By looking differently at the sources we know, or looking for them in other repositories, new information can still be discovered. Perhaps one day we'll be able to fill in the blank spots and voids in Jewish history.

In other words, it's about looking at things from the bottom upward rather than the top downward. Yes, I admit there's a fundamental problem and I completely agree. It interests me a lot, but as far as I'm concerned, I wouldn't favor this method, although I don't criticize it because I believe it's useful. Besides, you know that in Italy, even the smallest town has archives in which are sometimes found hundreds of documents about the Jews. But nothing there is catalogued, so it is necessary to look, and look some more. A whole army would be needed to catalogue it someday.

In my old age, I'm mostly concerned that an alternative way of conceiving and writing history should appear. Ultimately, it hardly matters whether literary sources or archives are drawn from. My academic path has changed, even if I haven't had time to write about this new conception of historiography. For this reason, I applaud *Mythistory* by Joseph Mali.[5] In my opinion, after this book we can no longer write history as we did before. This work's method consists in taking one idea per chapter and studying the way authors such as Jacob Burckhardt, Aby Warburg, Ernst Kantorowicz, and Walter Benjamin treated it. It's extremely interesting. Before knowing Mali's work, I had thought of writing a book of this kind and making it the theme of my lectures in Jerusalem. I even jotted down the compound word "mythistory" in my notebook. One day I saw an advertisement from the University of Chicago Press in the *New York Review of Books* about a new book, *Mythistory*. I ordered it immediately.

It's a method for handling thematics, but what about sources?

I believe that scholars from the time of Wissenschaft des Judentums, and even those from post-Wissenschaft until today, assumed that when a text or historical source is discovered, it must be legitimately approached with a "hermeneutic of suspicion," as Paul Ricoeur remarked about Freud.[6] Thus we are modern critical historians, because each text and document is a priori considered to be suspect. We start by reading, demonstrating, and adding other texts. In any event, we discover that the story or text or documents don't embody absolute truth. Perhaps there are a few specks of history, but everything else refers to the legendary or mythological. We shed this mythology, proud to have discovered that there are so many legends and mythologies in what previous generations considered absolute truth.

All told, today we no longer believe in the truth as a principle. We only think in terms of relative authenticity, perhaps as an avatar of the Einsteinian revolution?

I agree with your analysis. But now I aspire to use these mythologies and legends in writing Jewish history. One day I suddenly realized it, thinking to myself, "You've studied Jewish history for so many years and what do you really know about Jews of the past? Almost nothing. You had a grandmother who was born in Pinsk. But what do you really know about life, thought, and imagination of these Jews from Pinsk, how they perceived the city and the world? Almost nothing." The story is hidden in myths and legends. That's not to say that historical facts are unimportant. The first step of any investigation must undoubtedly consist of verifying anything mythological. But it shouldn't be immediately rejected. Ordinary people had these beliefs, and, as far as they believed, their lives were guided accordingly. We don't understand it because we are too far from it all and we don't think it's part of our job. So don't arbitrarily choose between myth and history. We should develop history that gathers and considers myths.

Can a parallel be drawn to the controversy over history, memory, history or memory, as well as history and memory?

There is so much to say about historical and collective memory. But it isn't the same question as with mythology. In Tübingen, I gave a press conference that took an odd turn when a complete ass of a reporter inquired: "Herr Professor, would you kindly tell us how you plan to spend your money?" I automatically replied that first of all, half would go directly to the state coffers and that I hadn't decided about the other half. Then a second journalist asked, and this relates to the question you just mentioned, if I had seen the new Memorial to the Murdered Jews of Europe in Berlin. Basically, he wanted to know if I thought this memorial was necessary. I evaded the question, which is really about how and what exactly to remember, not just remembrance. Two years ago, an association of museum curators invited Leon Wieseltier and myself to speak on the theme, "The Museum and the Jewish Past." I improvised on what a Jewish museum is or should be, what is the function of a Jewish museum? what to display and how? It's not enough to say that tourists walking around New York should visit a museum just because it is Jewish, they have to understand something too.

10

A JEWISH KID FROM THE BRONX AT HARVARD AND COLUMBIA

Let's return to your career. How did you become a professor?

When the 1964–1965 academic year was over, I wasn't sure that my research was finished and I could buckle down to writing the thesis. I was thirty-four or so, old enough by American standards. I think I could've easily waited another three years before starting to write the thesis if two events hadn't occurred during the summer of 1965. I was in the countryside when I received a postcard from Baron, stating: "I am retiring at the end of the next academic year. If you still want your thesis to be accepted under my supervision, now is the time to finish it." When I returned to campus in September, I was told that suddenly and unexpectedly, Harvard was going to create an assistant professorship in Jewish History and was willing to hire me starting in June or July, under the express condition that I had received the doctorate. I believe that Baron had been in touch with them.

Never in my life had I worked so hard or so fast. I thought to myself, "In seven months, I must do seven chapters." I took all my notes and organized them into chapters. I must admit that since then, I've never written as fluently. I hardly had to make any corrections. After seven months, I gave Baron six or seven hundred pages. About two weeks later, Baron returned my text with a single spelling correction, which in practical terms meant that I had my doctorate. Incidentally, Columbia University Press awarded a prize for best university thesis from all faculties, which included publication. I won the award and wanted to add two chapters to the published thesis; it took two years to write them.

You've had careers at Harvard and Columbia, two of America's most prestigious universities. Can you explain this flawless academic progress?

The first thing to emphasize is the personality of Isadore Twersky,[1] who brought me to Harvard. Wolfson's successor, he incredibly managed to represent two distinct, and usually opposed, worlds. He held high university positions and was also heir to the Tolna Hasidic dynasty as a descendent of Rabbi Menachem Nochum Twersky of Chernobyl. The very morning in 1972 when his father died, he became Talner Rebbe[2] of the Boston synagogue; this didn't prevent him from teaching concurrently as professor of Jewish literature and philosophy.

That he recruited someone like me, a Jew who, although not antireligious, was obviously not Orthodox either, shows a certain tolerance on his part. Baron's recommendation cannot fully account for it. I like to believe that we were somehow complementary. For many years, we handled the doctoral seminar together, without any hitches about choice of theme or allocation of sessions.

After only four years, I was promoted from assistant professor to full professor. Such good fortune was only possible because Harvard is Harvard. I'm not even sure that it would be possible at Harvard today. Needless to say, the intellectual and material wealth of Harvard makes the Widener Library the best university library in the world, even if it lacks the thousands of Hebrew manuscripts that Columbia owns. It's a marvelous place for every field of research, just incredible.

What's the defining feature of each university?

First, although they both established chairs of Jewish Studies, in 1925 at Harvard and 1930 at Columbia, before the Holocaust and the revival of Ethnic Studies, they have inherently different approaches to the field. At Harvard, all areas of Jewish Studies, including Jewish history, philosophy, Hebrew literature and language, form a single section within the same department of Near Eastern Languages and Civilizations. This may seem odd, since most of what I taught there has nothing to do with the Middle East. On the other hand, at Columbia, the study of Jewish religion is done within the framework of the Department of Religion, Jewish history in the Department of History, Yiddish in Germanic Languages and Literatures, and so on.

This difference is due to their historical background. Until the Second World War, Harry Wolfson was the sole professor at Harvard, directing a division called, as at many other universities, Semitic Studies. After the war, the use of the term "semitic" became problematic, and at some point it was replaced by "Near Eastern." Therefore, I was linked administratively to the Near Eastern Languages and Civilizations department, but in the Harvard course catalog, my class was affiliated with History. It made little difference to me, except on a symbolic level. When the École pratique des hautes études[3] in Paris awarded me an honorary doctorate as professor of the History of Judaism, I had the audacity to write to the École pratique's administration, asking them to change one detail. I explained that a distinction is made in America between Jewish history and the history of Judaism. I never got any reply.

Getting back to Harvard, what was it like to collaborate with Twersky?

The only significant difference in opinion that Twersky and I ever had was when we established the Center for Jewish Studies at Harvard after long years of negotiation with the university. The question arose of what specialty to choose for the Chair of Hebrew Literature. Given student expectations, I thought we needed a chair in modern Hebrew literature; Twersky believed that it must be in medieval Hebrew literature. In and of itself, I didn't disagree, but a choice had to be made and it seemed more urgent to have a chair of modern literature first. I don't remember any other basic dispute with him. I think that a chair in Hebrew literature was established without further specification.

As part of fundraising to create the center, I recall that Twersky and I traveled across the country. We visited Texas, San Francisco, places where I would never have set foot otherwise, and neither would he, for that matter. One day, at the top of a San Francisco skyscraper, someone pointed to the city below and said, "Do you see the people around you? All this belongs to them." I asked myself, "What am I doing here?" Fortunately, we were always accompanied by a university vice president, more experienced than ourselves in this kind of activity.

During my career at Harvard, I experienced other incongruous situations of this type, including lunches at the home of the mother of Derek Bok, Harvard's president. She lived in Bel Air, one of the most upscale Los Angeles neighborhoods. I knew chic areas of New York, which are already quite luxurious, but this! On the way there, the taxi driver said to me: "Oh, you're going there. I drove there last week. We had to send two taxis." I asked, "It's a big family?" He replied: "No, the second cab was just for luggage." When I met Derek Bok's mother, you know what she asked me? "How is my son coping with things?" Again I asked myself, "What am I doing here?"

In fact, I often asked myself this question at Harvard, as I identified it with what historically represents Anglo-Saxon New England, even in its architecture. I sometimes told myself: "Your class will be lamentable. What can you possibly do here?" I used to pinch myself and ask, "How did you get here? A little Jewish kid from the Bronx, with a name like yours, too." I never experienced any resentment, discord, or discrimination, God forbid. No, that all stopped at Harvard long before I got there. At the Harvard I knew, they used to say that in 1935, had a Jewish boy named Lenny Bernstein applied to Yale or Princeton, he probably would have been rejected, but Harvard accepted him.[4]

Nor was there any awkwardness with Arab colleagues in the department. The first time I was introduced to the department members by Twersky, he said, "This is Yosef Yerushalmi." One of them told me, "Oh, we have the same name!" Obviously, I didn't understand what he meant. He was an Arab, who left Harvard shortly after that. His name, George Makdisi, derived from Al-Quds.[5] So he was also a Yerushalmi or Hierosolymitan.[6] Our individual political views remained outside the university and departmental arenas, at least in my time. I left Harvard in 1980.

I often say to myself about my entire career that ironically, if I'd received a doctorate in English literature, I never would have been hired by Harvard because the competition is so tough in this field where there are so many candidates. There were far fewer students of Jewish history, and that's probably why I was lucky enough to land there. Anyway, having a full-time teaching position at Harvard meant my career was almost indestructible. Nothing could affect it unless I sabotaged it myself. When I was a doctoral student, I was already married and had to teach as part of my fellowship. Baron arranged for me get a job as an instructor, which is even less than an assistant professorship, on the main campus of Rutgers University in New Brunswick, northern New Jersey. At Rutgers, I used university stationery to write to publishers of interesting new books, asking for free copies. I never received one, I think, or perhaps only one. But when I wrote letters with the Harvard letterhead, I usually got all the books I asked for. Through this sort of tiny detail, I started to understand and appreciate the mythical value of Harvard. The university offered me everything I could have wanted. As was later the case at Columbia, my faculty friends were not generally from my department. Departmental colleagues were kind, but other than Twersky, I didn't make any real friends. Instead, I bonded with other people. So everything was fine until everything went too well.

What do you mean, "too well"?

I had a feeling, and my wife Ophra agreed, that Harvard would finally suffocate us. All of our lives revolved within the Harvard perimeter. From one point of view, Harvard suited Ophra better than New York, because there were the famous houses where students lived.[7] We were both connected with Eliot House, where she was a music fellow. So she could give recitals and lectures on music and narrative whenever she liked. She continued this activity in New York. But the fact was that our world was limited at Harvard.

In short, what else did I have to complain about? Two years before I left Harvard, a new chair was created. A Harvard alumnus friend of the well-known banker and philanthropist Edmond Safra convinced him to finance a chair in memory of his father. The Jacob E. Safra Chair in Jewish History and Sephardic Civilization was naturally attributed to me, given its title.

At the same time, I took over management of the Near Eastern Languages and Civilizations Department. So from a career perspective, there was absolutely nothing to complain about. We also had no shortage of friends. But I more or less felt a sort of indefinable feeling of immobility in this delicious situation.

In the past, Columbia had twice suggested that I return, but always at times when this was simply impossible. Still, the idea lingered. One weekend, Ophra went to New York to attend a friend's concert. On Saturday evening she phoned me, bursting with enthusiasm that was not just about the concert. She says, "Do you know who is here?" She began to recite a long list of friends who were dear to us, remaining so despite years of distance. I suddenly realized that we didn't have as many friends in Cambridge as in New York. So I immediately decided, because major decisions are made spontaneously rather than rationally, that when she returned on Sunday, I'd ask her directly: "Would you like to return to New York?" If she agreed, I was ready to immediately phone the chair of Columbia's History Department. And that's just what occurred. So what had to happen, happened.

Was it a sort of homecoming?

Indeed, I went "home," which surprised some people, because few choose to leave Harvard. But I didn't see this as an obstacle, especially since other professors left Harvard the year I did. It was quite odd. Not only was I returning to the university where I had spent a number of decisive years, but I was also going back to the same neighborhood of the Jewish Theological

Seminary, only six blocks away. Baron was still alive, as was his wife. I sensed the same maternal attitude in her that she had expressed, ever since the first time I visited her home to attend a seminar. It was pleasant.

How did you feel when you were back at Columbia to teach?

I felt what I often feel, a part of me can't get over the path my life has taken. I can see myself once more going up the lane toward Fayerweather Hall, to look at all those names on the doors. I never conceived that one day I could be at Columbia, or anywhere else, occupying a research chair as a professor, any more than I dreamed of teaching at Harvard. One might say that this return "home" was somewhat ambiguous, insofar as completing a circle by returning to the starting point raises the question of how little progress has been made in life. In the real world, I mean. On the other hand, our life has certainly changed in New York, becoming much more open. We spent time in groups well beyond Columbia, or even academia in general. That's how I was able to get involved with the group of psychoanalysts I worked with. That never would have happened had I stayed in Cambridge. It might have happened in Boston; but although Boston is just across the river, people from Cambridge don't often go there except for special concerts or social events, because Harvard and Cambridge are self-sufficient. Yes, when we left Boston for New York, our life changed for the better, and I have no regrets about returning to Columbia.

II

PROFESSOR YERUSHALMI

Do you guide your students' research
the same way that Baron guided yours?

Baron did not impose any epoch, subject, or even research theme on his students. Conversely, in recent years I have often seen PhD students, even among the brightest of them, visit me when it's time to write the thesis so that I can help them choose a subject. Generally, I always resisted such requests until I felt there was no way out.

Today's students may be different from those in the days when Baron was teaching, but I think I inherited from him a reluctance to impose a theme on someone else. I think that the only response to a research proposal is to ask if the chosen subject is warranted and productive. Baron would ask about that, but he never said, "Work on this or that." I witnessed only one exception, totally unrepresentative of his attitude. When I studied for my master's degree, he provided a thesis subject. I told him that I was interested in the South of France, and suddenly he suggested, "Why not research the question of relationship, or lack thereof, between the emergence of Kabbalah in twelfth-century Provence and Albigensian Gnostic heresies?" That's how I spent about nine months reading all the sources available. At the time, we had none of direct Albigensian or Cathar sources that have since been discovered. So I worked exclusively on sources deriving from their detractors. At the same time, I read everything to be found about the emergence of Kabbalah: Gershom Scholem's *Reshit ha-Kabbalah* (*Origins of the Kabbalah*) of course, which was later augmented in the edition published in German, *Ursprung und Anfänge der Kabbalah*,[1] and also *Sefer Ha-Bahir*.[2] After nine months of work, I found I was getting nowhere. Admittedly, I was able to draw a vague parallel between more- or less-pronounced Gnostic tendencies in Kabbalah and Catharism, but there was nothing to trace a direct relationship between the two. So I went to Baron and admitted, "I could write something, but all I'd be able to establish is that there was certainly 'something in the air,'" which I would later call turning "history into meteorology, and historians into weather forecasters."[3] He just said, "Very well," and let me choose another subject. This is only a detail, but it adds to the portrait of Baron's teaching.

How do you choose doctoral students?

Generally, I ask three questions. First, is the student linguistically equipped to do the research? Second, is the subject genuinely interesting? Which means, do unexamined sources or new perspectives remain to be discovered? Third, although a thesis topic is inherently limited, does the one chosen have wider implications? Can we learn from things that go beyond the subject itself? This third question is mainly intended to open a discussion.

Starting on the first day, I forbid my doctoral students to use the term "thesis." I explain, "When you start out writing a thesis, you end up writing a thesis. From the first moment, you must tell yourself that you are writing your first book not just for me and other jurors, but for interested and intelligent readers who, without being historians or even informed about your subject, should be able to read it with pleasure. All scholarship should be relegated to the notes, and the text itself should be legible. Even historical terminology should be considered from this viewpoint. Generally, I think I am rather successful. I believe that every single doctoral student published a "thesis" two or three years after graduation. And many, if not all, of these books have found readers.

Do you notice any difference between students you knew when you were a young teacher and the ones you meet today?

Absolutely. Whether at Harvard or Columbia, I was fortunate to have doctoral students who are undoubtedly among the elite of American students. This is obviously due to the universities, not to me. But I feel that there is a real difference. Of course, there are exceptions, and what I say now also applies to undergraduates, who are wonderful. They are no less intelligent than my first doctoral students, but they lack the general culture that we had in the 1960s. It's not their fault, it is due to education and the prevailing cultural climate. Today at Columbia I find a generation of students who generally don't value classical music. It's not a question of intelligence. Intelligence is there, witness the vast competition to enter these universities. But does culture still play an essential role?

Could this change be linked to ones more generally affecting the nature or position of the intellectual in society? If the intellectual and the academic are no longer much valued in society, symbolically speaking, does the wish to be an intellectual in the fullest sense of the term also recede?

This question involves several others. I must digress here to repeat that at Columbia, the situation is special; Jewish Studies never constituted a separate department, nor does it today. Each aspect of Jewish Studies may be approached in a particular department: Jewish history is found in the Department of History. For example, within the divisions of the history of Africa, China, and the Middle East, one can focus on the history of the Jews. I must be the oldest one in the department, and I don't think my new colleagues are less intellectual than those of my generation. On the other hand, they clearly have other conceptions and a completely different relationship to history.

Let's return to your students. Do the subjects they plan to study differ from those once handed in by their predecessors, in the direction and academic track guidance they suggest for Jewish Studies?

Yes, but that's also partly because I too have changed. Admittedly, I don't belong to the modernist avant-garde, but I also haven't been completely cut off from new trends emerging in historiography. For example, the history of women; when I started, such a subject didn't seem relevant to me. Today, this is no longer the case. Other questions are also arising.

I'd like to clarify a point that may be connected to the aforementioned issues of existential quest and objectivity. From when I started as a historian at the Jewish Theological Seminary, professors and students have all shared a certainty that insofar as there is a legitimate specificity of Jewish history, we all self-evidently accepted the rules of the game by adopting general historical methodology, or as we'd say today, different methodologies. In other words, it isn't justifiable or useful to develop a special methodology to study Jewish history.

This key choice was made by nineteenth-century positivist historians, and this is how Jewish history should be written, even when using resources of philological criticism, source criticism, or metacriticism. Likewise, it goes without saying that I'm happy when I see my students implementing new approaches in the Jewish Studies field. It has nothing to do with me individually, but with trends in today's historiographical environment that I've assimilated.

I'm thinking especially of the work of a brilliant young woman, who does "a history" rather than "the story" of something and addresses the important question of heresy in Judaism.[4] Starting with the salient theme of heresy, after much discussion, she defined and introduced the subject precisely. The theme is really new, even if for many years, one of my seminars has been on heretical messianic movements during the first centuries of Islam. Generally, we are doing a lot more social history than before. Social history was not invented either by the Annales school or postmodernists. However, we practiced another form of social history, a community history.

Conforming to what Baron did?

Yes, but we are touching on a central question to which I have no answer: should we consider that what Baron called "social and religious history" was really social history? In any case, it wasn't social history as we understand it today. Jacob Katz criticized Baron on this point.[5] What interests me deeply is the emphasis that Baron placed on the form of interaction that exists between the social and religious in Jewish history. In the title *A Social and Religious History of the Jews*, the term "religious" poses no problems, although the absence of the word "political" is troubling. I think that a political history of the Jews doubtless remains to be written.[6] And today we are starting to write this type of history.

I immediately think of the three volumes of source texts for use in a political history of the Jews edited by Walzer, Lorberbaum, and Zohar.[7]

Michael Walzer is indeed a great specialist in history and political theory. For example, one day it may be possible to write a history of Jewish diplomacy. Because what we call *shtadlanut*,[8] or intercession with a local power by certain individuals in favor of a Jewish community, is just a specific form of political diplomacy.

12

QUESTIONS OF HISTORY AND HISTORIOGRAPHY

You've worked alongside great masters of Jewish Studies. Can we discuss a few whom you haven't mentioned yet, such as Shelomo Dov Goitein?[1]

I did know him well, and I wrote one of many tributes to him when he died. His work is obviously monumental, and the title he gave it is of great importance as well as especially eloquent. He aptly entitled his work *A Mediterranean Society*, rather than *A Jewish Mediterranean Society*, because the sources he discovered in the Cairo Geniza[2] form a mirror beyond Jewish communities, revealing a mass of unknown information on all Mediterranean society of the time.

Earlier, you stated that Baron's idea of social history would not necessarily correspond to methodological criteria used in the sort of social history now being done. Would you say the same about Goitein's work?

No, probably because Goitein was limited to a specific region and time. But how can we speak of limits, given the scope of the work he did? He comprehensively studied all the aspects he had planned to explore in the Geniza materials. He also published a separate volume on education.[3]

And the fifth volume of A Mediterranean Society *is entirely devoted to the individual.*

To the individual, but somewhat indirectly. It can be said that much material exists relating to individuals among the social elite, but obviously there's much less about relatively unimportant individuals. Anyway, this book has so much insight into everyday life that it really doesn't matter. Not just elite lives are evoked, but the life of Jewish merchants in communities are discovered, as well as concerns about charity and the daily life of the poor.

Haim Hillel Ben-Sasson[4] *is another author I'd like you to discuss because I have the impression that he is a bit neglected today.*

I knew him too. Haim Hillel Ben-Sasson was an important historian, but sometimes problematic, in my view. Let me explain. He did good things, especially his monographs. His study of the Jews and the Reformation is superb.[5] But he sometimes tended to generalize a bit excessively, going far beyond what the data really permitted. Take a subject I know well, Jewish historiography in the Middle Ages. I insisted that, with some exceptions, historiography as a genre wasn't in use among medieval Jews. However, in *Historians and Historical Schools*, lectures delivered at the Historical Society of Israel, Haim Hillel Ben-Sasson divides medieval Jewish historiography into different eras.[6] I'll skip the details, but for example he proposed as periodization: "Tenth century: the *Chronicle of Ahimaaz* and *Yosippon*."[7] But there is no connection between the *Chronicle of Ahimaaz* and *Yosippon*. The latter obviously belongs to the historiographical genre, but it would be much more difficult to categorize the *Chronicle of Ahimaaz*. Officially, it's a family chronicle that also contains historical information.

This brings us back to debates following the publication of Zakhor. *Some said that what you call "history," or more precisely "historiography," was part of an approach that didn't exist before the nineteenth century, so it was logical that you didn't find any trace of it in medieval Jewish literature, for example.*

I never said that nothing historiographical existed during the Middle Ages. The works I've already mentioned—*Yosippon* and the four Jewish chronicles of the Crusades[8]—are obviously historiographical sources. To them we must add a genre that I highlighted particularly, the chain of tradition: so-and-so taught so-and-so, who then taught so-and-so. This genre, already present in the opening of *Pirkei Avot*,[9] lasts throughout the Middle Ages until the start of the eighteenth century. It's the only historiographical tradition that has remained alive, unlike the tradition of the Bible, which is a marvelous historiographical document. As for Flavius Josephus, his works were not even preserved by the Jews. The central idea of *Zakhor* was this: Jews didn't produce much historiography because they had no need to write history, insofar as History was self-explanatory, referring to the model of exile set in the Talmudic era. Exile could be better or worse, but remained exile.

You mentioned chronicles of the Crusades. Currently, the use of these chronicles as historiographical sources is questioned. Some researchers claim that they are essentially literary in genre and as such, dubious sources that should no longer be considered reliable historical documents.

Just because they are denied the status of works by *historians* doesn't mean that they should be denied all value as *historical* documents. For my part, historiography is also a literary genre, but I have an extremely broad definition of it. I am always wary of confusing reflections on history, philosophy of history, and meditations on history with historiography as such. There's an abundant Jewish literature in these areas, but I wouldn't call it historiography. For me, a work cannot be seen as historiographical if the author merely refers in detail to historical events in their time and place. For that matter, we don't need it to be a real chronicle. Dry chronologies and plain lists can be part of it. These lists, which may be boring, are a form of historiography in their own right.

By contrast, the works of the Maharal of Prague,[10] or Abravanel, which are full of deep reflections on Jewish history, do not fit into a historiographical framework. Abravanel announces somewhere that he has written, or is going write, a chronicle entitled *Yemot 'olam* [Days of yore]. We don't know if he ever wrote it or if it's been lost. In any case, we have no record of it. His introductions to biblical commentary remain in the category of exegesis, although he mentions events from his personal life and the time of the Expulsion as well as developing a theory about comparative merits of monarchies and republics in his reading of the Books of Samuel and Kings.

I once wondered where and when historical writing began. Trying to go back further than Sumer intellectually, I arrived at a slightly crazy theory: if writing history means leaving a tangible record of something that has happened, it's possible that this beginning is linked to death. But I didn't pursue the inquiry as far back as prehistory. I don't know where or when the first stones used to denote tombs were discovered, or the first cave paintings that recorded an event. Were the hands found in the earliest cave paintings intended to remind those to whom they had belonged? Were the hunting scenes a memory of an event? I don't know. But it's an idea in my head that annoys me from time to time, that the origin of history can be linked to awareness of death.

13
THE COLLECTOR

Over the years, you've amassed an impressive collection of rare books, making an invaluable library. How did it start?

My parents were great readers. They read all the time, in Hebrew, Russian, and Yiddish. But my father, who had a real passion for books, could never purchase a library worthy of the name, or even dream of having one, first of all because our apartment was too small, especially during the seven years when my grandmother lived with us. I'm convinced that in other circumstances, he would have accumulated a library as sizable as mine, but he had to settle for a wall of bookshelves. Our family's economic situation meant that buying books was a luxury. I remember that arguments broke out when he brought a book home. This environment probably determined my mad passion for books. I started buying books at around age ten. Not Jewish books, but all kinds of things I liked, which cost nothing in New York at the time.

Around the age of sixteen, I discovered the Judaica bookstores on the Lower East Side. At the time, the whole of Fourth Avenue up to Fourteenth Street was full of second-hand bookstores selling Judaica and other subjects. We went from one to the other, a bit like on the banks of the Seine in Paris. When I returned to New York after my stay at Harvard, I took the first opportunity to go for a walk on Fourth Avenue. I didn't recognize anything. There were no more bookstores, only luxury buildings.

In the great era, Judaica bookstores had quite extraordinary books in Hebrew and other languages. One in particular, Philipp Feldheim's, became dear to me, because there I started my collection.[1] Entering his bookstore on lower East Broadway was like walking into an enchanted forest. He had the most fabulous books, and there I started buying Judaica in other languages, especially German. He also had great things in Hebraica and the prices were incredibly low, even at the time.

Do you remember the first really rare book you bought there?

Absolutely. I bought a first edition in perfect condition of Naphtali Herz Wessely's *Shirei Tiferet* (*Poems of Glory*),[2] published in five volumes in eighteenth-century Berlin. I don't think I paid more than fifteen dollars, which was still a sum of money at the time. I bought sixteenth-century books with pocket money I earned working here and there after school. I wound up getting so many that I don't recall all their titles anymore. Among them, I managed to acquire a seventeenth-century edition of *Shevet Yehudah*,[3] a work I still read and reread.

I didn't wear a kippah,[4] but Philipp Feldheim, an ardent follower of Samson Raphael Hirsch,[5] never treated me with suspicion. On the contrary, during my visits we developed a friendly rapport. After several years, one day he gave me a present. It was a charming little pamphlet published in Germany in the 1920s by an organization of Jewish bibliophiles called Die Soncino Gesellschaft.[6] This company published texts in limited series for the exclusive use of its members. The little pamphlet in question, which I didn't even know existed, was a brief text by Agnon[7] written in German and entitled *Das Schass meines Grossvaters* (*My Grandfather's Talmud*). Feldheim dedicated it to me, and afterwards finally gave me all the Soncino publications.

That was when I became an incorrigible collector. Having left the family home, I transformed my former room into a rare book depository. Starting at age twenty-five, when I began to travel overseas, in every city I visited, I inspected the shelves of rare book sellers in Madrid, Lisbon, Italy, and of course Israel. I still can't understand how I managed to acquire so many invaluable rarities in all the areas that interested me: Judaica in Spanish and Portuguese; premodern Hebrew literature from before the nineteenth century; and finally, Jewish children's books.

I once learned a simple principle: to acquire a genuine rarity at a reasonable price, you must know more than the bookseller. So, I have an eighteenth-century book published in Amsterdam or Hamburg about circumcision, containing all the instructions, prayers, and blessings for the occasion. The cover of this fairly thin work is decorated with a beautiful woodcut. The bookseller had not noticed that the back cover had a list of circumcisers from all Sephardic centers in the world, including Hamburg, Bayonne, and Amsterdam, and as far away as Curaçao in the Lesser Antilles. A priceless document. In this way, and also by trading, I've amassed a collection of spectacular rarities. For instance, I own a legendary book, the Ferrara Bible.

The original one?

The original. I bought it from a bookseller who did not know Spanish and had found it in a kibbutz. He calls me one day from Israel, saying, "I have a book on which the word *Biblia* is written. And at the bottom of the page, Ferrara, 1553." I replied in the most indifferent tone possible that he just had to show me the book. I was able to exchange a much less valuable work for it. The craftsmanship was exceptional. The Ferrara Bible is the first printed Hebrew Bible in Spanish. It was translated in Ferrara between 1553 and 1554 by Spanish and Portuguese refugees. There are two versions of this Bible, with the much rarer one wrongly called the Jewish version, and the other the non-Jewish version. Mine was the "Jewish" version. It bears a dedication to Doña Gracia Nassi[8] and a colophon with the date in Hebrew. Probably because he lived in the sixteenth century, its first owner had unexpectedly written in his copy all details that differed from the other version published in the same year, including the dedication; so I had the two editions combined in one. The volume was worm-eaten in places. I daren't imagine the indignities suffered by this book between the sixteenth century and when it reached my hands. I entrusted it to a friend from Lisbon who left it with a book restorer for seven years before I could reclaim it. I have no idea what a Ferrara Bible is worth today.

Another pearl from my collection is the *Tehilim*, a book of Psalms printed in Genoa in 1517 or 1518. It is a multilingual psalter published in columns with a red-and-black cover decorated with arabesques. The text is in Hebrew, Aramaic, two Latin versions (the Vulgate and another), Greek, and also an Arabic translation printed in Arabic. It's one of the first books printed in Arabic, if not the first. Just for this detail, the book must be considered of high value. But it also has a Latin commentary on each page, which the bookseller couldn't evaluate because he didn't know the language. In one of the first Psalms, mentioning the "ends of the earth,"[9] the commentator interpolates the comment: "Nowadays, the ends of the Earth were pushed back because our compatriot Christopher Columbus . . . " Ten pages follow, constituting the first printed biography of Columbus.

One final example, which doesn't really belong to my areas of expertise since it is a history of medicine published in Spain in the 1480s. Two particular features of this book enticed me to buy it. The first is a Ladino inscription on the inside cover. The owner writes that he is in Safed and notes a date in the seventeenth century. How does this medical work make its way from Spain to Safed? Obviously, by the Sephardic historical trajectory of its owner. The second characteristic is that in the text, beautifully printed in Gothic letters, each time he happened upon the name of Jesus, the owner behaved like an inquisitor and crossed it out in ink. He censored the book for his own use. Since most inks decompose after centuries, it's generally possible to read what is underneath. That's how I could see that he was doing this every time the name Jesus appeared. This detail abruptly transforms a fifteenth-century medical book into a unique work of Judaica.

What book have you sought most persistently?

I've consistently looked for Ibn Verga's *Shevet Yehudah* in any edition or translation. I now own two editions from the seventeenth and eighteenth centuries of the Spanish translation published in Amsterdam; the one in Ladino published in Belgrade; some old editions in Hebrew, but neither of the two sixteenth-century editions, which are too rare. Nor are they the originals from Adrianople,[10] where only four copies were printed.

Can you explain your fascination with Shevet Yehudah, *which you have studied since your young years?*

Briefly, it's the first Hebrew text I know in which the phrase "natural cause" is used to refer to Jewish history and the catastrophes that have marked it. One day I'll have to figure out why, after living for almost forty years with this book, I've not yet published my edition. Sometimes I discuss it in seminars, and my translation is at home with an already written commentary, yet I never published it. It becomes stranger and stranger to me.

But you've lived with it, you know its every detail almost by heart; why does it look increasingly strange?

I wouldn't say that I know it by heart. Yitzhak Baer knew it well. He did fundamental research on the subject, including a fine book, *Untersuchungen* über *quellen und komposition des Schebet Jehuda*,[11] already published in 1923, and then some other articles. The text seems more and more strange because the author deliberately left things ambiguous, including his own identity.

14
GERSHOM SCHOLEM

You knew the great thinker Gershom Scholem. What was your interaction like?
I never researched Kabbalah, and never really studied messianic movements. Even so, although I didn't study with him, Scholem was a huge influence. Discovering Scholem was a turning point in my life. I've already mentioned our group of three or four Jewish Theological Seminary students who followed Scholem's work and met to discuss his latest articles in the Israeli journals *Zion* and *Tarbiz*.[1] Many years later I met Scholem, and as strange as it may seem, we became friends. A friendship that obviously couldn't compare to the one he enjoyed with his lifelong friend Walter Benjamin. I certainly cannot claim that status. But we'd meet when he visited New York, and when I went to Jerusalem, I always visited him.

Did you exchange letters?
Yes, and I deposited copies of them at the Leo Baeck Institute,[2] which published Scholem's correspondence. In my view, they published the most trivial letters they could find. The first letter I received from him was in English. My book on Isaac Cardoso had just been published, and the English translation of his *Sabbatai Sevi* by Werblowsky[3] was at the printer. He wrote to me to apologize that my book wasn't cited in the translation's index, although Werblowsky does mention it in a note. Scholem said he would like me to publish two letters in Spanish from Abraham Cardoso, but as he had already analyzed them in his book, I didn't do so. There's a note in the German edition of his letters that there was a similar project in German, which likewise never occurred. I kept the rest of the exchange. It's not vast, but we liked each other. We shared the passion of book collecting, even if I can't compare my library to his, and we would scour the bookstores of Jerusalem together.

When Yerushalmi meets Scholem, what do they talk about?
Everything and nothing. We gossiped and spoke of Jewish history. I remember I was tormented by a question that I never dared ask. In 1961,

Scholem gave a speech in Jerusalem on the occasion of Martin Buber's completion of the German translation of the Bible that he began with Franz Rosenzweig. Scholem told Buber: "Jews for whom you undertook this translation are no longer alive, and those among their children who escaped this catastrophe no longer read German." I don't remember now if Buber replied or reacted. It happened long before I met Scholem. But since I had read *Ursprung und Anfänge der Kabbala*, the augmented version of his *Reshit ha-Kabbalah*, I wanted to ask Scholem the same question: "Why did you write this book in German?" Why not simply add to his *Reshit ha-Kabbalah* in Hebrew, which then would have been translated into English? It has nothing to do with *From Berlin to Jerusalem*,[4] which had to be written in German. Besides, he once confided to me: "It's written in Berlin dialect, not just in German." Today, I no longer wonder about this matter because my own attitude toward the Germans has radically changed.

We also had lively discussions. The following story will offer a taste: During our 1966–1967 sabbatical year in Jerusalem, the time of Jungian round trips to Haifa, Scholem and his wife Fania visited us. Since my arrival, I had managed to buy an entire shelf of books. As is well known, the first thing Scholem habitually did upon entering someone's home was to go straight to the bookcase and inspect it. If he found a book that, as he put it, "had to belong to him," he borrowed it and the owner never saw it again. Obviously, it was impossible to refuse.

So as soon as he entered, Scholem stood in front of a shelf and took out a thin book, saying: "This one must belong to me." It was a brief work in English published in Bombay or Calcutta. I may have paid five dollars for it. At the time, I collected books of Indian Judaica and already had a nice collection. Most were written either in Hebrew or Judeo-Arabic, in Marathi, the language of the Bene Israel, or in Malayalam, the language spoken by the Cochin Jews.[5] At the time, no one was interested in this subject. The Indian author of this little book on the Kabbalah introduced himself as a "Hierosolymitan" rather than an Israelite, a term I'd never seen elsewhere. Its contents were insignificant, but because it was about Kabbalah, it must belong to him! We sat in the living room, and I said in a voice loud enough for everyone to hear, "Okay, take the book, but what will you give me in exchange?"

"Do you want reprints?" he asks me.

"No thanks, I already have all possible reprints."

"So what do you want?"

I knew his library, at least in part. So I replied, "If this book belongs to you, there's one in your library that must belong to me because you can't read Spanish." He opened his eyes wide and asked, "What book can that be?"

I replied with feigned detachment, "The *Mahzor Moguntia*."[6]

The *Moguntia* or *Mainz Mahzor* is doubtless one of the rarest surviving examples of Spanish Judaica. It's a mahzor written entirely in Spanish, obviously not really printed in Mainz. More likely it appeared in Amsterdam at the turn of the seventeenth century. At the time, Jews were uncertain and insecure about their status and played it safe by ascribing false publication places to books. I don't know how many other copies survive, perhaps five, all in library collections.

How did Scholem react to your request?

Fania sat next to him, speechless. With an embarrassed look, she said, "Go on, Gershom, give it to him." Suddenly his expression grew solemn:

"I can't, and I will explain why," he says. Indeed, he had an excellent reason for not parting with it: "This *Mahzor Moguntia* belonged to David Shaltiel,[7] who led the Jewish Brigade[8] to Jerusalem in 1948. The book belonged to his family, who were of Sephardic origin. I saw the book at his home and asked for it. Shaltiel replied, 'One day, if Jerusalem is reunified, I'll give you this book.'"

In 1967, Shaltiel did so. There was such an emotional charge associated with the book that I didn't insist. So I made do with a rarity of lesser importance, but a rarity all the same: *Be-'Iqvot Mashiyah*[9] ("In the footsteps of the Messiah"), a collection of texts by the Sabbatean prophet Nathan of Gaza[10] that Scholem published at the end of the war in a limited edition of 104 numbered copies, who knows why. When I took Scholem home to Abravanel Street[11] late that evening, he located the book, wrote a nice long dedication, and presented it to me. That's how I got this book.

Can you explain why reading Scholem's work was a turning point in your life?

First of all, *Major Trends in Jewish Mysticism* opened a world of Kabbalah that I was unaware of. No one mentioned Kabbalah in the schools I'd attended. It wasn't rejected, it was just completely outside the scope of traditional Talmudic study which had to be the sole focus. Then there was Scholem's other essay, "Mitzvah haba'ah ba'averah" ("Redemption through Sin"), which I read in the original 1937 edition.[12] This was taken by all to be a revolutionary essay, and even more so for me at the start of my journey. "My God," I said to myself, "this is what Jewish history can be. Such things can be written."

Before that, the only image I had of Sabbateanism was the uninspiring one by Heinrich Graetz. Now I discovered that Sabbateanism was not just a delusional movement, and that this phenomenon had its own internal logic. At the time, I scarcely knew what dialectical philosophy meant. Never before had I encountered anyone capable of such profound understanding of the Jewish spirit. It should be added that Scholem was a great writer. We were won over by his writing style as well as subject matter, since he took care with both. So I became, and have remained, a follower of Scholem's, despite all the revisions subsequently made to his work.

After all the debate sparked by his research, how would you characterize Gershom Scholem's vision of Jewish history?

I'm afraid he's basically right. I don't mean about a specific point, like his debate with Jacob Katz[13] over the influence of Sabbateanism on the Reformation and Haskalah. Let's say that I share Scholem's point of view, except for one point of only relative importance. I probably lack the expertise to accurately gauge the role that mysticism has played in Jewish history. Scholem's work proves that it was important, but I'm not persuaded that European and world Judaism were essentially Kabbalistic from Sabbatai Zevi in the seventeenth century forward.

I really disagree with Scholem's ideas on another point, but I'm not sure how to express it. He published an essay on Kabbalistic rituals, drawing a radical distinction between Kabbalistic rituals on the one hand, and rabbinic and Talmudic rituals on the other. According to him, rabbinic and Talmudic rituals are rituals of remembrance, producing no effect.[14] Conversely, the performance of Kabbalistic ritual is directly effective, with something happening as a result. This statement appears incorrect. Not because I reject what he says about Kabbalistic rituals, but because I think that, despite his immense respect for rabbinic Judaism, his understanding of Talmudic Judaism did not match his grasp of mystical Judaism. I think this was due to a simple reason: rabbinic and Talmudic Judaism have not yet found a Gershom Scholem. In my view, despite the tremendous progress in scholarly knowledge of rabbinic Judaism since the creation of the Wissenschaft,[15] no one has achieved with rabbinic and Talmudic texts what Scholem did with Kabbalistic texts.

However, Scholem never claimed to provide access to experiences of the mystics. He would tell this anecdote: when he first arrived in Jerusalem, the last members of an authentic Kabbalistic circle still survived in the Old City. He met their leader and asked if he could study with them. According to Scholem, this Kabbalist peered at his forehead and refused.

Even if he failed to reproduce the mystical experience of the Kabbalists, which is impossible by definition, his penetrating descriptions allow us to access a much deeper understanding of Kabbalah. Nothing like this exists for the Talmud. That's not what interested Lieberman,[16] any more than his predecessors such as Louis Ginzberg, whom I studied with for six weeks before his death, nor even Jacob Nahum Epstein, Lieberman's mentor at the Hebrew University.[17] One small example comes to mind. Today we have a good knowledge of these charismatic Kabbalistic figures. Yet we never refer to a great rabbinic scholar as a charismatic figure, even when citing the influence and reputation of a certain central rabbinical character; yet this charisma did exist.

I observed this phenomenon belatedly—since everything that can be observed is belated—when I was on vacation. Rav Joseph Ber Soloveitchik[18] delivered his annual public lecture at Yeshiva University, and Jews of all kinds came from everywhere, not just yeshivot. In addition to rabbis and Talmudic students, some of those present seemed quite undistinguished. But Soloveitchik was with them all. He usually spoke for three or four hours at a time, as inspiration dictated. Talk about charisma. Just seeing the way the audience looked at him showed that something was genuinely happening between them. How to account for it? This isn't the image we have of someone who teaches a lesson about the Talmud. I'm convinced that the same is true with rabbinical rituals; who ever really discussed their emotional dimension? Scholem may have been right in saying that rabbinical rituals lack the power or aim to change the exterior world the same way that Kabbalistic rituals do. But rabbinical rituals have the power to transform an individual at the very moment he performs them. I can say that, because I've experienced it.

15
THE RITUAL EXPERIENCE

You mention experiencing the effectiveness of rabbinic rituals, although you generally don't practice them. What does that mean?

I'd like to share this experience, just as a personal story. In December 1941, when the United States went to war, I was nine years old. Soon afterwards, a maternal uncle and an aunt—I never knew my father's family—who had settled in Washington, DC, earlier, suggested that my parents join them there and purchase a grocery store. At the time, Washington was teeming with people. It was a good time to earn a little money, which my parents were never able to do. So we left for Washington. It was the only time my parents took me out of Rabbi Israel Salanter Yeshiva.

Housing was too expensive in overcrowded Washington, and we could only afford a single large room close to the grocery store my parents had bought. I was sent to a secular Catholic school where the teachers were studying for the priesthood. My parents had heard that it was an excellent school where there would be no pressure to convert. This establishment was presented as the best school in the area. So I went there, and encountered the only experience in my whole life of real anti-Semitic aggression. Starting with the first lesson, the teacher entered the classroom and said:

"Let us pray."

So, like in the Plaza Mayor at Salamanca, everyone kneels, and I sit like the well-behaved boy I was. I like to think that the teacher hadn't been informed that I was Jewish. She asked me, "Why don't you get down on your knees?"

I replied that I didn't kneel because I'm Jewish, and Jews don't kneel. A few hours later, it was time for recess. I sat in a corner of the courtyard, and a boy who looked to me like the biblical giant Goliath dragged me to a place shielded from view and pushed me against a wall. Holding me against the wall with one hand, with the other he started hitting me, not the way children fight, but methodically hammering me countless times while chanting, "Christ killer! Christ killer! Christ killer!" When I returned home that day, I was black and blue. My mother was furious. Never afraid of authority, she rushed to school the next morning to see the principal and tell him what had happened. The latter babbled some apologies, and I even received a prize for the sufferings I'd endured; I was appointed traffic monitor, which made me proud because I was given a white belt and badge. My job was to stop cars, letting schoolchildren to cross the street. Nothing like that ever happened again. I don't recall what became of that boy. I believe he was in my class and must have been given a talking to by the teachers. Anyway, that was the background of our Washington stay.

Everything there was strange. I was left to myself most of the time, because my parents were entirely busy working at the store. That's how the stories began. I saw my parents working so hard and I got the perverse impulse to steal a few pennies here and there from the cash register. I used to save them until I filled a little bag and presented it to my parents, saying that I'd earned it by selling pencils. They knew that was a lie, but never told me. Then I started to steal more seriously. In retrospect, I must have been terribly affected emotionally by everything that had happened. I committed one of these thefts at my aunt's house. She had a collection of seashells. One day, I saw one of the beautiful shells and without saying anything, I took it.

A bit later, with my parents still busy elsewhere, I walked to a Woolworth's five-and-ten-cent store. I browsed the shelves and suddenly saw something extremely desirable, a small plastic compass priced at twenty-five cents, which obviously I didn't have. I looked at it, examined it, put it back, and all of a sudden took it and put it in my pocket. At this precise moment, I felt a hand grabbing my neck. And this huge invisible hand pushed me to the store manager's office. "I caught this kid pilfering." He left me alone with the manager: "You look like a damned scoundrel. How could you do such a thing? What's your address?" I gave it to him, of course. After a while, he said:

"It's okay, I'll let you go home, but we'll come and get you because we're probably going to take you to a reformatory."

I can't describe the thoughts that were running through my mind, but I was obsessed with the idea of getting my mother out of the store before the police arrived. On the way home, I saw that the local movie theater was showing an old American patriotic film about the Marines, *From the Halls of Montezuma*.[1] I got to the store and told my mother, "You must take me to the movies now." She said, "But I'm working!" I was so insistent that she must have suspected something. She finally took off her apron, and we went to see *From the Halls of Montezuma*. At least I had managed to delay the inevitable by two hours. After that, I had no plans. I had to be prepared for what was going to happen when we got home.

Of course, the police never came, but fear of the police turned into deep guilt over the theft. I was a *goniff* (thief). After less than a year, realizing that the move to Washington had been a big mistake, my parents closed the store and we returned to New York. This story continued to haunt me. I couldn't stop thinking that I had stolen, and especially that I'd stolen a shell from my aunt. One evening when my mother came to my room to say good night as usual, I confessed it all: the pennies, the seashell, and the reason why I had dragged her to the movies. Being my mother and the person she was, she just tried to console me, saying it was all due to circumstances. She gave me absolution, so to speak.

Why bring up this memory when we are discussing rabbinical rituals?

You'll understand when you hear the rest of the story. We were in the Bronx, across from Crotona Park, and in the middle of the park was a real lake where my father often took me to row and catch small fish. And on Rosh Hashanah, all the neighborhood Jews used to meet around this lake for *Tashlikh*.[2] I was going too. Although my mother had absolved me, a residue of guilt remained that year. I put the seashell in my pocket and approached the lake. I told myself that I would wait for a moment when everyone was busy and I'd throw the seashell into the lake. Of course, I never considered returning it to my aunt, who lived far away in Washington. So I took the shell out of my pocket and threw it into the water. By this simple action, the remaining weight of my guilt disappeared.

So I have my own evidence about the effectiveness of rabbinic ritual: the lake. Because it wasn't just a remembrance ritual, and in general, rabbinic rituals aren't pure remembrance rituals. That's the story. I once told this to my friend the poet Yehuda Amichai,[3] who said, "You should write a short story about it."

16

TRUTH IN HISTORY AND ITS AVATARS

Have historiographical methods changed since you started as a historian? In the field of history, many things have changed. That's inevitable and doesn't necessarily lead to repeating the banal observations that history isn't an exact science and each generation must rewrite it in its own way. This has been true since the origins of modern historiography. However, as I witnessed during my lifetime, some developments probably surpass the classic process by which new generations discover original things in history, because they find a special significance in them and focus on trends that speak directly to them. I note two major developments, with the second seeming the more complex. The first change happening at the levels of general history and Jewish history was the desire and concern to write history as seen from below, rather than from above. In other words, history shouldn't only be written starting with the elite and victors, but must also account for the fate of lower classes and the vanquished. Even so, in the past, attempts have been made to write history from this point of view, even in work by the Wissenschaft des Judentums.[1] Among the most striking ones are by Moritz Güdemann[2] and Israel Abrahams in *Jewish Life in the Middle Ages*.[3]

Yet despite these attempts, I think that around the second half of the twentieth century marks the first determination to seriously study popular culture or popular religion, whichever you call it. This is the first significant development, posing a real problem for historians of the Jews. On the one hand, we fight to convey the idea that Jewish history is part of general history. On the other hand, if we address the question of a gap between popular culture and the culture of the elite, I am convinced, although others disagree, that the paradigm of a cultural gap, or religious practice, between the elite and the people is less valid in the case of Jewish history than in non-Jewish history. One of the questions this creates—going beyond what

I'm talking about—is how to balance between general paradigms and specificities of Jewish history.

The second level leads to the study of a genuinely neglected aspect of Jewish history that really had to be saved from oblivion, the history of Jewish women. This oversight was repaired. There is now a mass of work already done and being done in this area. In principle, I defend all this innovative work because I'm convinced that the field has been ignored for too long in Jewish history. I don't want to give out grades. However, it must be admitted that although certain published books and articles are genuine historical writings of the highest level that will undoubtedly prove decisive, they often remain submerged under a flood of texts written in a spirit deeply tinged with ideology and based on mediocre knowledge and limited linguistic, or other, skills. I discover cases like this all the time. In this category, I would gladly put the mass of work accumulated on American Jewish history, although it should be remembered that this direction started in the 1930s and that even Baron wrote on this subject. Avoiding generalization, today there are still so-called historians of American Judaism who have little linguistic proficiency, who think that all they need to know is English, or at most English and a little Yiddish, who think that all they really need to know to understand the history of Jews in the United States is American history, and who know almost nothing about European Jewish history, when in fact all these Jews came from Europe.

As for postmodernism, with all the problems presented by this term, including that of "deconstruction," I must admit that my position remains ambivalent. I can't and won't wholly reject what is catalogued under the vague and complex term of postmodernism, calling it all worthless when it isn't. I'm deeply worried that all these "post" somethings often defend two principles: the first is an unprecedented break with modern historiographical tradition as we know it in all its variations; the second goes far beyond the framework of history and returns to the culture in which we live. It's a question about the limits of interpretation. While being aware that this is not a new problem for historians, I feel that most, if not all, of the work done under the banner of "post"—including postmodernism and postcolonialism—too often lead to ideological distortion of history or unprecedented relativization of history.

This brings us to another side of the question, more directly related to the ways of writing Jewish history. It is generally agreed that the first structures in Jewish history were arranged by the Wissenschaft des Judentums to bolster the fight to emancipate the Jews. Then it was said that the Jerusalem School bolstered the founding of the State of Israel, providing it with a homogeneous national history. Today, some claim that deconstructionism and postmodernism are linked to post-Zionism. Do you situate all of these approaches in a similar ideological or political perspective?

Certainly, links can be established between certain works of postcolonial historiography in Israel and some essential aspects of so-called postcolonial historiography. But I don't think we need to get deeper into the issue at present. We have more important things to talk about. Relativism or objectivity are old and recurring problems. I always like to remind so-called postmodernists that they didn't discover these problems. In the field of American historiography, suffice it to mention the wonderful book by Peter Novick, *That Noble Dream*,[4] which takes its title from a speech at the American Historical Association about the noble dream of objectivity.[5] Struggles and debates over objectivity have existed since the end of the nineteenth century.

All this does not date from today, or even yesterday, and precedes postmodernism by far. But I think the issue is taking a different turn today. How to say it? It's grown considerably because it affects all our culture and existence. It's the question of the truth. Can we approach truth? Is it legitimate to use the expression "historical truth"? We mustn't forget the maxim that facts are not history. As long as facts haven't been filtered out by historians and written down, they can't be used as "facts." A document in an archive isn't a fact in itself. It's simply an artifact. I'm trying to find the words to express my feelings about this . . .

If I claim that snow is white, does that fall into the category of "truth" or "fact"?

There you venture into the fields of philosophy and psychology. I'm currently interested in these subjects. I'm thinking especially of recent studies of consciousness. Nicholas Humphrey[6] gave a series of lectures at Harvard that have just been published by the university press. During one of these, he stood before a screen upon which he projected the color red and asked, "What is red? Is it on the screen, in the eye, or in the optic nerve?" It would be extremely perilous to enter this field. I remain at a much more basic level. What I'm talking about is the current tendency to use terms like "construction" or sentences like "This is a narrative construction."

The problem appears in the same context in France, where the question of the "disappearance of the object" frequently arises.

Precisely. That's the French way of saying it, the disappearance of the object. But I'd like to return to two things about the Wissenschaft des Judentums and the so-called Jerusalem School. I say so-called Jerusalem School, because I don't think the name Jerusalem School is really relevant. Before Jerusalem, there were schools of historians in Tel Aviv, Haifa, Be'er Sheva, and Bar-Ilan. Let me explain: what can Scholem's work have in common with works by others, except perhaps Yitzhak Baer—who, moreover, best understood the importance of Scholem's work for Jewish history? How could we ever liken the work of Baer to Ben-Zion Dinur?[7] They are such different historians. Without even going back to the origins, with Joseph Klausner.[8]

Let's return to the two things that seem representative of the way we've evolved. It's true that from a certain angle, the Wissenschaft des Judentums was linked to the fight for emancipation. But in my old age, I'm trying to remind younger historians that despite all the criticisms they deserve, this doesn't invalidate what Wissenschaft des Judentums members were and what they accomplished. It's true that historians at the Hebrew University of Jerusalem thought they were writing a new form of history, to the great displeasure of Scholem, who expressed his despair in a celebrated article written at the end of the war: "Some Reflections on the Scientific Study of Judaism."[9] Let's accept that its members somehow tried to write the history of a nation or people rather than a religion. Very good. But that doesn't dispel the work these people have done as historians.

In various contexts, I often cite a highly impressive book by Thomas L. Haskell, an American historian. It's a collection of essays significantly titled *Objectivity Is Not Neutrality*.[10] In my view, this theme's importance hasn't been perceived, since it hasn't been discussed at all. We can have a project—like the Wissenschaft des Judentums or let's say, the Jerusalem School—but that doesn't keep us from honestly trying to approach a certain form of objectivity, as far as humanly possible, in the daily hands-on work that we do as historians.

Today, the question of objectivity in history no longer seems controversial. Historians have a duty to be as objective as possible, but no one believes in total objectivity or absolute neutrality.

True. Today, historians no longer claim to be objective in the sense of nineteenth-century positivism,[11] but the question of relative objectivity still arises.

We tend to think that if it's possible to deconstruct the work of a historian by showing that he has recourse to narrative processes, or even to discover an ideological project in the background, we then may affirm: "This is just a story that the historian has composed in a narrative form, spurred by personal motives, conscious or unconscious ones." From this point of view, the objective validity of what the historian writes vanishes in an ad hominem attack. This seems to me a new phenomenon, at least in the extreme form we see it today, and the phenomenon is widespread. The permeation is total, and not just with history. This is the negative side of "postmodernism."

I won't dwell on another significant change, which I know the founders of the Wissenschaft would welcome, that Jewish history has taken root in universities, at least in the United States and Israel. I couldn't even say how many American universities offer Jewish Studies courses, and the movement is growing exponentially. Instructors produce PhDs, who in turn train other students, and so on. There's a real explosion in absolute numbers of research and publications in Jewish history by Jews and for the first time, by non-Jews, sometimes with excellent results, like in Spain traditionally and Germany recently. I've personally experienced this. German students have studied with me, and I'm currently supervising a young doctoral candidate who is finishing her thesis in Düsseldorf. She obtained a Fulbright scholarship to spend a year under my supervision at Columbia. They are well-trained students, good historians with the necessary linguistic skills. Not to mention the growth and accretion of everything written in every sector of research concerning the Jews.

Why is it so surprising? We currently have the wherewithal in every field, which we wouldn't have dreamed of thirty years ago.

I'm surprised now when just as I discover a potentially interesting subject and do a bit of research about what's already been published, just on a single theme, I find so many publications that if I had to read them all, I wouldn't have time for anything else. Of course, I know that we're supported by all kinds of electronic machines that we didn't have before, but I still don't think we have more time to use them. But that's another story.

In any case, this situation has huge implications. As I said, I never considered myself the heir of Baron in the sense that like him, I would've mastered the whole history of the Jews. It never occurred to me; I never dreamed of it and never believed I had the ability to write a complete history of the Jews as he tried to do and largely achieved. Had he been allotted more time and had his wife survived longer, he would have completed the project. But with the sort of training I received, before and from Baron, I always believed that I could deal with any period or historical theme that I wanted.

In other words, in 1980 when I wrote *Zakhor*, covering a period from biblical times to the modern era, I still felt that I could penetrate biblical times, the Talmudic era, the Middle Ages, modern history, and so on. I knew I had the bibliographic skills and knowledge to do so, and the few books I hadn't yet read were available to me. Today, that kind of certainty is gone. I've simply lost my footing. I can't keep up with the pace of publications in Jewish historiography; there are too many. How can you read everything written in scholarly journals around the world, not to mention books? We are no longer at the time when the only publications were *Zion*, *Tarbiz*, and the *Jewish Quarterly Review*.[12] And the phenomenon became far-reaching. If I consider my special fields, the history of Spain and Portugal or medieval history, the floodgates are open wide. If I were to try to read everything that is published in just one year about medieval Spanish Judaism or Sephardic Judaism, I would do nothing else all year. And I'm not even talking about my own research; I wouldn't have time to read theses, either. And even then, I doubt I'd have time to read everything.

There's no reason to think that this phenomenon will diminish; with new possibilities for online publication, resources become unlimited.

Anyway, who knows what the future holds. If the world doesn't destroy itself, maybe science will develop a pill that allows us to read everything in no time. It reminds me of the old joke of a fellow who takes a course in speed reading. His friend asks him, "So, how was it?"

"It was great!"

"Really? What did they teach you?"

"What did they teach me? I read *War and Peace* in an hour."

"Is that so. What's that about?"

"Russia."[13]

Whether it's a pill, or something genetic or computer based, condensation is necessary. Of the three points I've discussed, the last mentioned is the least important. The other two really matter, the generally positive development of research in neglected areas and the disturbing influence of "postmodernism."

I could also cite the example of postcolonial studies, so popular today. Edward Said undeniably opened up a basic field of research with *Orientalism*. It was indeed necessary to study the relation, or possible relation, between academic work and politics. In Said's case, it was a question of analyzing academic work by Western orientalists through the prism of their relationship to the needs and ambitions of empires. But is that all Western Orientalist studies accomplished? Did orientalists only serve imperialist interests of Great Britain, France, and Germany in a purely political fashion? For example, Said completely overlooked Ignaz Goldziher,[14] one of the greatest nineteenth-century Islamologists, as already mentioned. Goldziher was an assimilated Hungarian Jew who practically converted to Islam. How could it be argued that Goldziher did his research in pursuit of colonialist objectives? In a recent issue of the *New York Review of Books*, I read an article by Maya Jasanoff with a completely original point of view about the British Empire and its presence in India.[15] She sought to tell the story of British officials who settled in India and became collectors. And this is important: Although these people openly served the Empire, the author doesn't believe that this fact alone explains their conduct as collectors, intellectuals, or even historians in one of the cases discussed.

Seen from today, colonialism is abominable, although it's necessary to distinguish between colonial regimes, because the English in India were not the same as the Belgians in Africa. Based on this, are we entitled to dismiss as irremediably hollow and manipulative the words of colonizers who saw, or tried to see, themselves as benefactors? I imagine that the question is much debated in France, relating more specifically to immigration issues.

The discussion in France was incited by new dictionary definitions for the word colonialism. Some saw it as a defense of positive aspects of the colonial enterprise, which supposedly didn't have only harmful effects. The controversy expanded further when politicians sought to pass an amendment requiring that the "positive effects of colonization" be added to the curriculum.

It's easy to say retroactively that colonists had no right to educate peoples in lands where they settled. In theory, I completely agree with this view. In no way do I defend colonialism, either in its past forms or the modern

American manner. I reject the approach inherently. I simply want to suggest that the historian's duty is to contextualize things, situating them in the contemporaneous climate of opinions and beliefs. In that case, it's impossible to totally ignore altruism as one motive of the colonial enterprise, although surely a secondary one. I believe that colonization was a historical mistake, but evaluating it cannot be reduced to a moral judgment.

The fact is, a nineteenth-century middle-class Englishman, educated at Oxford or Cambridge, who goes to India to serve the British government, may first be considered as a British civil servant. But it may just as easily happen—I'm not saying in all cases, but examples do occur—that after arriving in India, he identifies sufficiently with local populations to campaign for them and try to help them. That's what I think. Once the historical context of the existence of empires has been established, the fact remains that the motivations of empire weren't entirely repressive or exclusively aimed at increasing the power of the homeland. That's what I believe, and if it be heresy, then I accept the status of heretic. I think that a colonial enterprise of this nature would generate a different history if it were launched today. Let's take the example of the founding of the State of Israel. Had Israel been created in the sixteenth century, at the time of the discovery of the New World by the Spanish, or the seventeenth century, when the English and Dutch conquered North America, instead of in 1948, no one today would say, "Get out and give the land back to the indigenous population." Well, of course Israel couldn't be born before the historical processes leading to the emergence of Zionism, and it was obviously unimaginable that Jews of the sixteenth or seventeenth centuries should embark on a colonial adventure of their own.

17

MESSIANISM AND ZIONISM

In the preface to the French translation of Yitzhak Baer's Galut,[1] *you claim that "in its author's mind," this book must have been a "tragic history of the exile of the Jews." Moreover, in one of your articles on exile, you identify a "dialectic of exile and domicile" that involves "feeling at home within exile itself."[2] Have you anything to add?*

One can say extremely profound things about *galut* (exile) without necessarily being a historian. That doesn't mean that exile is outside the scope of historical investigation. The same may be said of messianism. One might wonder why, despite all the messianic belief inherent in Judaism, there have been so few practical historic attempts to return to *Eretz Yisrael*. No doubt individuals and even groups tried, but there was no genuine overall movement before the saga of Sabbatai Zevi.

That's debatable. In the tenth century, the Karaites went up from Babylon to Eretz Yisrael *and two centuries later, sources describe a similar movement from northern Europe.*

Certainly, the nascent Karaite movement strongly encouraged settling in *Eretz Yisrael*. But in my opinion, this aspect of Karaism has nothing to do with a messianic impulse.

So don't you think that Karaism was part of the messianic movement from its beginnings?

Let's take the most interesting example of this point of view, by Daniel al-Ḳumisi,[3] which I've discussed several times in my seminar. For two reasons, it's questionable to claim that his appeal, or manifesto, calling for leaving the diaspora and returning to *Eretz Yisrael* is really messianism. First, we must agree on definitions. What do we mean by messianism? What is a messianic movement? What is messianic activism? All these can be defined in different ways. Are the various groups of *Avelei Tziyon* (Mourners of Zion) messianic movements?[4] Is the real idea of a messianic movement that it's insufficient to pray in exile and we should really be within Jerusalem's walls to weep and pray together? Daniel al-Ḳumisi doesn't genuinely pose as a messiah or herald of return.

The second problem is to determine the content of the reason invoked. Reading Daniel al-Ḳumisi carefully, we find another decisive motivation: he was convinced that if they remained in Babylon, Karaites would assimilate in the medium term to the Rabbanites.[5] In this perspective, joining Fatimid Palestine[6] was an obvious and realistic solution, confronted by probable future extinction of the movement. In Palestine, the Karaites would be free and independent. They managed to get support from the Fatimid caliphate in Egypt, which itself had broken with the Abbasid caliphate of Mesopotamia.

Let's go back to messianism. You said that the first great messianic movement was Sabbateanism.

I'm not saying it's the first big movement. We know there have been others, we just lack details about them. During the Umayyad Caliphate at the beginning of the eighth century, it's known that there was a movement led by a man named Serene the Syrian (Sirenus), so important that its echo resounded in Muslim Spain, which speaks volumes about its power.[7]

Sources also claim that some waged real war, such as the insurgency started by Abu Isa[8] of Isfahan, whose tragic memory was still vivid almost five centuries later, as evidenced by Maimonides's *Epistle to Yemen*.[9] Despite the scarcity of sources, it is clear that there were indeed messianic movements of certain importance before the Sabbatean episode. But on the one hand, none of them ensnared most Jewish people and in the overwhelming majority of cases, they amounted to strictly local unrest. So we don't debate over whether these movements were marginal or significant. On the other hand, we see from most descriptions of these messianic movements, not just by their Jewish opponents, but also by neutral observers such as Arab historians, that these movements are generally limited to certain classes of individuals, usually the lower classes. This is also one of the elements that led Marxist historians to conclude that a class struggle exists.

In this way, although the Sabbatean movement wasn't the first messianic movement, it was the only geographically unlimited one; it really sparked a world movement and spread with incredible speed. Incidentally, this shows how news circulated quickly, even in the seventeenth century. It's also the only messianic movement that we know for sure involved all classes of Jewish society, including the wealthy and elites. Thus, we have minutes from meetings held by Hamburg community notables, families who became rich through international trade, deciding how they should liquidate their assets, pack their belongings, and depart. It was unprecedented.

In terms of foreshadowing what would happen later, we must debate Scholem's conclusions, which Jacob Katz disagreed with. But it's uneven ground. I have serious doubts about the relevance of any form of what some people call precursorism.[10]

What do you mean?

I mean that in Zionist historiography in particular, there's a clear tendency to find precursors of Zionism in ever more distant times. It's enough to refer to books by Sokolow[11] or Ben-Zion Dinur, which I haven't reread for a long time. At this rate, we can easily make Spinoza a precursor of Zionism. Certainly, he writes in a passage from the *Theologico-Political Treatise*[12] and I paraphrase: "Who knows? Perhaps one day the Jews will regain their political independence if they renounce outdated superstitions." But he's absolutely not a precursor of Zionism and this passage seems to be, why not, the precursor of tension between understanding the Jewish religion and Jewish nation building. Spinoza conceives of the notion that if Jews keep their religion, they cannot establish a state. But he isn't at all sure; all this remains conditional. It would be interesting to know to what extent he was inspired by witnessing the Sabbatai Zevi movement.

Which brings us to the present day. How do you view the existence of a Jewish state?

We are currently experiencing this tension. It's another question in itself, as you know. The fact is that until modern times, one key to all Jewish history is the unique fusion of national phenomena and religion. There are no other such examples among all the rest of the world's great religions. This was Baron's thesis, which others have accepted. Fusion here doesn't mean that it's about assembling two separate entities. It's about interlacing, as in upholstery. I don't see why we should start modern times with Jewish emancipation, just because it's simpler for everyone to adopt the same division into historical phases. Besides, despite vast pressure exerted from the start of the Emancipation in France for Jews to free themselves completely by abandoning their Jewish national identity and be defined just by religion, the process failed up to a point. That point was where the two conflicted; and sometimes Jewish national references were abandoned externally in the classic Reform movement, to merge into the national entity that Jews dwelled in.[13]

But in practice, this doesn't really work. So far, national identity and religion haven't been entirely separated. By the time of Israel's founding, the issue had become so acute that it was thought that this tension would inevitably be resolved by the emergence of a Jewish state. However, the solution was never really planned. This was the subject of a lecture I gave in Tübingen, that the founding of a Jewish state was *never* anticipated in Jewish tradition, which could only envisage two states, one in ancient times before the Exile, and the other that would exist at the end of days, when the Messiah comes. But a state now, between the two? It was inconceivable. All the extreme polarization and tension seen today in Israel was inevitable, because even Israelis failed to completely separate the two notions. All national holidays in Israel, except for new ones like *Yom ha-Shoah* or *Yom ha-Zikaron* are Jewish religious holidays.[14] This is so, even if they are secularized or celebrated differently; Passover remains Passover, whether or not haggadot are printed by a kibbutz. Everything's the same.

Isn't the same true in Christian countries? Doesn't Christmas remain Christmas? Easter hasn't lost its status as a religious holiday by becoming a public holiday on the civic calendar.

Certainly, but there are two essential differences. The fundamental, original difference is that no religion, neither Christianity nor Islam nor Buddhism, identifies with a single people and destiny. We celebrate Christmas in a secular way around a tree and offer gifts, but there's no connection with being French, Italian, or Zulu. Israel does the opposite; the notion of the Jewish people is part of the fabric of the Jewish religion, whether in daily prayers or the Passover ritual, even if celebrated on a [secular] kibbutz. Passover isn't the memory of an exodus by a religious sect out of Egypt, but the birth of a people who become a nation during their wanderings in the desert. It doesn't matter whether things "really" happened that way. It's how Jews represent them in their collective consciousness until today. Of course, we can change things a little and make Passover a springtime festival, but the historical foundation remains identical.

Nevertheless, this turns it into a secular event, depending upon historical conditions.

That's irrelevant. It's only superficial secularism. The holiday contains within itself an invisible link. Passover transcends that. It's not just part of history, but explicitly the remembrance and updating of an event of historical, not mythical, character. Because of this, the Passover story links today's Israelis to ancestors who weren't secular. The seder table is arranged by placing food that can be seen in a secular and secularized way, but all the symbols conveyed by it have Jewish and religious roots. That's why this situation is unique, and remains so. The whole question of the unique nature and singularity of Jewish history has been discussed in splendid books, so there's no need to dwell on it at length.

But beforehand, when stressing this unique nature, we must know what we're talking about. Obviously, every nation is unique, and yet Jewish history stands out amidst this uniqueness. When Jewish history is studied in depth, elements are discovered that, despite links with world history in general, place it distinctly apart from other histories in a truly specific way, even if each history has its own identity. The specificity of Jewish history lies precisely in this matter of persistent historical interlacing of religious and national elements. Therefore, does the uniqueness of the "chosen people" have a pragmatic or metaphysical nature?

And contemporary history isn't over yet. Had the Jews been wiped out, or if one day they will be, there'd be no Judaism in the world. Whereas if Italians or Spaniards were wiped out, Catholicism would continue nevertheless; or if all Syrians or Moroccans died out, there would still be Islam.

18

THE STATE OF ISRAEL AND MESSIANIC SIGNIFICANCE

Do you remember the day that the State of Israel was proclaimed?[1]

Do I remember? My parents and I were at home. I was sixteen and when we heard the news of the United Nations vote and Ben-Gurion's announcement, we danced the horah.[2] It's very clear in my mind. I also remember buying all the Yiddish newspapers and others the following day. All the newspapers, except *Morgen Freiheit*,[3] the Communist newspaper I never touched, had headlines in blue and white. We were disoriented. I was raised with Zionism and at that age was certain that what had occurred was justified and flawless. It's an awful thing to admit, but I wasn't thinking about Palestine. I believed everything, that the Arabs had fled after being asked to do so by their commanders, that Tzahal[4] was a comparatively virtuous army, which I continue to believe in part. Clearly, I didn't know what would happen next. I imagine if I'd been asked in 1948, and even a few years later, if Palestinians deserved a state, I probably would've said no.

What do you think today?

My ideas today aren't new; I decided quite early. I believe I was one of the first Jews, at least in the United States, to assert that Palestinians had the right to a fully sovereign state. The problem is how to resolve the territorial question. I never doubted the right of the Jews to have a state, but I didn't really consider all the difficulties involved. What Israel did was so spectacular that at least until the June 1967 war,[5] it was easy to be swept away with enthusiasm. The June War transcended anything imaginable, for me and other Jews. I even remember wondering why it took so long. *Life* magazine printed a special postwar issue[6] showing an Israeli army commander in Sinai, a tough-looking fortyish man. The editorial declared, "Now the Arabs have no choice but to make peace."

My wife and I were in Israel during the summer immediately after the war. We saw people who were surely neither right-wing nor particularly fanatical, saying: "What we conquered, we keep. Without rights over Hebron, we have no rights over Tel Aviv." Needless to say, I personally think we're entitled to Tel Aviv, but not to Hebron and all the problems that entails.[7] I don't know exactly when this turning point occurred, but it had already started it in the early 1970s. God forbid, I hadn't begun to think in any anti-Zionist way. I have no sympathy for New Historians or post-Zionist historians.[8]

Did you distance yourself from the policy of occupation even before the 1982 Lebanon War?[9]

In October 1973, at the time of the Yom Kippur War,[10] I was still at Harvard. As sometimes happens when an important problem arises, shortly after the war, the university organized a public debate among professors, to which students were invited. Stanley Hoffmann[11] and I debated the subject in front of a crowd of students. All I remember from Hoffman's presentation are his unacceptable comments, like "From the perspective of long-term American interests, Israel is a liability, not an asset." Well, I admit that this argument may be defended purely on the basis of political science considerations. But that's politics. For my part, I stressed that political considerations weren't enough to understand what was going on in the Middle East. Another element had to be added: religion. I remember as if it were yesterday that I said publicly during this meeting, and I don't know how I reached this conclusion: "The Palestinians have been a nation since long before 1973, and, as a nation, they are fully entitled to have a state." I remember this statement because immediately after the meeting, two young Harvard students from Libya came up to me. They said that I was the first Jew that they had heard argue that Palestinians had the right to a state, adding that we could become friends.

It's often said today that since the War of 1967, Judaism has experienced a new messianic moment. Would you agree?

I've always had difficulty with this claim. In essence, all this is problematic, even if we ignore the Zionist-religious movement. When I started studying Jewish history, it was clear to me, and still is, that Zionism represented an absolute revolution and break in Jewish history. Although underpinned by continuities, it marks a fundamental break. Besides, I've always been embarrassed by the prayer for the government[12] recited in synagogues internationally, and especially the one recited in Israel, because it isn't addressed to the state. If I'm not mistaken, Agnon proposed the formulation: "*Reshit tsemihat geulateinu*" ("the beginning of the flowering of our redemption"), which seems to me problematic from every point of view, including semantically.[13]

You ask if I think the War of 1967 sparked a messianic moment. I would reply by asking more generally, did the founding of the State of Israel create a messianic moment in itself? To which I would vehemently reply, no! I know that some people as intelligent as I am see 1948 and 1967 as the start of the redemption of our nation. Jacob Katz is one of them. In an article that I didn't read at the time it was published in *Commentary*,[14] Katz tries to explain the attitude of Jews who see a sort of beginning of redemption, and incorporates the dramatic victory of the June War. Please note that I avoid calling it the Six-Day War, because this formula also has symbolic meaning.

The six days of Creation.

Exactly. Personally, I don't believe that anything about the State of Israel marks the beginning of redemption. It's the start of a purely secular redemption that has nothing to do with messianism. Beyond the different opposing currents in the history of Jewish messianism, one definition is accepted: a messianic state will be a perfect state, ruled by a perfectly just king, and the Jews will do only absolutely perfect things, essentially studying the Talmud, or philosophy according to Maimonides, without any disturbances. So they will not need the IDF (Israel Defense Forces), because there will be peace on earth. Not only do I disbelieve the messianic validity of the State of Israel, but I think that to believe it means misunderstanding all that Israel really is, as well as what it means and *should* mean.

Only after we see that Jewish tradition conceives of two states, at the beginning and the end, with Israel being an unforeseen and unexpected state, can Israel's host of problems in domestic and foreign policy be explained.

What specific problems do you have in mind?

For example, the hot issue of returning captured territory in exchange for peace. I understand settlers from an ideological and human level. Sometimes their families have settled there for three generations; these are their homes. It's where they grew up, got married, and buried their loved ones. I understand that. But on an ideological level, their definition of *Eretz Yisrael* is fundamentally a messianic one that has never corresponded to historical reality. We never owned such vast territories, not under Joshua, David, or the Hasmoneans. If we stick to the literal text, the original promise made to Abraham pertains to a region extending from the Nile to the Euphrates. In that case, taken to its logical extreme, the present territories don't correspond to this promise either. What's the basis for these claims? A cursory reading of the Bible, that's all. The political polarization resulting from this definition is a glaring example of an aforementioned internal problem. There are also secular extremists who express claims to Greater Israel in lay terms, as Betar members did whom I met in my youth; I can still hear them singing, "Two Banks Hath the Jordan." By Jabotinsky,[15] of course.

As for the outside world, although this isn't the only factor, because clearly a phenomenon can never be explained by a single cause, one reason for the vast tension and wave of anti-Israelism overwhelming many spheres, especially the one of Western intellectuals and academics that is closest to my heart, appears to be linked to a Jewish and Christian messianic legacy. This legacy is increasingly insubstantial, due to secularization. Let's set Islam aside for the moment, because Arab hatred against Israel differs from European hatred.

One millenarian Christian legacy, unlike Islam, subconsciously or subliminally spreads the idea of restoring Hebrew sovereignty in the Holy Land. But as in Jewish messianism, this perspective is transferred to eschatological times; what's more, it's inseparable from the Second Coming of Jesus and permanent conversion of all Jews to Christianity. That poses another problem. The whole American fundamentalist right wing that comprises Israel's most fervent backers, support it specifically, and often explicitly, with this in mind. Yet Israel's right-wing Jews accept this support and the money that goes with it, without being troubled by the fact that it's intimately linked to the conversion of the Jewish people, signifying the destruction of their identity.

Meanwhile, the left wing claims a certain heritage of socialism, Communism, and Marxism that was always opposed to Jewish nationalism in any form. Lenin didn't even want the Bund to be a separate socialist organization, as he clearly wrote.[16] But because a supposed place exists in Christian tradition for a messianic Jewish state dependent upon the Second Coming of the Messiah, the existence of an intermediate sovereign Jewish state between the old and messianic states has never taken shape in Christian consciousness.

But to use a cliché, double standards are applied to Israel. My question is why? I've never heard a call for another academic boycott like the one started in England and continuing there to this day, specifically targeting universities and instantly spreading to the whole world, ordering that all university relations be severed with Israeli academic institutions. Has anyone wondered why such a demand was never made against Hitler's Germany, the most tyrannical and genocidal regime? Who proposes today that all relations with the University of Khartoum be terminated because of what's happening in Darfur?[17] Nobody. So there's a double standard. And the question remains, why? The explanation for this phenomenon, which frankly seems to me increasingly less satisfactory, is that we expect Israel to behave not by Middle Eastern standards, but by Scandinavian standards. But what do we know about the Scandinavian situation? Danes, Swedes, and Norwegians are not in the position of the Israelis. When you go out to a cafe in the evening in Oslo, Stockholm, or Copenhagen, you don't usually have the idea that you might not come back; that's the case in Israel when you put your child on the school bus in the morning. It's unclear how Scandinavians would react if they faced an invisible enemy. I'm not talking about an army; when confronted by armies, Israel knows quite well how to proceed.

Why is that? As always, Jews are expected to behave better than others because they're the chosen people, even if they've not always been up to the task. I'm sure this is the crux of the problem. Anyway, why should it be otherwise if the Jews imposed these standards upon themselves? What people have been more self-critical than the Jews? We are proceeding between two extremes; on the one hand, we're better than the others because we are the "chosen people" (a biblical misreading), and on the other hand, as in Amos 3:2: "You alone have I distinguished among all the families of the earth, that's why I ask you to account for all your faults" (Rak etkhem yadati mikol mishpahot ha-adama al-ken efkod alekhem et kol-avonotekhem).[18]

Because I chose you. Textually, when Jews ask a question already present in the Apocrypha, "Why us, when other nations have done much worse than us?" God replies, "What do you mean, 'Why us?' I don't have anyone better. I've given the Torah to you, I've revealed myself to you, so you *must* be the best."

Besides, what other people on earth have a national book more critical about them than the Bible is about the Jews? Which national epic criticizes ancestors the way the Bible criticizes the Hebrews or Israelites, whatever they're called?

You mention the Bible. In recent years, biblical archaeology has experienced a fresh impetus, especially with the more or less radical questioning of the biblical text's historical reliability. How do you see this approach?

I think that today, critical Bible studies, of which archaeology is a part, are in a chaotic state. Each viewpoint develops into a school of thought, and some are so radical, like the Copenhagen school,[19] that the question arises if anything is left to study. There's a general trend toward a kind of ghetto archaeology, a sort of minimalism; what can't be proven doesn't exist or can be overlooked. When you add postmodern distrust of narrative, not much remains of what's called history, meaning facts that can be scientifically relied upon.

In my view, this minimalism we are talking about is specifically reflected in archaeology, because fundamentally it doesn't deal with texts. True, texts are sometimes excavated during digs, but archaeology isn't responsible for their content and doesn't approach them as texts, but rather objects pertaining to material culture. Instead of asking, as in the past, "What do discoveries demonstrate?" now biblical archaeology asks: "What can be concluded from what we haven't discovered?" Asking this question puts us in a delicate position, I think. An old Israeli joke goes: "How do we know that the Hebrews of antiquity had radio transmitters? Because after diligent searching, archaeologists found no telegraph cables."

I'm not an archaeologist, although I'm interested in the research. I only know that the Old City of Jerusalem isn't at the site of the Jerusalem Citadel,[20] that the latter is buried under one or more Arab villages, and that these villages cannot be razed to see what's underneath. I don't know, and I defy anyone to say, what's really under the Al-Aqsa Mosque and the Dome of the Rock,[21] except that it's sure to be damaged. For the rest, you know the old maxim, "No evidence exists because we haven't seen anything." That's a form of absolute disregard for all oral or written tradition. In a way, it amounts to saying, don't even imagine that there's the slightest bit of truth in these traditions and writings. Yet this position itself is based on a few presumptions that are rarely, if ever, examined.

Speaking of tacit presumptions reminds me of Yehezkel Kaufmann. I happen to have spent a lot of time studying the Bible critically with excellent specialists. Within the framework of my systematic reading, the volumes of Kaufmann's *Toledot Ha-Emunah Ha-Yisraelit* (History of the faith of Israel) had the same effect upon me as reading Scholem, namely certainty that I was dealing with a masterpiece, reading someone who grasped things that no one else had discussed before. Yet I strongly feel that in today's world of biblical studies, Kaufmann is relegated to the past and no one refers to him now, although there's a chair named in his honor at the Hebrew University.[22] One of Kaufmann's central ideas is that Israelite monotheism didn't gradually develop over a long time, but appeared suddenly. In this sense, it was a spontaneous phenomenon, a revelation, despite the term's religious connotations. Such things do happen in history; sometimes a radically new thing appears that doesn't bear the trace of the past, with each phase easily identifiable. An evolutionary bias exists behind almost all current biblical studies and the issue of the birth of monotheism. Things are considered always in flux, never occurring suddenly. Given this assumption, research consists in finding developmental stages, and by dint of looking only for that, one will inevitably be found.

A long time ago, I studied with Abraham Joshua Heschel.[23] I recall that he once said in the middle of a lecture, "What do you think would happen if an archaeologist suddenly discovered the original Tablets of the Law in the Sinai Desert, in scattered, perfectly engraved fragments of ancient Paleo-Hebrew script?[24] Would it change anything? Do you think that all Jews would abruptly start to believe?" In a nutshell, his answer was, "No, it probably wouldn't change anything. Some archaeologists would surely claim that while the fragments appear authentic, in reality they are fakes. We are beginning to historicize in every sense of the word."

By the way, I never became a Heschel disciple, but the story is highly pertinent. Heschel was an excellent actor and knew how to use grandiloquence when necessary. Another time, he told us: "One day when I was studying for my doctorate in Berlin, it was five o'clock in the afternoon and I was going to start *Mincha* and *Maariv*[25] prayers when I suddenly hear that a friend is being operated on at the university. I rush to the university, and it's true; I go into a big room, and they're operating on my friend. My friend was the Bible, and they were carving it up."

Of course, he was referring to German biblical criticism. For him, his "friend" was being operated on, with relatively slim chances of survival. I don't share this radical attitude. Even Heschel, who changed a bit after he emigrated to the United States, knew the critical method perfectly well, as reflected in the thesis that he delivered in Berlin, *Prophetic Consciousness*,[26] published many years later in English. I have a rare copy, published by the Polish Academy of Sciences.

Do you think that Judaism is being totally changed because of the founding of the State of Israel?

The question has become sensitive again. Do you mean inside or outside Israel?

All over, Judaism in Israel and elsewhere.

The general answer to these two questions is probably yes. The emergence of the State of Israel has obviously changed a lot for the Jews, both as Jews and in their relationship with the world. In this sense, Jews and Judaism are in a situation identical to that of all peoples and religions in today's world. These constant transformations occur today at a historically unprecedented speed, regardless of viewpoint. On a given day, I may think that I understand American Judaism, but the next day or week, events reveal that things are not as I believed. The same thing happens each time I visit Israel. Which is not to deny continuities.

In terms of total change outside Judaism, can we speak of new forms of anti-Semitism?

Do you mean the issue of anti-Zionism and anti-Israelism as new forms of anti-Semitism? I wouldn't be among those who equate the two by saying that essentially, any expression of anti-Israelism in the West is simply a manifestation, or disguised form, of anti-Semitism, with the proviso that in some cases, the link is quite clear. But this link isn't systematic, and I even believe that assimilating one to the other is false and dangerous for the Jews. By the way, Jews have always been vigilant against expressions of anti-Semitism, but I think it's as harmful for them to let down their guard as it is to see anti-Semitism where it doesn't exist. Much international criticism of Israel lashes out stringently against Israeli policy; on occasion, these are fully justified and sometimes even expressed in Israel. I'm not talking about "new historians" or post-Zionist historians, who are not necessarily tinged with anti-Semitism. The two things shouldn't automatically be confused.

However, are there new forms of anti-Semitism? Anti-Semitism has always existed; political and cultural conditions are changing. The type of anti-Semitism that prevailed in American universities, especially in elite universities, is no longer noticeable. The only anti-Semitic letter I received in my entire life was from someone who had read an article in the *New York*

Times about a conference at The Cathedral of St. John the Divine[27]—the only Holocaust conference I ever participated in[28]—and wrote to me, signing with his name and address. He wrote: "So you're a Harvard professor. How many Jews teach at Harvard? What is the percentage of Jews in the American population? Just remember that if you don't watch your step and stop being so arrogant and ambitious, it could happen again here as well." There's no need to construct major theories; this was an anti-Semite writing an anti-Semitic letter.

On the other hand, I think that Muslim anti-Semitism underwent an extremely radical change during the twentieth century because it imported and, more importantly, *internalized* Western anti-Semitism, Christian and otherwise. Today, part of Arab hatred is expressed in terms well known in the West, translations of *The Protocols of the Elders of Zion*[29] quoted in televised speeches, and accusations of ritual murder. I think it's always difficult to link modern anti-Semitism with medieval Christian anti-Semitism; but as far as Arab anti-Judaism is concerned, these elements aren't present at all in the Middle Ages, where no warning signs exist. The sort of racism that I described in Christian Spain didn't happen there. These are separate issues and on different levels. Therefore, it's better to separate the Muslim and Western worlds. Still, I couldn't precisely assess what has changed.

So anti-Semitism resists historical change?

Let's look at the hopes we had at the end of the Second World War and what's happened since then. Like everyone I know, and I don't believe it was because I was age thirteen, I thought that after what had happened, anti-Semitism was a closed chapter. It seemed obvious that anti-Semitism was so closely tied to all kinds of other disasters that it was finished. With my Zionist family culture, I too believed that the State of Israel's founding was going to end it, but paradoxically it apparently produced the opposite effect. In any case, the great changes that have occurred mean that instead of starting with less anti-Semitism in the world, there's more of it. Despite everything, different situations must be analyzed country by country; America isn't France, France isn't America, and both aren't Germany, which itself isn't the same as in bygone days.

19
AN AMERICAN JEW

You were born in America and still live there, amidst a culture and customs that are distant in many ways from the French psyche. For example, what about the idea of a "Jewish lobby" in the United States? Do American Jews identify with its positions?

Is there a Jewish lobby in France?

Probably, according to some people's delusions.

Here, there is indeed an Israel lobby, in Washington, DC, which has been violently attacked and remains powerful. Do you have something similar in France?

Not that I know of.

The problem isn't the Israel lobby, whatever its nature. I think the problem, perhaps a peculiarly modern one for communities, is as follows: Who is speaking on my behalf? What are the official Jewish organizations? There's no national Jewish community, no municipal communities, only synagogues and temples.[1] Nevertheless, nationwide organizations continue to express themselves: the American Jewish Congress, the American Jewish Committee, the Anti-Defamation League (ADL), and so on. So I wonder who these people are who are speaking on my behalf. Much to my dismay, I find that what they say is far from what I think. They may be representing a large number of Jews, but I still feel that what they say does not represent the views of those it is meant to express.

Here's an example. In an issue of the *New York Review of Books*,[2] Aryeh Neier, long-time president of Human Rights Watch,[3] spoke out vehemently against the accusation of anti-Semitism brought against this organization, saying that it was a maneuver intended to discredit him. What had happened? Human Rights Watch had published the report of an incident in which the Israeli army ordered the evacuation of a Lebanese village, and it turns out that the evacuation convoy suffered an attack in which an official and fourteen Lebanese civilians were killed. The president of the

ADL then attacked Human Rights Watch, accusing Neier not of anti-Israelism, but anti-Semitism. I find this accusation unfair, because it is precisely the role of an organization like Human Rights Watch to report such incidents, and Human Rights Watch has also spoken out against rocket attacks striking Israeli civilian populations. It's their vocation. It bothered me the most that the president of a large Jewish organization contributed to anti-Zionist propaganda, which delights in claiming that anyone who criticizes Israel is anti-Semitic. What is there to say? We're in this paradigm and here we remain.

In recent years, have you seen the image of America changing as well?

So many things have happened. The history of America can't be written today in the same way it once was. Most importantly, the great American myth, in the positive sense of the term, of "American newness,"[4] has collapsed with the notion that America represents a new beginning for humanity, with everything unprecedented and radically new, signifying a new type of human being, citizen, and democracy in addition to a new country. This myth, without reflecting reality, functioned from our nation's origins until the nineteenth century. Time and history exploded it, first gradually and then suddenly. We discovered that American history was muddied, even beyond its slaveholding past. In 1848, we went to war in Mexico to annex the California and Arizona territories; in 1898 we fought a war against Spain. All this didn't quite destroy the myth. Vietnam really wrecked it. But you can't write or judge nineteenth-century American history with Vietnam or the Bushes[5] in mind.

You mean it's necessary to consider another side as well?

It's probably inevitable that the mythical image of every great figure in American history has been torn to shreds or badly bruised. To cite only a few, Thomas Jefferson slept with one of his slaves,[6] and for practical reasons Abraham Lincoln wasn't in a big rush to free the slaves.[7] In the 1920s, Charles Beard,[8] among others, had produced revisions with his celebrated rereading of the American Revolution in terms of economic interests rather than the goal of survival. That may be true, but it doesn't mean that the American Revolution wasn't also about freedom. Just read the texts, unless you consider them evidence of the blind leading the blind.

There's a valid need to pay attention to historical participants' unconscious motives, as well as explicit ones, when we read the Declaration of Independence as well as labor union newsletters. Obviously, economic factors were at stake in the outbreak of the American Civil War. Slavery was an economic issue between the industrial North and agricultural South, as well as a moral question. But that doesn't mean that most Union soldiers risked their lives in the name of northern economic interests. When Lincoln started to mention the slaves, surely thousands, if not hundreds of thousands, of soldiers thought they were fighting for human freedom. I am certain of it. If we focus exclusively on negative, materialistic motives in the name of discovering hidden material, we do an injustice to history. It's as simple as that.

As a Jew, do you observe any noticeable change in self-awareness?

I think it's obvious that being a Jew in the Middle Ages was absolutely different from being a Christian or Muslim. Today, and for quite some time, everything has become much more indistinct than before. I imagine most American Jews see themselves both as Jews and different from non-Jews, without necessarily being able to substantiate this feeling. In a few generations, New York Jews, a category in themselves, produced intellectuals, writers, and novelists, to the point where it became customary to speak of the contribution of Jews to American literature and even of American Jewish literature. Philip Roth and Saul Bellow certainly played a crucial role in this sense. Bellow felt especially involved in this movement. He playfully translated T. S. Eliot's "The Love Song of J. Alfred Prufrock" into Yiddish with the sociologist Daniel Bell.[9] I saw the text briefly; it was wonderful.

Yet when Bellow returned from visiting Israel and published his travel account,[10] he was invited to speak by a Jewish organization, B'nai B'rith[11] or something like that, which introduced him as an American Jewish writer. He responded, "In what sense can you say that I'm a Jewish writer? I wasn't brought up with the Bible or Talmud; I grew up with Mark Twain and Edgar Allan Poe. That's my culture."

Of course, his family was Jewish. But I don't want to venture into the slippery terrain of defining what is, or isn't, Jewish literature. I don't see the point. Let literary critics or posterity decide the question. We are living in an age now where the definition of what is Jewish is so flexible that almost anything can be Jewish.

What about you and your identity?

I don't know if the question of my identity is of any interest. "Am I more Jewish or American?" This old question of double allegiance, as they used to say, seems totally outdated in our time, when an individual can hold several passports without seeming to be a spy. This is one of the problems of the European Union. Especially today, a European should be well situated to understand that a person can concurrently hold several allegiances. I also think that the issue of identity isn't just a Jewish problem, but one shared by many groups today, expressed in different forms. Who doesn't have an identity problem these days? There are only specific variations. I believe that for a long time, when I was a boy, I *knew* that I was American, but I didn't *feel* American. I didn't know how to experience being American.

How would the feeling of being American manifest itself?

Basically, it could be that English is your one and only language. And to be affected by a baseball game as much as those around you. I care about baseball today, but only belatedly. American identity lives in such small and big things. As a child, my only participation in American culture consisted in reading the same comic strips, Superman and Batman, as every other American kid. But my serious youthful readings included virtually no American literature, except Mark Twain and Edgar Allan Poe. In fact, in a rather stupid and ignorant way, I became a sort of European snob. In my view, there was no truly American culture or literature, only European culture and literature. Of course, I was American in many other ways. I grew up in a combatant America during the Second World War, and nothing could have shaken the strength of my American patriotism in the war against the Nazis and Japanese. On this point, I fully identified with the American people. But not culturally.

I discovered American literature belatedly. It happened long afterwards, in college, thanks to an English teacher who, incidentally, only taught British literature. I've tried to bridge the gap since then and now I habitually read works by American writers.

In addition to my cultural identification with Europe, I also intensely identified with the Yishuv[12] in Palestine and later, Israel. In 1948, I was sixteen. Through contacts at Zionist organizations I belonged to, I was offered the chance to leave for Israel. It happened either just before the war or during the war. I told my parents about the project, and my father told me that if I left, it would kill my mother. Anyway, I didn't leave. Was I serious at the time, or was it just a pretense? Today, I no longer know.

To be filed among your regrets?
I regret it, but my real regret is that I didn't move to Israel later to teach at the Hebrew University.

Did Gershom Scholem ever try to get you to move to Israel?
Indeed he did. During a sabbatical year, while we were chatting extemporaneously about one thing and another with Scholem and Fania, Scholem began to preach Zionism to me, much to my amazement. He asked, "Why aren't you here?" "Here" meant the Hebrew University of Jerusalem, although Scholem had already retired. I said, "Because nobody asked me." Then he said, "Do you know the students' symbol for the Hebrew University? A jackass. Do you know why? Because all teachers are jackasses."

Suddenly, without even asking, he picked up the phone and made an appointment for me the next morning with the university rector. So I went. The rector, who was a chemist, if I remember correctly, said, "Honestly, I have no idea who you are, but, since Scholem says that you must be part of this university, I've arranged for you to meet the chair of the history department." In fact, it was the Department of Jewish History, since there are two separate history departments at the Hebrew University.

I remember it as if it were yesterday. The meeting was set for the following day, not at the university, but in the city center at Café Atara.[13] I remember we drank coffee and he took notes on a paper napkin. He asked me in Hebrew:

"Do you know how the department is organized?"

I knew a little, but allowed him to tell me.

"This is how things work. Mikra period (of the Scriptures) is Professor *Aleph*; the Second Temple period is Professor *Bet*; Talmud period is Professor *Gimel*; the intermediary period until the mid-seventeenth century is Haim Hillel Ben-Sasson,[14] if I recall correctly; modern times, from the French Revolution onward, is Shmuel Ettinger."[15] After a quick calculation, I said to him with a big smile: "If I understand correctly, you're asking me to teach a period of one hundred and thirty-nine years, from 1650 to the French Revolution?"

I thought he would laugh, but instead he replied, "Yes, that's the important period of Sabbatai Zevi."

It was ridiculous. I said, "Wait a minute. You know I'm already a top-tier professor at Harvard. You can't offer me a lower position than the one I already have. Imagine if I accepted. I'd sell my house and move my wife and my son to Jerusalem, buy an apartment, settle down, and start teaching this one hundred and thirty-nine-year period at the university. A year or two goes by, and suddenly a dybbuk[16] takes ahold of me, and I feel like teaching something a bit later or earlier. What would happen, what would be the result?" I'll never forget his answer. He looked at me with concern and said, "Then you'd be encroaching on someone else's territory."

So I returned to Scholem and reported the conversation, concluding: "If I were a *tsabar*,[17] maybe I would have fairly tough skin, but I'm not prepared to live in such an atmosphere. All the delight I would experience in living and working in Jerusalem would fade daily if I had to be at this university and this department." That's how I declined the job. Between us, I should have followed the advice of my friend Moshe Greenberg,[18] who said after I told him the story: "Come anyway. Once you're here, just do whatever you want. After all, what can they do to you?" What could they have done to me? Ruined my life day after day. There it was, a missed opportunity. What's the use of dwelling on such regrets? But sometimes when I think back on my life, I tell myself how different it might have been. This is where I should have been.

In this regard, what do you think of the distinction made at the Hebrew University of Jerusalem between the Department of General History and that of Jewish History?

I understand that this distinction will be eliminated. Its origin may be explained in the way the university began. When in embryo form, *ha-Makhon le-Ma'adei ha-Yahadut*—literally, the Institute for the Sciences of Judaism—was founded on Mount Scopus, each professor of the future university was a department unto himself. That's how it all started.

Do you see any ideology implicit in this division?

I suppose that as departments became established and more staff arrived, it became a matter of ideology; Jewish history had to be studied in a specific way, even if it must be said that from 1920 to 1930, historians of the Jews did know general history. Honestly, I rather think that things were established like this, without too much forethought, and at some point these departments became institutions, even if everyone knew that fundamentally, the distinction wasn't relevant. However, it's difficult to transform institutions.

But it seems to me that the great historians' debate currently troubling Israel has little to do with the question of the relationship between general history and Jewish history. Instead, it's a conflict between the post-Zionist "new historians" and Israeli society. And these so-called "new historians" don't form a unified group; there are variations between them, just as there are variations between different universities. The one at Be'er Sheva is probably the most radical. Frankly, I consider what is written in these circles to have nothing to do with any integration of Jewish history and general history, but fundamentally shows a more or less conscious will to imitate the latest trends. Some of these people studied in England or America, where they swallowed the postcolonial potion. But it's an endless discussion. Of course, it's natural that a new generation revolts against the previous one. But I believe that this phenomenon is explained more deeply by the break in recent decades between a sense of the present and a sense of the past, which is more radical than ever.

Are you sure?

I'm not sure, but I feel that way. I have a feeling that this kind of post-Zionist history was written by people who had not really experienced 1948 and more importantly, what happened before. I believe that they have only the present as a criterion for judging the past. And it's obvious that we don't understand the history of Israel in the same way if we look at it from the present or the past. I would be the first to say that today, it's impossible to write and think as we did in 1948, 1950, or 1960.

20

FROM YESTERDAY TO TOMORROW

Looking back, how do you see your journey?

There was a time when I was young, when you could say I was religious in a traditional sense, even if I didn't follow all the rules. I was religious, I went to synagogue, I prayed. That lasted for a few years during my youth, then stopped. Had I remained religious in this way, I probably would never have become a historian. I believe that abandoning religion made historical research necessary. That's one thing. The second thing I wanted to say, to eliminate any doubt, is that I second Gershom Scholem's statement: "I am a *homo religiosus*." I too am a religious man, although I do not practice much. I don't eat meat from non-kosher animals, but I've done so in the past. I have no problem going to a non-kosher restaurant, but I won't order a meat dish there.

I wouldn't go so far as to say that I would've stopped being a Jew had I not studied Jewish history seriously. But what kind of Jew would I have been? My inner identity is so intimately mixed with my Jewish identity that I can't separate them. I wanted to try to understand the substance of my own Jewishness. In this regard, I'll tell you a story that I've rarely mentioned, which is about the question of the historian's personal motivation, a current and totally legitimate question. In the early 1960s, when I was writing my thesis on Cardoso, I had the privilege of finding a motivation that no one ever suspected and that I didn't tell anyone about, except my wife. I was completely buried in research amidst my archives, writing my manuscript by hand without a computer or typewriter. One night I had a dream, a real dream during sleep, not a waking daydream. It's one of the few important dreams that I can remember in its entirety. I dreamed that Jerusalem was reunited. This was a few years before the June War of 1967.

When I awoke, I thought about this dream a lot. I dreamed of the city of Jerusalem, and my name is Yerushalmi [the Hierosolymitan]. They have an

Old City and the new city there. For almost my entire life, I had a feeling of being divided, as if there were two Yerushalmis within me. One I know, my deep self, which isn't expressed socially, and the other one. I have a few personalities in public that aren't really "me." The reunification of Jerusalem seemed symbolic of my desire to unite the two aspects of my being. I don't know why I have this problem. Maybe because when I was young, between the ages of eight and fourteen, I was an actor, doing theater quite seriously, as already mentioned. Although I can't say how I was affected by a particular play or role, I do know that all that acting experience played an important role in building my personality, if only because it gave me the opportunity to pretend to be someone else. But I don't think that forcibly and fully explains the feeling I've always had of there being two people within me.

It might be added that as a professor,
you inevitably perform during lectures.

That's true. Some say that's why I'm a good teacher. But I also know fine teachers who seem to be themselves, whatever the circumstances.

I've spoken with close friends about this subject. When I asked them if they felt like they were always the same, they always answered yes, whether they were alone, or with me, or at a reception among a crowd of strangers. That's not how I feel. I don't know why this thing worries me so much, but it's part of my life.

Coming back to the dream, I suddenly realized that not only did it contain something personal, like any dream, but there was something in it that should shed light on a profound aspect of the research I was doing on Cardoso, a Marrano who fled to Italy to return to Judaism, who had lived two different lives simultaneously, one in Spain and the other in Italy. By leaving for Italy, he managed to reunite them. His double life was in Spain, whereas in Italy he had nothing left to hide, he no longer had to pretend to be Christian. The parallel seemed so striking that I told myself that when historians decide to question a researcher's motivations, they should be much more modest than they are. They believe that once they've studied a historian's life and environment, they understand what motivated him. But there are motivations that no one will ever grasp. This doesn't mean that we should stop questioning ourselves, but never forget that all individuals are separate worlds in themselves.

Today, how would you evaluate the work you've done?

I blame other causes for not having been more productive, and I'm not just talking about quantity. I have former students who write good books at the rate of one or two annually. It's the way I work or don't work, my doubts, or the number of times I must return to the text over and over again, telling myself one day that it's all right, and the next day that it's not.

That's because you don't settle for writing like a historian, you aspire to literature and pay special attention to stylistic matters.

Writing and style are important to me, but I also have writer's block. Writing has always been difficult for me. I can't say why this is so.

What have you gained personally from all these years spent in contact with Jewish history?

Although I've devoted myself to Jewish history for personal existential reasons, I don't think it has affected my objectivity in the least about subjects I've dealt with. But if you asked me point-blank if I've found what I was looking for, I would answer that all things considered, I've discovered many things that were, are, and will remain important for understanding myself and my situation over time. But I didn't truly find what I was looking for, at least not through history. Given that history impacted my life, it didn't produce the effects I had expected. In a way, becoming involved with history has turned out to be a muddled choice, because ultimately, I think I was looking for some sort of absolute.

Really? But all your work is opposed to that idea.

Certainly, and that's why my research as a historian couldn't quench my existential thirst for the absolute. I wanted to study history to understand what Judaism really is, in a way that can't be understood simply by studying the Talmud, the Bible, or sacred literature in general. I assure you that I'm not entirely defined by the fact of being a historian, but I've discovered that for the historian I am, neither the essence nor the absolute can exist. But if what I was looking for cannot be seen through history, it's possible to attain it by other means that need not be specified. Recently, I read an essay on the eternal question of the body-mind connection, which argued that it was a false problem, simply because the mind doesn't exist. Although I fully understand the approach of this theory and this type of scientific method, it doesn't satisfy me. It's the same with history, which everything mustn't be reduced to, despite its importance. And if that sounds mystical, well, too bad, it sounds mystical.

Is continuity the alternative aspect of history? As far as our subject is concerned, everything changes, to be sure, but Jews and Judaism remain, for the moment at any rate.

That question would bring us to another dilemma. If we start talking about continuity, I think we'll find ourselves in a tight spot. And I don't know anything about continuity any more.

Really? But you have a grandson.

Of course, I have a grandson, a wonderful grandson. I wasn't talking about that kind of continuity. Probably my grandson will be able to speak Hebrew someday, but I'm not sure that in terms of culture, religion, or psyche there will be any continuity between him and me. I know there is some continuity between me and my son; many of his values belong to the category of "continuity." But I also know from experience that my son will never live Judaism as I lived, perceived, and experienced it, which also represents a sort of breach in continuity. Because it's no longer possible to see things the way they were perceived when I was young. And I'm not saying that because he lives in Europe today. I would say the same thing if he lived in Israel. It's troubling, but I haven't fully clarified my ideas about this yet. I know it's easy to say that we're living in a period of transition. But by definition, we are still living in a period of transition.

This one in particular.

Especially this one. This one much more than others. In the 1950s, I don't remember so many important questions being asked about the future in general, of the world and humanity. Who had to face such dread before? Well, we were afraid that the Nazis would win, but that was a matter to be resolved by armies. Today, between terrorism, viruses, climate change, and environmental issues, there are enough reasons to be alarmed.

Today there's a new reality for America and Europe, since terrorism isn't fought the same way that armies are. I oppose Bush, the Iraq War, and the breaches of civil liberties seen on American soil. All this is appalling. On the other hand, I wonder how we are to fight invisible enemies like these; and I tell myself that maybe we have no choice, that sacrificing some of our rights to privacy is forcibly a necessary evil in the fight against terrorism. As for the Jewish people . . .

How do you see the future of the Jews and Judaism, now that a full range of choices for Jewish identity is available?

That's just one way of expressing it. The other is to say that most Jews no longer accept certain standards. Especially in terms of texts, no canon calls for obedience, and this isn't just a Jewish problem. I suppose if we asked Jews and non-Jews if the Bible is important, they would agree. But if we asked them why the Bible is important, how it should be read, or even if civilization arose between Athens and Jerusalem, to cite an old cliché, I don't know how most intellectuals would reply today, or even if they would try to answer questions of this nature.

Today, the fact remains that there's an infinite variety of ways of being Jewish, feeling Jewish, and acting as a Jew. One movement that is quite active right now calls itself "secular Judaism." I have nothing against these people, who include many American and Israeli academics and intellectuals, nor against their movement or this trend. I support any action taken in the name of affirming Jewish identity. The one thing that annoys me, and I don't think it's a sign of purism, is the name itself, "secular Judaism." Historically speaking, I find it distorting, misleading, and contradictory. Judaism is a religion, or at least it was. We can't artificially cancel this aspect.

It's also a way of life.

Above all, Judaism is a religion. By definition, every specifically Jewish way of life is anchored in one form or another to a religious connection to life.

Still, what "religion" means was defined belatedly.

No, it wasn't defined belatedly. Judaism is a religion in the same sense that Islam is a religion, and in other ways too. The *Halakhah*,[1] like *Shari'a*,[2] traditionally regulates all daily life and isn't limited to what we'd like to define as the strictly religious sphere of prayer, worship, and so on. Redefining Judaism in exclusively secular terms is an entirely artificial and misleading effort. Even more misleading is the urge to attach this definition to the Jewish past.

Because we started to look at the past in terms of the present, we rediscover Jews who wrote secular poetry, even during the Middle Ages. Of course, there was secular Jewish poetry in the Middle Ages, but that doesn't mean there was secular Judaism. Irreligious trends and fields of expression existed in a society that was deeply, irrefutably religious.

Young generations of historians who followed the great masters of the postwar era or my own generation, are part of currents perceiving far more multiplicity in Judaism than what we were used to. The very idea of normative Judaism appears to have become totally obsolete. I would be the last person in the world to condemn this development on the pretext that it wouldn't correspond to the form and content of what I was taught or the way I worked. Yet I think it poses an interesting historiographic or historiosophical problem: are these young generations moving in this direction because they are caught up in a trend in the culture around them—in America at least, multiculturalism is an indisputable fact—or is this due to the internal evolution of our discipline? Did a multicultural perspective allow them to see things that their "fathers" didn't see? I've no answer to this question.

I don't think that this way of doing history is blameworthy or bound to fail. Nor do I believe in what the Wissenschaft des Judentums aimed to define, namely the essence of Judaism. I'm not an essentialist and I don't think any historian can be today. Yet like an old stick-in-the-mud, I am not and probably never will be ready to discard the notion of norms in Judaism. By this, I don't mean to say that Judaism has remained static during any era. But I think that the consciousness that there is a norm to which the community's consensus was given and which saw deviation from the norm as heretic—in one way or another—has always been present, even if what the standard amounts to has varied in a more or less perceptible way. There's a fundamental difference between admitting that the norms may have evolved, and the modern, widespread phenomenon that consists in saying that individuals choose personal standards. It's quite possible that in our time, we can't help but subjectivize Judaism and claim that all are free to define their Judaism and Jewish identity. But to read history in the light of this modern outlook is to betray history and to misunderstand Jewish tradition.

However, Orthodox Jews continue to observe all the standards of Judaism.

By definition, I wasn't talking about Orthodox Jews, who are opposed to this subjectification of Judaism. But even today's Orthodox are far more problematic than their ancestors. The very notion of Orthodoxy is a modern one, because challenges to the standard against which it was ideologically and socially constructed emerged with modernity. What's more, there's a tremendous diversity within Orthodoxy inside and outside Israel, in which the subject of messianism plays an important role. For example, the Zionist-religious movement, in whatever form it takes, is inconceivable without a messianic dimension, because that's the source of its legitimacy. But I wasn't talking about the Orthodox. I was talking about the fact that it's become difficult and maybe impossible today, and for quite some time already, to define who is Jewish. I don't think that the difficulty was so great in the past, in the premodern era.

I don't remember if Baron said or wrote this, or simply passed it along to me as a bequest, but on the question of who is Jewish, my attitude is truly subjectivist. For me, Jews are any individuals who, since the Holocaust, have voluntarily identified themselves as Jews. End of story. Now, if we ask the question, what kind of Jew, we open endless debates. I'm afraid there's no other way of conceiving Jewish identity today than in this voluntarist and subjectivist way. Otherwise, we wind up getting into all kinds of hassles. And it's not just a theoretical question. To cite one example, long before the Intifada,[3] a Palestinian terrorist was arrested, and it turned out that his mother was Jewish and his father was Muslim. So, according to the *Halakhah*, he was fully Jewish. At the same time, there was a case in Israel of an Israeli naval officer who married a non-Jew who never converted to Judaism. She followed him to Israel, they lived in a kibbutz, and had several children. When applying for an identity card, the question arose of the children's identity for the card. I don't know how the case ended, but obviously, the rabbinical court clearly refused to consider them Jewish.[4]

In Israel, the problem is visible on a daily basis. I'm thinking particularly of military troops who die in combat without being Jews from the halakhic viewpoint. Where should they be buried?

Certainly, but it's also a critical problem for all those who have married in the diaspora and hope that their alliance will be recognized after they arrive in Israel. Yes, they will be granted Israeli citizenship, but that doesn't make them Jews, and their offspring won't be permitted to marry Jews. This discrepancy between Israeli identity and Jewish identity, more broadly a divorce between a perceived or claimed Jewish identity and Jewish identity based on halakhic standards, means that according to the *Halakhah*, a terrorist may be Jewish, but the son of an Israeli army officer may not be. This is intolerable, unliveable, and things must change. I don't know how they'll change. I'm convinced that finally, conversion will return to what it was originally, namely plain assimilation to the Jewish people. We find this model in the Book of Ruth.[5]

Not only was Ruth not Jewish, she was a Moabite, and the Bible commands that no Moabite will ever be admitted among the people of God.[6] Not only did she marry a "real" Jew, although the term didn't exist at the time, but when she followed Naomi, what could be termed "naomic" families emerged.[7] We aren't informed that she went through any conversion, she just integrated into Israelite society. I believe that in Israel at least, this will finally happen, once the Rabbinate[8] loses its grip on society.

Are you saying that rabbinic Judaism has reached its expiration date?

No, I believe that religious Jews are awaiting the arrival of another Yohanan ben Zakkai.[9] What Yohanan ben Zakkai and his inner circle accomplished by transposing Judaism of the Temple into standards that would ensure the durability of Judaism in exile, is now needed within the framework of the unexpected state and a diaspora that has nothing in common with historic diasporas. But who am I to speak on their behalf? Especially since I'm talking about a prospect that may only happen in five hundred years, if life still exists by then.

I would add something else, which I realized as I grew older, as mentioned in the lecture I gave at Tübingen.[10] At one point in my life, I read a lot of Spengler,[11] Toynbee,[12] and all those deterministic theories of history against which Isaiah Berlin[13] protested in his lecture *Historical Inevitability*.[14] One important thing I've learned is that history is still open and that this openness is linked to the issue of the future. History's openness means that it remains open to the best and worst. I don't believe in the old idea of progress. The only authentic consolation that I find in history, especially when I observe the current state of the world, is its openness. That's the only term that comes to mind. Things happen in history that have never been planned for or anticipated. We only learn about them retroactively. I wish that only one passage in what's called the "New" Testament had appeared in the Hebrew Bible, because I love it: "For now we see through a glass, darkly; but then face to face: now I know in part; but then shall I know even as also I am known."[15] And it's true; only at the end, after the fact, do things become illuminated. This thought consoles me. When the state of the world is largely depressing, I ask myself, "What do we know? Everything can change completely. Of course, it can also get worse, but everything can be overturned next year." It isn't quite "Next year in Jerusalem," but a sort of "Next year" wish.

Even when I think of the condition of the Jewish people, which isn't anything to be proud of, I've made it a practice to say two things. First, how would I have reacted at the time of the destruction of the Second Temple? Sources tell us about how most Jews of the time lived and felt about what was happening. The state of mind expressed in the *Apocalypse of Baruch*[16] is, let's stop sowing, plowing, getting married, and everything else, because it's all over. And yet, nothing's over, since we're here today to talk about it. The other example comes from a poem by Judah Leib Gordon,[17] whom I don't rank among the greatest poets, even if he occupied a key place in the development of modern Hebrew literature. His poem "*Le-mi ani 'amel*" ("For Whom Do I Toil?") inspired the title of a book by my colleague Michael Stanislawski.[18] Anyway—I quote from memory—the end of the poem states: "Who knows? Perhaps I'm the last Hebrew-language poet and you are the last readers." This poem was written in 1870, I believe. That's how Gordon felt at the time, with good reason. There was no way to predict that less than a century later, a Jewish state would be restored, in which Hebrew would become the daily language.

So that's all I have to say about the future. I don't believe in historical inevitability.

To sum up, what you wrote to me in August 2003 is reproduced here as a still-relevant conclusion, binding together the fabric of our conversations. Let the reader be the judge:

"So now I'm toying with a very heretical (and risky!) idea. I'm thinking of presenting a kind of intellectual-spiritual autobiography, of my path to Jewish history and as a historian, and where I feel myself today, when I am almost at the end of the road. If I do it, some will interpret it as arrogance, others may laugh. But I am virtually the last of my generation, and I think that what I have experienced and encountered may have more than personal implications. I certainly don't intend it as a defense of my work nor a critique of others. I want to talk of how I came to Jewish history, what I sought in it, what I found, and what I didn't find."

CLIO AND THE JEWS

Reflections on Jewish Historiography in the Sixteenth Century

YOSEF HAYIM YERUSHALMI[1]

The fiftieth anniversary of the American Academy for Jewish Research seems to me a propitious time, not only for celebration, but for pause and reflection. While, happily, research into all corridors and corners of the Jewish past has burgeoned far beyond what the small group that founded the Academy could have anticipated five decades ago, it is curious that a sophisticated history of Jewish historiography, one that would examine its theoretical underpinnings, its methods and goals, remains a desideratum. With but few exceptions there seems to be almost a reticence on the part of Judaic scholars to examine and articulate the latent assumptions of the enterprise in which they are engaged. The lag is especially striking at a time when, partly as a result of the ongoing crisis of the historicist view of the world, the general history of historiography as well as the theory and practice of the historian continue to be subjects of intense and widespread concern reflected in a vast and growing literature. If, as I am persuaded, modern historicism may be even more problematic when viewed within Jewish frameworks, the task of clarification becomes all the more urgent.

The following essay, then, is submitted to this *Festschrift*, not so much in an effort to offer a detailed account of sixteenth-century Jewish historiography per se, as in a spirit of introspection concerning the nature and place of Jewish historiography within the broader context of Jewish experience.

That the sixteenth century witnessed a noteworthy resurgence of Jewish historical writing has been, of course, long recognized, though the phenomenon has yet to be properly analyzed and evaluated. Within the span of a hundred years no less than ten important historical works were produced by Jews: Solomon Ibn Verga's *Scepter of Judah* (*Shebet Yehudah*); Abraham Zacuto's *Book of Genealogies* (*Sefer Yuhasin*); Elijah Capsali's *Minor Order of Elijah* (*Seder Eliyahu Zuta*), and his *Chronicle of Venice* (*Dibrey ha-yamim le-malkhut Veneziah*); Samuel Usque's Portuguese *Consolation for the Tribulations of Israel* (*Consolaçam as tribulaçoens de Israel*); Joseph Ha-Kohen's *Vale of Tears* (*'Emek ha-bakha*) and his *History of the Kings of France and of the Ottoman Turkish Sultans* (*Dibrey ha-yamim le-malkhey Zarefat u-malkhey bet Ottoman ha-Togar*); Gedaliah

Ibn Yahia's *Chain of Tradition (Shalshelet ha-Kabbalah)*; Azariah de' Rossi's *Light of the Eyes (Me'or 'Einayim)*; David Gans's *Sprout of David (Zemah David)*.

These works are of interest, not only for the historical data that can be extracted from them, nor even for the light they cast on the age in which they were written. In their ensemble they offer a valuable key with which to probe certain overarching aspects of the relation of Jews to historical knowledge generally, both before and after.

I

Any attempt to come to grips with sixteenth-century Jewish historiography must entail an assessment of what preceded it. This is no simple matter, for there are fundamental divisions of opinion as to whether one can even speak at all of Jewish historiography between Josephus Flavius and modern times. Some would deny its existence altogether. Others have argued that a ramified historical literature was created. Such debates often come to grief over essentially semantic issues. Very much depends upon how the term "historiography" is defined and conceived. On the whole it seems to me that the negators have proceeded out of a tacit modern bias that assumes that the only historiography worthy of the name must be, if not critical or analytic, at least vaguely secular. Clearly, however, such approaches merely enable one to dismiss almost any medieval historical work, and thus preclude any discussion at the very outset.

At the other pole are those who would broaden the perimeters of historiography to embrace any text that has a historical dimension, or that exhibits any interest whatever in history, with a blithe indifference to its avowed aim or its literary form. Here are two instructive instances of this approach:

To this day Moritz Steinschneider's *Die Geschichtsliteratur der Juden*, published in 1905, serves as the standard bibliographical guide to Jewish historical literature from the close of the Talmudic period to the early nineteenth century. But what is *Geschichts literatur?* In his introduction Steinschneider cautioned correctly that history is not to be confused with its raw materials. However, the book itself (several other hands were eventually involved in it) stubbornly defies this principle. It is, in essence, a listing of more than three hundred compositions and texts, most of which cannot properly be subsumed under even the most elastic definition of historiography. A handful of historical works are interspersed among such items as private letters, elegies, penitential prayers, Judah Halevi's *Kuzari*, folk tales and reports of miracles, communal statutes—it would seem almost as if no literary or documentary genre is absent. Like all the works of the master of Jewish bibliography, this one too is packed with information of importance for a variety of fields. For anyone interested in Jewish historiography, however, Steinschneider's list only serves, by its very nature, to blur the issues.

Some thirty-five years later there appeared in Jerusalem an edition of the "diary" of the famous sixteenth-century messianic adventurer David Reubeni (*Sippur David ha-Reubeni*) prepared by A. Z. Aescoly. This book bears also a preliminary title page, upon which the following is inscribed: *Historiographical Library of the Palestine Historical and Ethnographical Society, Volume I/II.* For the moment we need not pause to inquire whether Reubeni's so-called diary should be considered a work of historiography or merely a historical source. More germane to our concerns is the general introduction to the projected series, entitled "The Historiographical Library and Its Program," written by the historian Ben-Zion Dinaburg (Dinur) in the name of the Society.[2] "This historiographical library," he states, "belongs to the literature of ingathering. We want to gather into this library all the historiographical works from biblical times until the beginning of modern Jewish historiography." The formulation is instructive: "From biblical times until . . . " with no caesura along the way. There is here an obvious hint at continuity, as though somehow no significant interruption had ever occurred in the historiographical creativity of the Jewish people. I do not think I am mistaken in my impression. Coming to the Middle Ages, Dinur writes:

> As for Jewish historiography in the Middle Ages (until the Haskalah period), we are of the opinion that as a matter of priority there is need for a detailed bibliographic-literary survey that will present clear and precise information concerning the entire historiographical legacy which has reached us from this period embracing more than a thousand years. This historiographical legacy is by no means poor even in quantity. The number of historiographical works and fragments from this period may reach into the hundreds.

The claim for a medieval Jewish historiographical legacy of such dimensions must seem astonishing, until we read further and realize what is meant:

> The historical ideas which were active and influential in the course of the generations found expression and manifestation not only in the

historiographical literature. They frequently defined themselves with great clarity and fullness in other literary forms, in every age, from the prophetic literature of ancient times to the literature of mysticism and ethics, enlightenment and scholarship, in more recent times.

In short, the plan for a "historiographical library" traversed far beyond the bounds of historiography. The notion was to include not only the recorded historical recollections of the Jewish people, but also its meditations on its place among the nations and on its future destiny, as these expressed themselves in any and all literary forms. The details can be read in the Hebrew original and need not be repeated here. It was, in its way, a grandiose project, never executed. Perhaps it had its own intrinsic virtues. But once again we are confronted with a blatant tendency to stretch the concept of "historiography" to comprise phenomena that, whatever the definition, can hardly be squeezed into such a rubric without bursting it asunder and rendering it meaningless.

Now I am not prepared to offer a fixed definition of historiography, nor do the purposes of this essay require it. In the end, any such definition will prove, if not arbitrary, then either artificial or restrictive. However, if the term is to be used responsibly and not be allowed to turn into a random receptacle, one characteristic should be isolated without which I believe it altogether impossible to understand the phenomenon that the term is meant to represent.

The minimal condition to be satisfied emanates from the very word "historiography" in its literal and etymological meaning—and that is simply, the "writing of history"—in the sense of recording events out of the human past. Whatever its other aims, qualities, and contents, a "historiographical" work must be anchored in a recital of concrete events that possess a temporal specificity. Those events need not be political. They may be biographical, social, literary. But they must be there. This precondition, to be sure, does not tell us what historiography is. But at least it helps us to differentiate what is *not* historiography.

Historiography is not to be equated with "ideas of history," nor with an interest in historical processes, nor with attitudes and reactions to historical events, nor with efforts to unveil the "meaning" of history. Though any of these elements may be present in a historiographical work, none of them is a decisive feature. For historiography represents a very specific activity, not to be confused with others. At its source lies an impulse to record events of the past that, for one reason or another, are seen as worthy of remembrance.

By contrast, the quest for meaning in history can be pursued in various ways and through different literary genres that have an intrinsic connection with historiography. Indeed, this is largely how it has been pursued. Interpretations of history, whether explicit or implicit, can be found abundantly in works of philosophy, theology, exegesis, mythology, belles lettres, often without a single mention of historical events or personalities, and with no attempt to relate to them. The distinction would seem to be elementary, and yet it is consistently ignored. At an international symposium on medieval historiography held some years ago at Harvard, much of the discussion centered around Joachim da Fiore. Yet no matter how one may view the importance of Joachite ideas in the evolution of certain Western conceptions of history, I doubt that the admission of the Calabrian abbot to the agenda helped clarify the topic at hand which, one assumed, concerned the writing of history during the Middle Ages.

The same distinctions apply in the Jewish sphere as well. The prophets of Israel may have held highly articulate views about history, and some of the biblical historians may have absorbed those views and written their chronicles on prophetic assumptions, but the prophets were surely not historians, nor, then as now, were the historians prophets. If we leap momentarily to the sixteenth century and compare, say, Rabbi Judah Loew (Maharal) of Prague with his compatriot David Gans, we may easily agree that Maharal had by far the more profound views on the course and meaning of Jewish history. Nevertheless it is Gans, and not he, who was the historian. Similarly, we can often find important historical data in works belonging to various genres, yet the aim of these works is not at all historiographical, and it is not this that characterizes them. In the biblical commentaries of Isaac Abravanel, for example, as well as in his messianic treatises, there are scattered clusters of historical information whose significance is manifest, but this material remains incidental to the whole. Abravanel himself apparently understood the difference and, as is well known, he began to write a separate historical work to be called *Days of Yore* (*Yemot 'olam*).[3]

These observations, tentative and incomplete as they are, will suffice to orient us toward the subject at hand.

2

We possess, in all branches of Jewish literary creativity in the Middle Ages, a wealth of thought on the position of the Jewish people in history, of *ideas* of Jewish history, but comparatively little interest in *recording* the mundane historical experiences of the Jews since they went into exile. In light of what has been said thus far, the paradox is only apparent. As to whether a Jewish historiography existed before the sixteenth century—such a sharp formulation of the question can only obscure the real problem, which is of a more subtle order. For two things seem to me equally clear: Historical works were certainly written by medieval Jews, although, taken together, they do not constitute a historiographical phenomenon of the sort that is to be found among other peoples in whose midst Jews lived. *Iggeret Rab Sherira*, *Yosippon*, the Hebrew chronicles of the Crusades, and other known works, are certainly historical compositions, not to be removed arbitrarily from the category of "historiography" because of criteria alien to the times in which they were written. Nevertheless, no historiographical tradition ever emerged out of these, no genre with fixed conventions and continuity. The historical works that were written appeared only sporadically. By and large the distance between them in time and space is significant, the periods of silence long. Only in one well-defined area can one speak at all of a genre, and that is the literature of the so-called "chain of tradition" of the Oral Law (*shalshelet ha-kabbalah*), which dealt with the transmission of rabbinic law and doctrine, and with the luminaries who were its bearers through the ages. Only this type of historiography achieved legitimacy and found a home within Judaism, and here alone can one discover a certain continuity of effort, from the anonymous *Order of Mishnaic and Talmudic Sages* (*Seder tanna'im va-'amora'im*) in the ninth century, to the *Order of the Generations* (*Seder ha-dorot*) of Yehiel Heilprin in the eighteenth. Yet for all the variations they exhibit, and despite their significance as historical sources for us today, most of the many compositions of this type did not come into being out of a desire to write the history of the Jewish people. Their chief impulses lay elsewhere, in response to those heretics and antagonists who denied the validity of the Oral Law, in the practical need to determine points of law according to earlier and later authorities, and in a natural curiosity about the evolution of Jewish jurisprudence. Biographical details concerning the rabbis who were the links in the chain of tradition are generally scanty at best, and historical events are scattered about almost haphazardly. At any rate, if we except the literature of the "chain of tradition" there is no historiographical genre in medieval Judaism, only isolated historical works, but these hardly add up to a "legacy."

What I have sketched here is not a retrospective construct. There were Jews in the Middle Ages who understood that such was the situation. Already Moses Ibn Ezra complained about "indolence" and even "sin" on the part of Jews in the neglect of both the Hebrew language and the writing of history:

> [A]nd they did not succeed to polish their language, to write their chronicles, and to remember their history and traditions. It would have been fitting that they should not have ignored and despised such matters. Behold . . . all the other nations have exerted themselves to write their histories, and to excel in them.[4]

This written in the twelfth century, and by a Jew living in the midst of a Muslim culture. At the end of the fifteenth century Solomon Ibn Verga, who grew up in Christian Spain, concludes the third chapter of his *Shebet Yehudah* as follows:

> Thus is it found in the chronicles of the kings of Persia which were brought to the king of Spain, according to the custom of the Christians, for they seek to know the things that happened of old in order to take counsel from them, and this because of their distinction and enlightenment.[5]

Significantly, for Ibn Verga it is a *Christian* custom to read historical chronicles, and here there is a note of envy that is at the same time an implicit criticism of his fellow Jews.

Nor is it possible to agree with those who would find an organic connection between various Jewish historical compositions merely because they happened to be written within a certain span of time. One hears, for instance, about "epochs of historical creativity" in the tenth and twelfth centuries,[6] but such an artificial periodization does not convince. Other than a rough chronological coincidence, it is hard to discover a unifying factor around which to group the recital of the events of the Second Commonwealth in *Yosippon*, the description of the affairs of the Babylonian exilarchate in *Sippur Nathan ha-Babli*, and the history of the Talmudic and Gaonic sages presented in *Iggeret Rab Sherira*, though all three were written in the tenth century. Again, there is no discernible link between Ibn Daud's *Sefer ha-Kabbalah*, written against a background of the collapse of Jewish life in Muslim Spain, and the Hebrew Crusade chronicles in Germany, that would justify the suggestion of an "epoch of Jewish historiography" in the twelfth century. At best one may view the Crusade chronicles as a discrete unit, flowing out of a great catastrophe and a common spiritual outlook. Even so, no similar phenomenon is known to us from other times and places in the Middle Ages.

I must emphasize that in what I have outlined thus far, no criticism is intended or implied against the Jews of the past. I do not happen to be among those who would fault medieval Jewry for not writing more history. Quite to the contrary, I can conceive that there may yet arise a future generation that will demand of us why we were so preoccupied, not to say obsessed, with history. The writing of history is far from a natural and ubiquitous human activity to be found in every age and in every culture. If Jews in the Middle Ages wrote relatively little history, that does not point to a flaw or lacuna in their civilization, nor, as has sometimes been alleged, that they lived "outside history." It merely shows that they did not regard historiography as vital to themselves. There were three highways of religious and intellectual creativity among medieval Jews—Halakhah, philosophy, and Kabbalah, each of which offered an all-embracing worldview, and none of which required history in order to be cultivated or validated. These alone led to ultimate truths, to spiritual felicity, and to self-knowledge. In comparison, historical works were at best a form of diversion or, at worst, a waste of time.

It is not that Jews felt the past to be irrelevant to the present. But the relevant past was, for them, the distant, ancient past, the periods of the First and Second Temples. What had happened then had determined what had occurred since, and even provided the explanation for what was now transpiring.

With this in mind we can perhaps better understand why it was that *Yosippon* loomed as the single most important chronicle in the eyes of medieval Jews. Apart from the Bible itself, this was the only available work that offered a detailed account of ancient events in the fateful period whose repercussions were felt to extend to all subsequent generations. When, in the thirteenth century, Judah Mosconi enumerates the many virtues of the book, he writes: "For we can read in it the deeds of our ancestors because of whose sins our city was destroyed . . . and they ate the sour grapes, but our teeth are set on edge."[7] And when, in the generation of the Spanish and

Portuguese exiles, Tam Ibn Yahia sponsored a new edition of *Yosippon* published in Constantinople in 1510, he stated in his introduction:

> And I, in the midst of the exile, wallowing in the blood of the upheavals that are overtaking my people and nation, was roused by my soul and spirit to be among those who have helped to print this book, for this is the one that has laid bare the source of the misfortunes of the House of Judah.[8]

Moreover, the book had the good fortune to be accepted as an original work written by Josephus Flavius in the aftermath of the destruction of the Second Temple. Thereby *Yosippon* acquired a halo of authority in the eyes of Jews that was vouchsafed to no other medieval historical work, and that would have been denied it altogether if it had been regarded as the work of a Jew living in southern Italy in the tenth century. Much of the attitude toward *Yosippon* in particular and, by contrast, to historiography in general, is revealed in the following statement by Tam Ibn Yahia:

> Although it is characteristic of historical works to exaggerate things that never existed, to add to them, to invent things that never were, nevertheless this book [*Yosippon*], although it is part of the same genre, is completely distinct from them, and it is the difference between truth and falsehood. For all the words of this book are righteousness and truth, and there is no wrong within it. And the mark of this is that of all the books written after the Holy Scriptures this is [chronologically] the closest to prophecy, having been written before the Mishnah and the Talmud.[9]

In the same manner we begin to understand why, besides the literature of the "chain of tradition," whose very aim necessitated a survey of all the generations of halakhic endeavor in order to argue their unbroken continuity, there is not a single medieval Jewish chronicle that attempts to give a continuous history of what had occurred since the destruction of the Second Temple. The chronological span is generally short, with most compositions confined to contemporary events or those close to the time of the author, usually relating what happened during a persecution. There is little or no attempt to bridge events from one generation to another. More significantly, in most cases there is little search for specific explanations of what had occurred, and in fact the events described are not regarded essentially as novelties. Only in two instances can one detect a full consciousness that something genuinely new has happened and that there is a special importance to the events themselves. In Ibn Daud's *Sefer ha-Kabbalah* there is a keen awareness of certain processes as a result of which, in his view, spiritual and cultural hegemony among the Jews passed first from Babylonia to the Iberian Peninsula, and in his own time from Muslim to Christian Spain. In the Crusade chronicles there is a palpable sense of the terrifying shift in the relations between Jewry and Christendom, and an expression of astonished awe at this first instance of Jewish mass martyrdom on European soil. But Ibn Daud and the authors of the Crusade chronicles are, in this sense, exceptional rather than exemplary. On the whole, medieval Jewish chronicles tend to assimilate events to old and established conceptual frameworks. Persecution and suffering are, after all, the result of the conditions of exile, and exile itself is the bitter fruit of ancient sins. It is important to realize that there is also no real desire to find novelty in passing events. On the contrary, we find a pronounced tendency to subsume major new events to familiar archetypes, perhaps because even terrible events are less terrifying when viewed in patterns rather than in their bewildering specificity. Thus the new oppressor is Haman and the court-Jew is Mordecai. Christendom is Edom or Esau, and Islam is Ishmael. Samuel ha-Nagid is David, and the Andalusian landscape is biblical. The essential contours of the relationship between Israel and the Gentiles have been delineated long ago in the Aggadah, and there is little or no interest in the history of contemporary nations. In periods of acute messianic tension there may be a spurt of interest in global events and so, for example, we have texts stemming from the first century after the rise of Islam as a world power out of which we can reconstruct minute details of the progress of the Arab conquests.[10] But there is no historiography here, only a desperate apocalyptic equation. The Arab conquests are seen, in essence, as the wars of Gog and Magog which are to bring an end to history.

Not that there was a waning in the vitality of Jewish collective memory in the Middle Ages, but that it did not express itself or function through historiography. Jewish historical memory had other channels: synagogal poetry (*selihot* and *piyyutim*); *Memorbucher*, whose lists of martyrs were kept by the community; special fast days; "Second Purims." That which was placed into such vessels, that which was transfigured liturgically and ritually, was endowed with a chance for survival and permanence. Ordinary chronicles and historical texts were neglected and forgotten, unless (and here again I refer to the literature of the "chain of tradition") they were of halakhic significance, or were embedded in halakhic or theological works. Most medieval Jewish historical writings went down to oblivion, and they are in our hands today only because they were rediscovered and published by scholars in modern times. Should one desire to know what was the medieval historiographical "legacy" available to Jewish readers after the year 1500, it is only necessary to glance at the development of Hebrew printing. In addition to the ever-popular *Yosippon*, only four historical works out of the past were printed in the course of the sixteenth century: *Iggeret Rab Sherira*, *Seder 'Olam Rabba* and *Seder 'Olam Zuta*, and the *Sefer ha-Kabbalah* of Ibn Daud[11] (which usually included his brief sketches of the history of the Second Commonwealth and of the Roman emperors). This was, in effect, the entire "historiographical library" that remained in general circulation from all the preceding generations.

Even if we take into consideration everything that had been written, in the final analysis the Jewish historiographical literature of the Middle Ages was sparse enough, and modern attempts to inflate its dimensions only prove how important historiography is to us. Here I must stress once again that if medieval Jews generally did not write history it was not out of lack of talent, nor even for lack of knowledge, but primarily because they felt no need to do so. It just was not sufficiently important to them, for reasons I have suggested. None of the other explanations usually advanced will suffice. It has been said that sufferings and persecutions numbed the historical creativity of the Jews, that they wrote no history because, lacking a state and political power, they had no history to write about, or that it was because they had neither royal chroniclers nor monks who could devote themselves to historical writing. Such explanations are, however, no more than a form of second-guessing, and they are ultimately self-liquidating. All the aforementioned factors were equally true of the Jewish people in the sixteenth century. Yet in that time a corpus of Jewish historiography was created that surpassed, in scope and quality, all that had come before.

3

Only in the sixteenth century do we encounter, for the first time, a cultural phenomenon within Jewry that can be recognized with little hesitation as genuinely historiographical, though each book that was produced was quite different from the other. As we noted at the outset, ten major works were written. Of their eight authors, five were either exiles from Spain and Portugal or descendants of exiles (Ibn Verga, Zacuto, Usque, Joseph ha-Kohen, Gedaliah Ibn Yahia). One, Elijah Capsali of Crete, was profoundly influenced by Spanish refugees. Only two, Azariah de' Rossi and David Gans, emerge out of a non-Sephardic ambiance (Mantua and Prague, respectively), and their books present special problems. Patently, the primary stimulus to the rise of Jewish historiography in the sixteenth century was the tremendous catastrophe that had overtaken the Jews in the Iberian Peninsula. That is to say, for the first time we encounter a ramified historiographical response to a great historic event. So far as we know, no event in the Middle Ages, not even the Crusades, engendered a comparable literature. In addition to the historical works proper, almost all branches of sixteenth-century Jewish literature are replete with accounts of the Spanish Expulsion of 1492, of the forced conversion that followed in Portugal only five years later, and of the sufferings of the exiles on land and sea. Yet this had hardly been the first expulsion of a European Jewry. The expulsion from France in 1306, while not of the same dimensions, had been no paltry affair. Gersonides had written of the number of French exiles as "twice those who emerged from Egypt."[12] But except for the passage in his commentary on the Pentateuch, there are almost no references in fourteenth-century Jewish texts to that great upheaval. The contrast is glaring.

Certainly there must have been more than one reason for this. But above all, there is a highly articulated feeling among the generations following the expulsion from Spain that something unprecedented had taken place. Not only that an abrupt end had come to a great and venerable Jewry, but also something beyond that. Precisely because this expulsion was not the first but, in a sense, the *last*, it was felt to have altered the face of Jewry and of history itself. When Abravanel enumerates the various European expulsions that began from England in 1290, he perceives the expulsion from Spain as the climax and culmination of a process that has shifted the Jewish people, globally, from the West to the East.[13] The larger significance of the Spanish Expulsion is that because of it, Western Europe has been emptied of Jews. When Abraham Zacuto compares the expulsions from Spain and Portugal with the earlier French expulsion, he understands the radical difference. Relating that a forebear of his had been among the Jewish refugees from France who had found an immediate haven across the border in Spain, he exclaims: "And from France they came to Spain. But we faced the enemies on one side, and the sea on the other!"[14]

That historical crisis should stimulate historical writing comes as no surprise. To take but one pertinent instance, Hans Baron has shown the nexus between the rise of Italian humanist historiography and the breakdown of the republican system in the Italian city-states.[15] The resemblance ends there, however. Except for Azariah de' Rossi, we do not find that the spirit of Italian humanist historiography was absorbed into sixteenth-century Jewish historiography, though some Jewish historians drew information from it. The elements of humanist culture that crop up in the works of Joseph ha-Kohen or Gedaliah Ibn Yahia should not mislead us in this respect, for in the end they remain external trappings. Nor, as is commonly supposed, does the *Shebet Yehudah* of Ibn Verga betray influences of the Italian Renaissance.[16] Recent research has shown that Ibn Verga never came to Italy, but died in Flanders shortly after fleeing from Portugal.[17] If there are external influences in his book they should be sought, as I have long supposed, in the Iberian cultural milieu that was closest to him. But in general, the dynamics of Jewish historiography after the Spanish Expulsion are imminent to itself and related to what had happened within Jewry. Jews who were "wallowing in the blood of the upheavals" wanted to understand the meaning of those upheavals and, as Ibn Verga put it, "Why this enormous wrath?"

4

Jewish historiography in the generations following the expulsion from Spain does not only constitute a novum, but was felt as such. The awareness of novelty is expressed most vividly by Joseph ha-Kohen, in an exultant passage that deliberately echoes the biblical Song of Deborah:

> All my people is aware that no author has arisen in Israel comparable to Yosippon the priest, who wrote of the war of the land of Judea and of Jerusalem. The chroniclers ceased in Israel, they ceased, until I, Joseph, did arise, until I did arise, a chronicler in Israel! And I set my heart to write as a remembrance in a book the bulk of the troubles that have been visited upon us in Gentile lands, from the day that Judah was exiled from its land until the present day.[18]

For all the hyperbole in this passage, it deserves special attention. Joseph ha-Kohen was acquainted with the Jewish historical works of others and drew from them ("I gleaned among the sheaves after the harvesters, whatever my hand could find"). Nonetheless, he considers himself a new creature. Since Yosippon (and let us remember that for him Yosippon was Josephus Flavius of the first century), "the chroniclers ceased in Israel." He states this as something of common knowledge ("all my people knows"), and in terms of the psychology revealed, this testimony is impressive. There is here a consciousness that to write history is something new for Jews, a new beginning after a very long hiatus. Yet if, as he has tacitly admitted, there were historical works in former ages, whence does this feeling arise? What is there about his manner of writing history that enables him to style himself the first Jewish historian since Josephus? Indeed, since we are concerned here not with Joseph ha-Kohen alone, we may well broaden the question. What, in essence, are the novelties within sixteenth-century Jewish historiography as a whole?

To begin with, these works cover a temporal and geographical span far beyond anything that can be found previously. They do not focus merely upon this or that persecution or set of events, but attempt, within the limits of the data available to their authors, a coherent and consecutive survey of many centuries, in an expansive and detailed narration.

A new element is the prominence assigned to postbiblical Jewish history. For the first time we sense a keen interest in the entire course of Jewish history from the destruction of the Second Temple down to the authors' own time. The *Shebet Yehudah* is concerned almost exclusively with events that have occurred since the loss of Jewish independence and especially during the Middle Ages. Joseph ha-Kohen begins his *'Emek ha-bakha*: "And it came to pass *after* all the glory had departed from Jerusalem." If he opens his *Dibrey ha-yamim* with "Adam begat Seth," it is only in order to establish the genealogies of the nations, and after half a page he plunges the reader into the seventh century of the Common Era and the rise of Islam. In Usque's Portuguese work there is a clear triple periodization based, not upon the literary history of scholars and sages, but upon the larger rhythms of Jewish history: the periods of the First and the Second Temples, and a third period that comprises "all the tribulations Israel has suffered since the loss of the Second Temple, destroyed by the Romans, until this day." To this third period he devotes as much space as to the other two combined.

This points also to a new attitude toward the history of Jewry in exile. While, by and large, the Jewish historians of the sixteenth century believe, no less than prior generations, that "for our sins were we exiled," and that "the fathers ate sour grapes and the teeth of the sons are set on edge," they do not regard this as a warrant to gloss over the history of those very sons. On the contrary, they lavish their attention upon it. Thus they bestow a new value upon the events that have transpired over the entire course of the Middle Ages. They seem to recognize implicitly that these events too have a meaning for the present and the future that cannot be grasped merely by focusing attention on ancient times, and that they are therefore worth recalling. All this marks a significant change in outlook.

A final novelty is the renewed interest in the history of the nations, especially of the contemporary nations, in which a desire to know various aspects of non-Jewish history combines with an incipient recognition that Jewish destinies are affected by the interplay of relations between certain of the great powers. To these categories belong such books as Capsali's *Chronicle of Venice*, and large portions of his *Seder Eliyahu Zuta*[19] that are devoted to the history of the Ottoman Empire. In fact, for all its archaic theological presuppositions, the latter work may properly be regarded as a first attempt to write Jewish history within the framework of general history. From Joseph ha-Kohen we possess not only the chronicle of the kings of France and Turkey, but his Hebrew translations (with insertions of his own) of Francisco Lopez de Gomara's *Historia general de las Indias* (*Ha-India ha-hadashah*) and *La conquista de Mexico* (*Sefer Fernando Cortes*).[20] On another level mention should also be made of the various sections dealing with general history in Zacuto's *Sefer Yuhasin* and Ibn Yahia's *Shalshelet ha-Kabbalah*.[21] And of course the entire second part of David Gans's *Zemah David*, although, as already indicated, this book arises out of a different cultural setting.

Taken together, the features enumerated thus far are impressive enough, and for that very reason there is no need to inflate their proportions. Jewish historiography in the wake of the Spanish Expulsion marks a leap forward when viewed over and against what had preceded it. Within other perspectives its stature tends to diminish. It never reached the level of critical insight to be found in the best of general historical scholarship contemporary with it. Moreover, although ten full-fledged historical works following so closely upon one another mark, for Jews, a period of relatively intense historiographical activity, they do represent but a tiny fraction of the sum of sixteenth-century Jewish literature.

Yet these reservations do not absolve us of our primary duty, which is to evaluate this corpus of historiography within its own context, as one among a gamut of Jewish responses to the trauma of the expulsion from Spain. From this vantage point the work of the sixteenth-century Jewish historians may properly be seen as a significant attempt, however tentative, to pave the way among Jews toward a concern with the historical dimension of their existence. In itself this phenomenon was laden with potential for future development and, had it continued, who knows where it might not have led. Seen in retrospect, however, we must conclude that it was an attempt that failed.

It was not, essentially, a failure of the historians, though their limitations are obvious in themselves and deserve to be spelled out.

For all their innovations, they could not free themselves from conceptions and modes of thought that had been deeply rooted among Jews for many ages. We have said that events since the destruction of the Second Temple received a new appreciation, and so they did. But in general these events are perceived as important, not because of any causal connection between them, but because the historians seek to find within them hints, configurations, and meanings that lie beyond them. The historical episodes that Usque narrates derive their significance, not from any intrinsic links they might have to one another, but from his conviction that these events are fulfillments of biblical prophecies that predicted what would happen to the Jewish people in exile. By his own time, Usque believed, even the most dire of biblical prophecies had come to pass, and hence redemption was imminent. All that was lacking was that the Portuguese Marranos return openly to Judaism.

Messianic impulses are discernible in both the *'Emek ha-bakha* and *Dibrey ha-yamim* of Joseph ha-Kohen, even though his messianism is generally restrained and often veiled. He himself hints at the messianic framework in a passage repeated in both books, declaring: "The expulsions from France as well as this exceedingly bitter exile [i.e., from Spain] have roused me to compose this book, so that the Children of Israel may know what [the Gentiles] have done to us in their lands, their courts and their castles, *for behold the days approach*."[22] Behind the *Chronicle of the Kings of France and of the Ottoman Turkish Sultans* there hovers a venerable apocalyptic tradition. Although, characteristically, Joseph ha-Kohen does not allow apocalyptic elements to erupt into the foreground, his book is not a mere exercise in French and Turkish history, but an attempt to trace the age-old struggle between Christendom and Islam, whose leading contemporary standard-bearers were perceived by him as France and the Ottoman Empire. The explicit history remains that of the French and the Turks; the tradition, however muted, that of Gog and Magog.

The messianic theme of the *Seder Eliyahu Zuta* is so dominant as to leave no doubt of Elijah Capsali's intentions. The entire book is messianic history at its most exuberant. It is saturated with biblical messianic language and typologies, and the Turkish sultans are cast in the redemptive image of Cyrus the Great.

In Ibn Verga's *Shebet Yehudah* there is, by contrast, not a trace of messianism, and in several respects its boldness and originality are impressive. Ibn Verga alone transfers the concept of "natural cause" (*ha-sibbah ha-tib'it*) from the sphere of philosophy and science to history and, as Yitzhak Baer has shown, it is he who went farthest in exploring the mundane causes of Jewish historical suffering generally, and of the Spanish Expulsion in particular. Still, it remains a fundamental error to consider Ibn Verga, as some have, to be merely a rationalist with a precociously secular conception of Jewish history. The truth is that his use of "natural cause" by no means precludes or contradicts the notion of divine providence. A close reading of the book will also reveal to what extent Ibn Verga was still bound by attitudes that had crystalized ages ago among the Hispano-Jewish aristocracy and no longer corresponded to the historical realities of his time.[23]

All of these features, however regressive they might seem to modern eyes, do not detract from the essential achievements of the historians. A mixture of old and new is to be expected in the initial phases of almost any cultural development. The fate of sixteenth- century Jewish historiography was ultimately determined by an inheritance of a different order—the attitude among Jews toward historical works generally.

We have noted that historiography had never become a legitimate and recognized genre in medieval Judaism. This meant that except for Zacuto and Ibn Yahia, who continued to write within the familiar and accepted mold of the chain of tradition, the Jewish historians of the sixteenth century found no available slot into which to fit their work. Each, in fact, had to create his own individual forms. But though it made their task more difficult, it is not even this that ultimately defeated them. Something else had passed over from centuries gone by, namely, the relatively low esteem in which historical works of any kind were held by most Jews. Despite their own occasional disclaimers (we shall examine these shortly), it can hardly be doubted that the sixteenth-century historians felt themselves engaged in something that was of high seriousness and purpose. Whether they were taken by the Jewish public as seriously as they deserved, or even correctly understood, is questionable.

Though the reading public of the past is silent almost by definition, there are indirect ways of gauging the attitudes with which our authors had to contend. Most of the historical works under consideration are preceded by introductions filled with apology for the very fact that the writer is dealing with history at all, and offering a host of reasons to justify such a concern. Why was all this necessary? Because the historian knew very well the nature of the audience that awaited him. If even Zacuto, writing within a literary tradition in which distinguished rabbinic scholars of the past had already participated, still feels called upon to declare with a self-deprecatory shrug—"I cannot presume to say that it is a deep science, for because of my sins, as a result of the many persecutions and the want of a livelihood, I have neither strength nor wisdom"[24]—then how much more is there need for special pleading when David Gans presents his detailed chronology of the Gentile nations. These and other apologia go far beyond conventional literary protestations of modesty. Here it is not really the authors' capacities that are at issue, but the value of the enterprise itself. All the introductions sound a common note. It is as though the historian were saying in the same breath: "Dear reader, although both of us know that what I am writing is unimportant, nevertheless it is important."

A somewhat whimsical but revealing example of another kind can be found in the first edition of the *Dibrey ha-yamim* (Sabbionetta, 1554). We recall the exultant cry of Joseph ha-Kohen in his preface to the work: "The chroniclers ceased, they ceased . . . until I arose." But in old printed books it is worthwhile to read all the preliminary matter. In this instance, along with the author's introduction, the following verses are inscribed:

> When the author's nephew, Zerahiah Halevi,
> Saw the glory of this book, and the nectar of its honeycombed words,
> The Lord lifted his spirit and he began to speak.
> So he opened his mouth with song and hymn, and declared:
> Let anyone who delights in a time that was before ours
> *Take this chronicle and read it when his sleep wanders,* [italics mine]
> For in it he will see the history of the nations,
> And should he merit to witness the end of our exile,
> He will understand the difference between the destiny of the Gentile kings and of our Messiah.

Leaving aside the somewhat curious ending, we may focus upon the lines I have placed in italics. Faint praise this, one might say, in a poem purporting to extol the book. After all, even Bach's "Goldberg Variations," though composed expressly for a case of insomnia, were not intended exclusively for nocturnal performances. Certainly we understand that there is a biblicism lurking behind Zerahiah Halevi's lines (Esther 6:1, "On that night the king's sleep wandered, and he commanded to bring the book of records and chronicles"). But it is also more than a neat turn of a biblical phrase, and deserves to be taken seriously. Historical chronicles are to be read "when sleep wanders" (*bi-nedod shenah*), for otherwise such reading is *bittul Torah*, a waste of time that could otherwise be devoted to the serious study of sacred texts. In fact, Zerahiah's attitude is by no means unusual. Despite Tam Ibn Yahia's veneration for *Yosippon*, he is at pains to add in his introduction to the work that especially "the merchants who are immersed in temporal successes, and who have not turned to the Torah in their leisure time, will delight in reading it."[25]

Of all the historical works, Ibn Verga's *Shebet Yehudah* was to enjoy the widest popularity. I have examined no less than seventeen different editions printed from the mid-sixteenth century to the end of the eighteenth, and there may be others. What was at the heart of this extraordinary success? How was the book read, and what did its readers see in it? I think one may safely assume that only isolated readers grasped Ibn Verga's intentions in exploring the Spanish Expulsion and the situation of Jews in Christian society. There are sufficient indications that what seems central to us in the book was not what attracted most readers, but rather other matters. It is interesting, for example, to follow the metamorphoses in the texts of the title pages of the *Shebet Yehudah*, for these were aimed at focusing the reader's attention on what were considered the highlights within. Already in the title page of the first edition (Adrianople, 1553), published more than four decades after Solomon Ibn Verga's death, the following description of the book is given (the words are not of the author, but of the editor, Joseph Ibn Verga, or the printer):

> This is a book of the generations of Israel, and of the many misfortunes that have come upon the Jews in the lands of the nations. . . . And so it tells of the blood-libel, how many times its falsehood was revealed and made public, and Israel emerged delivered. Similarly,

> it speaks of religious disputations that were held in the presence of kings, as well as the ceremony of installing the princes [i.e., the exilarchs] in various periods. . . . Finally, it depicts the structure of the Temple and its inner precincts, the service of the High Priest when he came to his chamber before the Day of Atonement, and the order of the Passover sacrifice, which we shall yet see with our own eyes, as we were promised by our Creator, the lord of compassion.

What is so frustrating about this harbinger of the modern publisher's blurb is the fact that technically each detail is correct, yet the total impression is so far removed from the inner spirit of the book. By the time we come to the third edition, a Yiddish translation printed in Krakow in 1591 "for ordinary householders, men and women" (*far gemayne baale-batim, man un vayber*), we can see from the title page that the *Shebet Yehudah* has been transmuted perceptually into a standard piece of edifying folk literature:

> One will find in it marvelous stories of what happened to our fathers in exile, and how many times they underwent martyrdom, the book also specifying in which times and in which countries it all happened, so that a person's heart will be roused to the fear of God. May the Blessed Lord in His infinite mercy and grace continue to keep His people from all evil calamities, and send us the redeemer, Messiah son of David, speedily and in our own days.

More examples could be adduced, but the point remains. The attitude toward historiography among sixteenth-century readers was no different, by and large, from what it had been in prior ages. A historical work was regarded as something pleasant and diverting in moments of leisure, and at best a source of moral uplift. Works concerned with the history of Gentile nations were still described generically as "books of wars" (*sifrey milhamot*), and in halakhic literature opinions continued divided about whether one is permitted to read them, and when, and in what language.[26]

5

Still, one Jewish historical work of the sixteenth century, though not a chronicle, was received with sufficient seriousness to produce some very interesting repercussions. I have in mind Azariah de' Rossi's collection of historical and antiquarian essays, entitled *Me'or 'Einayim* and first published in Mantua in 1573–1575. Unlike the other books with which we have been dealing, the *Me'or 'Einayim* has no links to the Spanish Expulsion and the spiritual crisis it provoked. It is rather the fruit of a creative encounter, in the mind of an Italian rabbi, between Jewish tradition and Italian Renaissance culture. Unlike so many other books written by Italian Jews that display a veneer of humanistic learning, here the humanist spirit has penetrated the very vitals of the work, and only here do we find the real beginnings of historical criticism. The *Me'or 'Einayim* remains the most audacious Jewish historical work of the sixteenth century. Its essential daring lies in Azariah's reluctance to set up predetermined boundaries between his general and Jewish knowledge, in his readiness to allow a genuine confrontation between the two spheres, and in his acceptance of the conclusions that seemed to flow out of it.

For our present purpose the most instructive aspect of the book lies in what it reveals about the audience and the spiritual climate of the time. Throughout his writing Azariah shows himself particularly sensitive to public opinion. He writes with utmost care, and is even prepared to make certain compromises so long as they do not involve basic principles. Time and again he interrupts his discussions in order to comment on the objections he anticipates from his potential readers. Thus, in speaking of various Talmudic references to the massacre of Alexandrian Jewry:

> Let us now turn back to the city of Alexandria. Our eyes behold three different passages concerning it, for the Jerusalem Talmud has stated that the evil murderer was Trajan . . . and the Babylonian Talmud in tractate Sukkah said it was Alexander of Macedon, while in tractate Gittin it changed its opinion to write that it was Hadrian. And if we have now begun to investigate the [historical] truth of these matters, that is not because of the thing in itself, for what was—was [*mai de-havah havah*], but only because we are concerned that the words of our sages in relating well-known events should not appear to contradict one another.[27]

Later on, in the same chapter:

> At any rate, even were we to admit that some stories reached the ears of the sages with some distortion, and that this is how they related them to us, that in no way diminishes their stature. And even though

> this chapter consists mostly of inconsequential investigations [*hakirot shel mah be-khakh*], for it will be said "what was—was, and there is in it no relevance to law or observance," still, the refined soul yearns to know the truth of everything.[28]

And again, in his strictures on the computation of the traditional Jewish era of Creation:

> Before we leave this subject it will become clear that the manner in which they, of blessed memory, computed the years was considered a noble science whose worth was known and proclaimed by every enlightened person. However, I can foresee that you will say to yourself, dear reader: "But surely such an investigation is completely far-fetched [*hilkheta de-meshiha*, literally, "law for the time of the Messiah"] and even worse, for what have we to do with all this, considering that what was—was, several thousand years ago or more?"[29]

There are many such passages in the *Me'or 'Einayim*, and they demonstrate vividly the reactions that Azariah expected from his readers. He was wary of them on two counts. His overall concern was that they had a low opinion of any historical investigation. "What was—was." This phrase seems to sum up for him the prevalent Jewish mood, and it surfaces so frequently in the book as to be almost a leitmotif. More specifically, however, he suspected that some of the contents of the book would be construed as a denigration of the Talmudic sages.

As it turned out, his worries were not in vain. The book was printed and immediately attacked. In various Italian Jewish communities it was placed under rabbinic ban.[30]

Rumblings were heard from Prague and from Safed in Palestine.[31] Some rose in defense of the book. But the question remains—what, in essence, stirred up the tempest? Azariah was no heretic, but a respected physician-scholar whose personal piety was not in question. Mantua was a center of Jewish intellectuals well attuned to the cultural currents of the time. Indeed, most of the Italian rabbis who signed the ban were not obscurantists, but men of fairly broad secular culture.

Could it really have been Azariah's debunking of the rabbinic legend about the gnat that entered Titus' head through the nose and finally killed him?[32] Azariah himself relates that there were Jews who sharply criticized this passage in his book and regarded what he had done as an insult to the sages. But could the critique of such an *aggadah* really have seemed like a novelty in the sixteenth century? Did there not already exist long and recognized traditions within Judaism, whether philosophical or kabbalistic, which could not accept rabbinic *aggadot* literally, and which strove to reinterpret them rationally or mystically, at times to the most radical extremes? In what manner, then, had Azariah de' Rossi transgressed?

I would suggest that the answer lies, not in the fact of Azariah's criticism, but in its source, method, and conclusion. Philosophic and Kabbalistic critiques and reinterpretations of *aggadah* possessed an age-old legitimacy even though, to be sure, there still remained Jews in Azariah's time who would not accept even these.[33] The essential innovation in Azariah's approach lay in his attempt to evaluate *aggadot*, not within the framework of philosophy or Kabbalah, each a source of truth for its partisans, but by the use of profane history that few, if any, would accept as a truth by which the words of the sages might be judged. Worse than that, Azariah ventured to employ non-Jewish historical sources for this purpose, drawn from Greek, Roman, and Christian writers. Above all, he did not flinch from the conclusions that emerged out of the comparison, even when these affected so sensitive an area as calendar computation. As for Titus's gnat, Azariah would not reinterpret the legend metaphorically or allegorically, nor did he spiritualize it in any way in order to salvage it. Citing Roman and other historians as to the actual date and cause of Titus's death, he dismissed the story as historically untrue. Such historical critiques could not yet be tolerated, let alone assimilated, by Azariah's Jewish contemporaries. On the contrary, it is perhaps a token of the flexibility of Italian Jewry that the ban upon the book (it was not pronounced against the author, and only required that special permission be obtained by those who wanted to read it) was not always enforced stringently, and there were some who continued to read it in subsequent generations. Azariah's experiment, however, remained his alone. There were no heirs to his method.

In a vital sense that is true of sixteenth-century Jewish historiography as a whole. In retrospect we see it as a sudden flowering, and an equally abrupt withering. It produces no real continuity and has no parallel for the next two hundred years. At the end of the sixteenth century those who still sought the meaning of Jewish historical suffering and of the length of exile found it in the Kabbalah of Isaac Luria and his disciples, and it is surely more than coincidence that a people that did not yet dream of defining itself in historical categories should find the key to its history in an awesome metahistorical myth.

I do not mean by this to imply in any way that sixteenth-century historiography and Lurianic Kabbalah stood in a consciously competitive relationship in which the latter was "victorious." Though both were ultimately related to the Spanish Expulsion, each represented a separate response with its own inner dynamics. If I juxtapose the two, it is not in order to suggest an organic lateral relationship, but because of what the juxtaposition reveals about the mentality of Jews. That the historiographical effort proved abortive, while the Lurianic myth permeated ever-widening circles in Jewry, seems to me a datum of no small consequence for an understanding of important facets of that mentality. Whatever Lurianic Kabbalah may have meant to Jews (and Gershom Scholem has unveiled for us both its conceptual audacity and overwhelming pathos), its rapid reception by the Jewish world is significant in itself. Clearly, the bulk of Jewry was unprepared to tolerate history in imminent terms. It is as though, with the culminating tragedy of the expulsion from Spain, Jewish history had become opaque, and could not yield a satisfactory meaning even when, as among most of the historians, it was viewed religiously. Patently, however, Jews were spiritually and psychologically prepared for that which Lurianic Kabbalah offered them: a mythic interpretation of history that lay beyond history, and endowed the individual with the power to participate actively in hastening its messianic liquidation.

For us, both the Jewish historiography and the Kabbalah of the sixteenth century have become "history." Not only are we equidistant from both; we also study both—historically. But if we style ourselves historians and do not aspire to be kabbalists, that should not indulge us in the illusion that we have salvaged the one over the other.

There is no continuum between sixteenth-century Jewish historiography and Jewish historical scholarship as we know it and practice it in modern times. The rupture has been complete and decisive. To the degree that we have become historians (and there is no Jewish scholarly discipline today that is not historical), our roots lie in other soil. The fact that, in 1794, the *Me'or 'Einayim* was republished by the *Maskilim* in Berlin should not mislead us in this respect. At that time the *Historisches Journal* had already appeared in Gottingen for more than two decades, Barthold Niebuhr was eighteen years old, and Ranke would be born a year later. We are not the heirs of Azariah de' Rossi, but of these men and others, and the mode whereby we came into this inheritance has implications of its own. If the historical consciousness of the modern West is the result of gradual and coherent developments within European culture, Jews absorbed it abruptly when they plunged into that culture in the nineteenth century. The quest for Jewish history inaugurated by *Wissenschaft des Judentums* emanated from the convergence of a religious collapse from within and assimilation from without.[34] These observations involve neither judgment nor regret, both irrelevant in face of what seems, in retrospect, to have been inevitable.[35] In the measure that we have become modern Western men and women, the historical outlook is now part of our innermost selves.

As a result, Jewish scholars since the nineteenth century have been building, at an ever-accelerating rate, a vast edifice of historical research. Whether, despite what has been achieved, one can say even now that historiography has found a home within Jewry at large is another matter. Whether contemporary Jewry, having lived through its own unparalleled cataclysm, looks to history for meaning, or awaits a new myth, will also bear discussion. These and other queries arise, unsummoned, "when sleep wanders," even though one knows that the work will continue in the morning.

NOTES

FOREWORD

1. David N. Myers and Alexander Kaye, eds., *The Faith of Fallen Jews: Yosef Hayim Yerushalmi and the Writing of Jewish History* (Lebanon, NH: Brandeis University Press, 2013); Elisheva Carlebach, John M. Efron, and David N. Myers, eds., *Jewish History and Jewish Memory: Essays in Honor of Yosef Hayim Yerushalmi* (Hanover, NH: Brandeis University Press, 1998).

2. Salo W. Baron, *A Social and Religious History of the Jews*, 18 vols. (New York: Jewish Publication Society, 1952), 7: 197.

3. Ahad Ha'am, *Selected Essays by Ahad Ha-'Am*, trans. Leon Simon (Philadelphia: Jewish Publication Society of America, 1912), 309.

4. Job 38:2, 38:4.

INTRODUCTION

1. *Proceedings of the American Academy for Jewish Research* 46/47 (1979–1980): 607–38.

2. École des hautes études en sciences sociales (EHESS). S. A. Goldberg, "Interview with Yosef Hayim Yerushalmi," *Communauté nouvelle* (December 1987): 202–7.

3. Another interview exists in Hebrew with Shulamit Volkov and Yosef Kaplan, published in *Historia* 16 (2005): 5–19.

4. For an overview of the scope of Yerushalmi's interests and publications, see *Jewish History and Jewish Memory: Essays in Honor of Yosef Hayim Yerushami*, edited by Elisheva Carlebach, John M. Efron, and David N. Myers (Hanover, NH, and London: Brandeis University Press, 1998), 457–59.

1. *Zakhor*, FROM MEMORY TO READING HISTORY

1. Pierre Nora, *Les Lieux de mémoire* (Paris: Gallimard, 1984–1992, Quarto, 1997), translated as *Realms of Memory: The Construction of the French Past, Volume 1: Conflicts and Divisions* (New York: Columbia University Press, 1996); *Realms of Memory: The Construction of the French Past, Volume 2: Traditions* (New York: Columbia University Press, 1997); and *Realms of Memory: The Construction of the French Past, Volume 3: Symbols* (New York: Columbia University Press, 1998). All three volumes in English were edited by Pierre Nora and Lawrence D. Kritzman and translated by Arthur Goldhammer.

2. Amos Funkenstein (1937–1995), *Theology and the Scientific Imagination from*

the Middle Ages to the Seventeenth Century (Princeton, NJ: Princeton University Press, 1986); *Perceptions of Jewish History from Antiquity to the Present*, in Hebrew (Tel Aviv: Am Oved, 1991); in English (Berkeley: University of California Press, 1993).

3. Amos Funkenstein, "Collective Memory and Historical Consciousness," *History & Memory* 1 (Fall–Winter 1989): 5–26.

4. Heinrich Graetz (1817–1891), a graduate of the University of Jena and director of the rabbinical seminary in Breslau, was the first to write a global history of the Jews: *Geschichte der Juden*, 11 vols. (1853–1875; Leipzig: O. Leiner, 1905–1906).

5. Salo Wittmayer Baron (1895–1989), born in Galicia, received rabbinical ordination from the Jewish Theological Seminary (hereafter JTS). He taught at Columbia University. His monumental *Social and Religious History of the Jews* (17 vols., 2nd ed., Columbia University Press, 1952–1983) and *The Jewish Community* (3 vols., Jewish Publication Society of America, 1948), are among his major publications.

6. The term Jerusalem School refers to historians at the Hebrew University of Jerusalem during the 1930s.

7. Yitzhak Baer (1888–1980), born in Germany, studied in Berlin, Strasbourg, and Freiburg before emigrating to Palestine in 1929, where he became one of the pioneers of Israeli historiography: *A History of the Jews in Christian Spain*, in German, 1929–1936; in Hebrew (Tel Aviv: Am Oved, 1945–1959; in English (Philadelphia: Jewish Publication Society, 1961–1966).

8. [Tr. note] Gershom Scholem, *Major Trends in Jewish Mysticism* (Jerusalem: Schocken Publishing House, 1941; repr., New York: Schocken Books, 1946 and subsequently).

9. Gershom Scholem (1897–1982), born in Berlin, emigrated from there to Jerusalem in 1923, where he became one of the major figures of the Hebrew University. His masterful work on Jewish mysticism has transformed the general approach to Jewish history. His "Mitzvah haba'ah ba'averah," *Keneset* 2 (1937): 347–92, was translated by Hillel Halkin in G. Scholem, *The Messianic Idea in Judaism: And Other Essays on Jewish Spirituality* (New York: Schocken, 1971).

10. Sabbatai Zevi was at the origin of a messianic movement that traversed the entire Jewish world and aimed to return the Jews to Palestine. In 1666, Ottoman authorities, suppressing all revolutionary fervor, offered Sabbatai the choice between conversion to Islam or death. Sabbatai converted. Despite this conversion, interpreted as a stage in his messianic work, the movement continued, taking on an antinomian turn, in which to transgress a law was to accomplish it in the highest degree. This transgressive theology was brought to its apogee in late eighteenth-century Poland by Jacob Frank.

11. Saul Lieberman (1898–1983) taught at JTS for four decades. His work fo-

cuses in particular on critical editions of the texts of the Jerusalem Talmud, Tosefta, and Midrashim. His works have become classics: *Greek in Jewish Palestine* (New York: Jewish Theological Seminary, 1942); *Hellenism in Jewish Palestine* (New York: Jewish Theological Seminary, 1950); *Texts and Studies* (New York: Ktav, 1974).

12. Shalom Spiegel (1899–1984), *The Last Trial: On the Legends and Lore of the Command to Abraham to Offer Isaac as a Sacrifice*, trans. Judah Goldin (Philadelphia: Jewish Publication Society of America, 1967).

13. Harold Louis Ginsberg (1903–1990) was a specialist in Semitic languages, pioneer of Ugaritic studies, and professor of rabbinic literature at the Jewish Theological Seminary.

14. Paul Oskar Kristeller (1905–1999) was a pupil of Martin Heidegger before fleeing Nazi Germany. Among his works on the Renaissance: *The Renaissance Philosophy of Man* (Chicago: University of Chicago Press, 1950); *The Classics and Renaissance Thought* (Cambridge: Harvard University Press, 1955); *Die Philosophie des Marsilio Ficino* (Frankfurt am Main: Klostermann, 1972); *Humanismus und Renaissance*, 2 vols. (Munich: Fink, 1974–1976).

15. *The Civilization of the Renaissance in Italy* [Die Kultur der Renaissance in Italien, 1860] is a work about the Italian Renaissance by the Swiss historian Jacob Burckhardt. Together with his *History of the Renaissance in Italy* [Die Geschichte der Renaissance in Italien, 1867], it is counted among the classics of Renaissance historiography.

16. Johan Huizinga (1872–1945), *Herfsttij der Middeleeuwen* (1919), translated in 1924 as *The Waning of the Middle Ages*. Newly translated by Rodney J. Payton and Ulrich Mammitzsch as *The Autumn of the Middle Ages* (Chicago: University of Chicago Press, 1996).

17. Ernst Kantorowicz (1895–1963), *The King's Two Bodies: A Study in Mediaeval Political Theology* (Princeton: Princeton University Press, 1957) with new edition from Princeton University Press in 2016; and *Kaiser Friedrich der Zweite* (Georg Bondi, 1927), translated as *Frederick the Second, 1194–1250* (New York: Frederick Ungar Publishing Co., 1957).

18. [Tr. note] The Annales school is an influential group of historians associated with a style of historiography developed by twentieth-century French historians to investigate long-term social history. It is named after its scholarly journal, *Annales d'histoire* économique *et sociale*. Cofounders were Lucien Febvre (1878–1956), Henri Hauser (1866–1946), and Marc Bloch (1886–1944), with a second generation including Fernand Braudel (1902–1985), Georges Duby (1919–1996), Jacques Le Goff (1924–2014), and others.

19. Braudel's major work was *La Méditerranée et le Monde Méditerranéen à l'époque*

de Philippe II (3 vols., 1949), later published as *The Mediterranean and the Mediterranean World in the Age of Philip II* (2 vols., 2nd rev. ed., trans. 1972 and 1973 by Sian Reynolds).

20. Lucien Febvre, *Le problème de l'incroyance au XVIe siècle. La religion de Rabelais* (Paris: Albin Michel, 1947; new edition 2003). Translated as *The Problem of Unbelief in the 16th Century: The Religion of Rabelais*, trans. Beatrice Gottlieb (Cambridge, MA: Harvard University Press, 1983).

21. Lucien Febvre, "La sensibilité et l'histoire" [Sensitivity and history], *Annales d'histoire sociale* 3 (1941): 1; repr. in *Combats pour l'histoire* (Paris: Armand Colin, 1953), 236.

22. Américo Castro, *España en su historia; Cristianos, Moros y Judíos* (Buenos Aires: Editorial Losada, 1948). Substantially edited and revised in the translation by Edmund L. King, *The Structure of Spanish History* (Princeton, NJ: Princeton University Press, 1954).

23. For more details, see Yosef Hayim Yerushalmi, "L'antisémitisme racial est-il apparu au XXe siècle? De la *limpieza de sangre* espagnole au nazisme" [Did racial anti-Semitism appear in the 20th century? From limpieza of Spanish blood to Nazism], Esprit (March–April 1993): 5–35; also *Assimilation and Racial Anti-Semitism: The Iberian and the German Models* (New York: Leo Baeck Institute, 1982).

24. Claudio Sanchez-Albornoz (1896–1984), *La España musulmana: Según los autores Islamitas y Cristianos medievales*, 2 vols. (Buenos Aires: El Ateneo, 1946).

25. Marcel Bataillon, *Erasme et l'Espagne. Recherches sur l'histoire spirituelle du XVIe siècle* [Erasmus and Spain: Research on the spiritual history of the 16th century] (Geneva: Librairie Droz, 1937); translated into Spanish as *Erasmo y España, estudios sobre la historia espiritual del siglo XVI* (México, Buenos Aires: Fondo de Cultura Económica, 1950).

2. CHOOSING HISTORY

1. Conservative Judaism, known as Masorti Judaism outside North America, is a religious movement that regards the authority of Jewish law and tradition as emanating primarily from the assent of the people and the community through the generations, more than from divine revelation. The Conservative rabbinate employs modern historical-critical research, rather than only traditional methods and sources, and lends great weight to its constituency when determining its stance on matters of practice.

2. Narrative passages.

3. Documents written in a cuneiform syllabary, discovered on the site of the ancient city of Ugarit, on the Syrian coast. These texts, written in a language close

to Hebrew, bear witness to a Canaanite culture. Their proximity to biblical language has shed light on the meaning of many obscure terms in the Bible.

4. Abraham Halkin (1904–1990), who taught for thirty years at the Jewish Theological Seminary, produced a critical edition of the Yemen Letter written by Maimonides and sent to the Yemenite Jews (*Moses Maimonides' Epistle to Yemen: The Arabic Original and the Three Hebrew Versions*, New York: American Academy for Jewish Research, 1952).

5. Zvi Ankori (1920–2012) was a specialist in the history of the Jews of medieval Byzantium and Crete, and author of *Karaites in Byzantium: The Formative Years, 970–1100* (New York: Columbia University Press, 1956; repr. New York: AMS Press, 1968). Also *Chestnuts of Yesteryear: a Jewish Odyssey*, trans. from the Hebrew by Evelyn Abel (Jerusalem: Gefen, 2003).

6. Garrett Mattingly (1900–1962), professor of European History at Columbia University, was author of *The Defeat of the Spanish Armada* (London: Jonathan Cape, 1959).

7. Gerson D. Cohen (1924–1991), author of *Jewish History and Jewish Destiny* (New York, Jerusalem: Jewish Theological Seminary, 1997); *Messianic Postures of Ashkenazim and Sephardim (Prior to Sabbethai Zevi)*, the Leo Baeck Memorial Lecture 9 (New York: Leo Baeck Institute, 1967); *A Critical Edition with a Translation and Notes of the Book of Tradition (Sefer Ha-Qabbalah) by Abraham ibn Daud* (Philadelphia: Jewish Publication Society, 1967); *Studies in the Variety of Rabbinic Cultures* (New York: Jewish Publication Society, 1991).

8. Revised nine years later and published as "The Inquisition and the Jews of France in the Time of Bernard Gui," *Harvard Theological Review* 63 (1970): 317–76.

9. Isaac ben Judah Abravanel (1437–1508) was a Portuguese Jewish statesman, philosopher, Bible commentator, and financier. He exercised leading responsibilities with the Spanish and Portuguese sovereigns before the expulsions of 1492 and 1497. After his departure from Spain he moved to Venice, where he produced an original biblical exegesis, in which the theme of redemption is in the forefront.

10. Cecil Roth, *A History of the Marranos* (Philadelphia: The Jewish Publication Press, [1932], 1947).

11. Literally, the Science of Judaism. A nineteenth-century movement premised on the critical investigation of Jewish literature and culture, including rabbinic literature, using scientific methods to analyze the origins of Jewish traditions.

12. [Tr. note] Hasdai ben Abraham Crescas (c. 1340–1410 or '11) was a Catalan Jewish philosopher and renowned halakhist. Along with Maimonides, Gerson-

ides, and Joseph Albo, he is known as one of the major practitioners of the rationalist approach to Jewish philosophy.

13. Harry Austryn Wolfson produced a considerable body of work, including *Philo: Foundations of Religious Philosophy in Judaism, Christianity and Islam* (Cambridge, MA: Harvard University Press, 1947); *Crescas' Critique of Aristotle: Problems of Aristotle's Physics in Jewish and Arabic Philosophy* (Cambridge, MA: Harvard University Press,1929); and *The Philosophy of the Church Fathers. Volume I: Faith, Trinity, Incarnation* (Cambridge, MA: Harvard University Press, 1956).

14. A specialist in medieval scholastics, Étienne Gilson (1884–1978), a French philosopher and historian of philosophy, taught at the Collège de France and in Toronto. Gilson originally specialised in the thought of Descartes, yet also philosophized in the tradition of Thomas Aquinas, although he did not consider himself a Neo-Thomist philosopher.

3. BACK TO CHILDHOOD

1. Rabbi Israel Salanter Yeshiva on Washington Avenue in the Bronx, New York, named after Rabbi Yisrael ben Ze'ev Wolf Lipkin, also known as Israel Salanter (1809–1883). He was the father of the Musar movement in Orthodox Judaism and aimed to spread in the yeshiva world a spirituality based on ethics, righteous self-effort, and caring for others.

2. [Tr. note] Today's Holoskiv, a village in the Letychiv Raion district of the Khmelnytskyi Oblast in western Ukraine.

3. [Tr. note] Givat HaShlosha (Hill of the Three) is a kibbutz in central Israel located about four kilometers east of Petah Tikva, near the Yarkon River. The kibbutz is named after three workers from Petah Tikva who were accused of espionage during the First World War (when Palestine was under Ottoman rule), imprisoned in Damascus, and tortured to death in 1916.

4. A traditional elementary school teaching the basics of Judaism and the Hebrew language.

5. Lighting a match for any reason, let alone to smoke a cigarette, is prohibited on Shabbat.

6. The General Jewish Labour Bund in Lithuania, Poland, and Russia (*Algemeyner yidisher arbeter-bund in lite, poyln, un rusland*), generally called The Bund (federation or union) or the Jewish Labour Bund, was a secular Jewish socialist party in the Russian Empire, active between 1897 and 1920.

7. Habonim (The Builders). A Jewish Labour Zionist youth movement organization founded in London in 1929, advocating agricultural establishments of the kibbutz type.

8. Hashomer Hatzair (The Young Guard). A Socialist-Zionist, secular Jewish youth movement founded in 1913 in Galicia, Austria-Hungary, promoting the concept that Jewish youth could be liberated by moving to Palestine and working on kibbutzim.

9. Bnei Akiva (Children of Akiva) is the largest religious Zionist youth movement in the world, extending over forty-two countries. It was established in 1929 in Mandatory Palestine with the motto, "Torah and Work."

10. *Haggadah and History: A Panorama in Facsimile of Five Centuries of the Printed Haggadah* (Philadelphia: Jewish Publication Society, [1975] 1997).

11. *From Spanish Court to Italian Ghetto. Isaac Cardoso: A Study in Seventeenth-Century Marranism and Jewish Apologetics* (New York: Columbia University Press, 1971).

12. Abraham Yaari (1899–1966), *Bibliography of the Passover Haggadah from the Earliest Printed Edition to 1960* (in Hebrew) (Jerusalem: Bamberger & Wahrman, 1960).

4. THE PATH TO CARDOSO

1. [Tr. note] *Shulamith or The Daughter of Jerusalem* (1880) by Abraham Goldfaden (born Avrum Goldnfoden; 1840–1908), a Russian-born Jewish poet, playwright, stage director, and actor considered the father of modern Jewish theater.

2. [Tr. note] Shloyme Zanvl Rappoport (1863–1920), who published under the pen name S. Ansky (or An-sky), was a Jewish author, playwright, and folklorist. He is best known for his play *The Dybbuk, or Between Two Worlds* (1914).

3. [Tr. note] In *The Dybbuk*, Khanan, a poor yeshiva student who is in love with Leah, is rumored to practice the forbidden Kabbalah.

4. [Tr. note] Maurice Schwartz, born Avram Moishe Schwartz (1889–1960) in Galicia, was a producer, director, and actor in the United States, where he founded the Yiddish Art Theatre and its associated school in 1918 in New York City.

5. [Tr. note] Israel Joshua Singer (1893–1944) was a Polish-born American novelist who wrote in Yiddish. He was the brother of authors Isaac Bashevis Singer and Esther Kreitman. His novel *Di mishpokhe Karnovski* (1943) was adapted for the stage in its year of publication, but the play was less successful than his *Yoshe Kalb* (1932), a hit in New York's Yiddish theater.

6. The United Jewish Appeal (UJA) was a Jewish philanthropic organization that existed from its creation in 1939 until it was folded into the United Jewish Communities, which was formed from the 1999 merger of United Jewish Appeal (UJA), Council of Jewish Federations, and United Israel Appeal, Inc. In 2009, United Jewish Communities changed its name to The Jewish Federations of North America.

7. Joshua Finkel (1904–1983) was an orientalist and scholar born in Warsaw, who studied the relationship of Islam to Judaism. Starting in 1937, he taught Semitic languages at Yeshiva University. Among his publications was *Maimonides' Treatise on Resurrection* [Maqala fi teḥiyyat ha-metim] (New York: American Academy for Jewish Research, 1939).

8. [Tr. note] Albrecht (Albi) Gabriel Rosenthal, music scholar and antiquarian bookseller, born in Munich (1914–2004), founded the Oxford, UK-based firm A. Rosenthal Ltd., specializing in Judaica and Hebraica.

9. Reprinted in Gershom Scholem, *The Messianic Idea in Judaism and Other Essays on Jewish Spirituality* (New York: Schocken Books, 1971).

10. [Tr. note] Today, the Arquivo dos Registos Paroquiais in Lisbon has been renamed the Arquivo Distrital de Lisboa.

11. [Tr. note] *The Jews in Modern and Contemporary Spain* (Madrid: Ediciones Arion, 1961–1962), by Julio Caro Baroja (1914–1995), a Spanish anthropologist, historian, and linguist, weighed the national impact of the Alhambra Decree, an edict issued in 1492 by the joint Catholic Monarchs of Spain (Isabella I of Castile and Ferdinand II of Aragon) ordering the expulsion of practicing Jews from the Kingdoms of Castile and Aragon.

12. Fernando was the baptismal name of Cardoso, who chose to be called Isaac after leaving Portugal and returning to Judaism.

13. [Tr. note] Trivium, an introductory curriculum at medieval universities involving the study of grammar, rhetoric, and logic.

14. According to canon law, baptism automatically and irreversibly confers the status of Christianity. Someone who has been a Christian and subsequently practices Judaism, even if he is of Jewish origin, is therefore not a Jew who pretended to be a Christian, but a Christian who practices Judaism. As such, he is guilty of Judaic heresy and falls under inquisitorial jurisdiction. At the end of the sixteenth century, the Republic of Venice, in conflict with the Papacy, decreed that it would not ask new immigrants from Spain what religion they practiced before their arrival, and that they were free to openly be Jews, even if officially no Jews lived in Spain after 1492.

5. THE MELODY OF HISTORY

1. Yosef Hayim Yerushalmi, *Freud's Moses: Judaism Terminable and Interminable* (New Haven, CT: Yale University Press, 1991).

2. "Series Z: An Archival Fantasy," *Journal of European Psychoanalysis* 3–4 (Spring 1996–Winter 1997): 21–31.

3. [Tr. note] Léon Bloy (1846–1917) was a French novelist and essayist. Jorge Luis Borges (1899–1986), the Argentine short story writer, essayist, and poet, wrote in his prologue to Emanuel Swedenborg's *Mystical Works* in *The Total Library: Non-Fiction, 1922–1986*, ed. Eliot Weinberger, trans. Esther Allen, Suzanne Jill Levine, and Eliot Weinberger (London: Allen Lane, Penguin Press, 2000), 456: "Thomas Carlyle would state that universal history is a text we must continually read and write, and in which we, too, are written."

4. Yosef Kaplan, *From Christianity to Judaism: The Story of Isaac Orobio de Castro* (London: Oxford University Press, 1989).

5. Hayden White, *Metahistory: The Historical Imagination in Nineteenth-Century Europe* (Baltimore: Johns Hopkins University Press, 1973).

6. [Tr. note] Jacques Derrida (1930–2004) was an Algerian-born French philosopher who developed a form of semiotic analysis known as deconstruction in the context of phenomenology.

7. Carlo Ginzburg, *History, Rhetoric, and Proof*, The Menahem Stern Jerusalem Lectures, (Waltham, MA: Brandeis University Press, 1999).

6. FROM *Zakhor* TO *Freud*

1. [Tr. note] Robert Faurisson (1929–2018) was a British-born French academic who became notorious for his publications denying the historical reality of the Holocaust.

2. [Tr. note] *Zakhor: Jewish History and Jewish Memory* (Seattle: University of Washington Press, 1982), 98.

3. [Tr. note] Elie Wiesel (born Eliezer Wiesel, 1928–2016) was a Romanian-born American novelist, essayist, Nobel laureate, and Holocaust survivor.

4. [Tr. note] *Yedioth Ahronoth*, a national daily newspaper published in Tel Aviv, founded in 1939 in Mandatory Palestine.

5. In 1954, Elie Wiesel completed an 862-page manuscript in Yiddish about his concentration camp experiences, published in Argentina as the 245-page *Un di velt hot geshvign* [And the world remained silent]. The novelist François Mauriac helped Wiesel find a French publisher. Les Éditions de Minuit published 178 pages as *La Nuit* in 1958, and in 1960, Hill and Wang in New York published a 116-page translation as *Night*.

6. Jan Assmann, German Egyptologist, author of *The Search for God in Ancient Egypt*, trans. David Lorton (Ithaca, NY: Cornell University Press, 2001); *Cultural Memory and Early Civilization: Writing, Remembrance, and Political Imagination* (Cambridge: Cambridge University Press, 2011); *Moses the Egyptian: The Memory of Egypt*

in *Western Monotheism* (Cambridge, MA: Harvard University Press, 1997; 1998); and *From Akhenaten to Moses: Ancient Egypt and Religious Change* (Cairo: The American University in Cairo Press, 2014).

7. Rivkah Schärf Kluger (1907–1987); see *Satan in the Old Testament* (Evanston, IL: Northwestern University Press, 1967); *Psyche and Bible: Three Old Testament Themes* (Zürich: Spring Publications, 1974); and *The Archetypal Significance of Gilgamesh: A Modern Ancient Hero* (Einsiedeln, Switzerland: Daimon, 1991).

8. [Tr. note] In Hebrew, *aliyah* means immigration by Jews from the diaspora to the Land of Israel.

9. [Tr. note] The *I Ching* or *Yi Jing*, usually translated as *Book of Changes* or *Classic of Changes*, is an ancient Chinese divination text and the oldest of the Chinese classics.

10. Mortimer Ostow, *Myth and Madness: The Psychodynamics of Antisemitism* (New Brunswick, NJ: Transaction Books, 1996).

11. *Jokes and Their Relation to the Unconscious* [Der Witz und seine Beziehung zum Unbewußten] is a 1905 book on the psychoanalysis of jokes and humour by Sigmund Freud, translated in 1960 by James Strachey and published by W. W. Norton. *Moses and Monotheism* [Der Mann Moses und die monotheistische Religion] is a 1939 book by Freud, translated the same year by Katherine Jones and published by Alfred A. Knopf.

12. Marthe Robert, *From Oedipus to Moses: Freud's Jewish Identity* (Garden City, NY: Anchor Books, 1976), translated by Ralph Manheim from *D'Oedipe à Moïse: Freud et la conscience juive* (Paris: Calmann-Lévy, 1974).

13. [Tr. note] The Berlin-born American literary agent Georges Borchardt (b. 1928) found an American publisher for Elie Wiesel's *Night* in 1959, following repeated rejections from publishers who considered Wiesel's book too morbid for American readers. Borchardt has also represented the literary estate of Hannah Arendt, among many other writers.

14. [Tr. note] *Freud's Moses* discusses a copy of the Bible presented to Freud by his father on the former's thirty-fifth birthday, with an inscription in Hebrew. Also see Benjamin Goodnick, "Jacob Freud's Dedication to His Son: A Reevaluation," *Jewish Quarterly Review* 82, no. 3/4 (Jan.–Apr. 1992): 329–60.

15. [Tr. note] Theodor Reik (1888–1969) was a psychoanalyst who trained as one of Freud's first students in Vienna.

16. [Tr. note] *Fragment of a Great Confession: A Psychoanalytic Autobiography* (New York: Farrar, Straus and Company, 1949).

17. Wilhelm Fliess (1858–1928) was a German Jewish otolaryngologist who practiced in Berlin.

18. Yosef Hayim Yerushalmi, *Freud's Moses: Judaism Terminable and Interminable* (New Haven, CT: Yale University Press, 1991), 55.

19. [Tr. note] *Totem and Taboo: Resemblances Between the Mental Lives of Savages and Neurotics*, or *Totem and Taboo: Some Points of Agreement between the Mental Lives of Savages and Neurotics*, translated by Abraham Brill and James Strachey respectively, from *Totem und Tabu: Einige Übereinstimmungen im Seelenleben der Wilden und der Neurotiker*, a 1913 book by Sigmund Freud, dealing with the fields of archaeology, anthropology, and the study of religion. Freud wrote a preface dated December 1930 for a projected Hebrew edition of *Totem and Taboo* in 1934 from the publishing house of Abraham Joseph Stybel (1884–1946). Freud's preface was first published in German in his collected works in 1934, but the Hebrew translation was not published until 1939 by Kiryat Sefer, Ltd. See *The Standard Edition of the Complete Psychological Works of Sigmund Freud*, vol. 13 (1913–1914): *Totem and Taboo and Other Works* (London: The Hogarth Press and the Institute of Psychoanalysis, 1955), xv.

20. [Tr. note] Latin, "by way of denial."

21. [Tr. note] Anna Freud (1895–1982), an Austrian-British psychoanalyst, was born in Vienna as the sixth and youngest child of Sigmund Freud and Martha Bernays.

22. Yohanan ben Zakkai (first century CE) was one of the Tannaim, an important Jewish sage in the era of the Second Temple, and primary contributor to the core text of Rabbinical Judaism, the *Mishnah*. See Freud, *Moses and Monotheism*, 124. Also Moshe Gresser, "Sigmund Freud's Jewish Identity: Evidence from His Correspondence," *Modern Judaism* 11, no. 2 (May 1991): 225–40.

7. DERRIDA

1. [Tr. note] Jacques Derrida, *Archive Fever: A Freudian Impression*, trans. Eric Prenowitz (Chicago: University of Chicago Press, 1996); translation of *Mal d'archive* (Paris: Galilée, 1995).

2. [Tr. note] Editions Galilée is a French publishing house located in Paris, founded in 1971 by Michel Delorme. It specializes in philosophy, French literature, arts, and human sciences, focusing on the deconstructionist thought of Jacques Derrida.

3. [Tr. note] In 1957, *Le colloque des intellectuels juifs de langue française* started meeting in Paris every two years.

4. See *Mémoire et Histoire. Données et débats, Actes du XXVe colloque des intellectuels juifs de langue française* [Memory and history: Data and debates, proceedings of the 25th colloquium of French-speaking Jewish intellectuals] (Paris: Denoël, 1986).

5. An account of this gathering is found in Leonard Lawlor's "Memory Becomes Electra," *Review of Politics* 60, no. 4 (Autumn 1998): 796–98. Another version of the colloquium by one of its organizers is in Michael Molnar, "Le Freud de Yosef," in *L'Histoire et la mémoire de l'histoire* [History and the memory of history], S. A. Goldberg, ed. (Paris: Albin Michel, 2012), 151–61.

6. [Tr. note] Ludwig Philippson (1811–1889) was a German rabbi and author, the son of Moses Philippson, a printer, writer, teacher, translator, publisher, and member of Haskalah, an intellectual movement dedicated to the modernization of Jewish life and culture. In 1839, he began an annotated German translation of the Hebrew Bible, which he completed in 1853, with on each page the original Hebrew text in one column and a German translation in another column.

7. [Tr. note] Emmanuel Levinas (1906–1995) was a French philosopher of Lithuanian Jewish ancestry known for his work on Jewish philosophy, existentialism, ethics, phenomenology, and ontology.

8. These meetings are mentioned by Derrida in *Derrida* (2002), an American documentary film directed by Kirby Dick and Amy Ziering Kofman.

9. [Tr. Note] Richard Bernstein (b. 1944) is an American journalist and author.

10. *Pirkei Avot* [Chapters of the fathers] is a compilation of ethical teachings and maxims that form a tractate in the Mishna.

11. [Tr. Note] Jacques Derrida, *Adieu à Emmanuel Lévinas* (Paris: Galilée, 1997), translated by Pascale-Anne Brault and Michael Naas as *Adieu to Emmanuel Levinas* (Palo Alto, CA: Stanford University Press, 1999).

12. [Tr. Note] Jacques Derrida, "Circonfession: Cinquante-neuf périodes et périphrases *écrites*," translated by Geoffrey Bennington under the title "Circumfession: Fifty-nine Periods and Periphrases," in Geoffrey Bennington and Jacques Derrida, *Jacques Derrida* (Chicago: University of Chicago Press, 1993).

13. [Tr. Note] Jacques Derrida, *Apprendre à vivre enfin: entretiens avec Jean Birnbaum* (Paris: Galilée/Le Monde, 2005), translated by Pascale-Anne Brault and Michael Naas as *Learning to Live Finally: The Last Interview. An Interview with Jean Birnbaum* (New York: Melville House, 2007; London: Palgrave Macmillan, 2007).

14. Derrida, *Learning to Live Finally*, 39.

15. [Tr. note] The Land of Israel (in Hebrew, *Eretz Yisrael*) is the traditional Jewish name for an area roughly congruent with two Jewish commonwealths.

16. Edward W. Said, *Orientalism* (New York: Pantheon Books, 1978).

17. Abraham Geiger (1810–1874) was a German rabbi and scholar and is considered the founding father of Reform Judaism, author of *Was hat Mohammed aus dem Judentume aufgenommen?* [What did Mohammed learn from Judaism?] (Bonn, 1833); translated into English as *Judaism and Islam* (Madras: Vepery, 1898).

18. Carl Paul Caspari (1814–1892) was a Norwegian Jew who converted to Lutheranism, author of *Grammatica Arabica* (2 parts, Leipzig, 1844–48; 5th German ed., by August Müller, Halle, 1887; English ed., by W. Wright, London, 1859–62, 1874–75; by W. Robertson Smith and M. J. de Goeje, Cambridge, 1896–98).

19. Ignác Goldziher (1850–1921), often credited as Ignaz Goldziher, was a Hungarian scholar of Islam. Author of *Der Mythos bei den Hebräern und seine geschichtliche Entwicklung* (Leipzig, 1876; English trans., R Martineau, London, 1877) and *Vorlesungen* über *den Islam* (1910; 2nd ed. revised by Franz Babinger, 1925); English trans. by Andras and Ruth Hamori, *Introduction to Islamic Theology and Law* (Princeton, NJ: Princeton University Press, 1981).

20. The four-volume *Passion of Al-Hallaj* is one of the major works of Western orientalism, translated by Herbert Mason as *The Passion of Al-Hallaj, Mystic and Martyr of Islam*, Volume 1: *The Life of Al-Hallaj* (1986); Volume 2: *The Survival of al-Hallaj* (1972); Volume 3: *The Teaching of al-Hallaj* (1972); Volume 4: *Biography and Index* (1979), as well as in a one-volume abridgement edited and translated by Herbert Mason, *Hallaj: Mystic and Martyr, Abridged Edition* (1994), all from Princeton University Press.

21. [Tr. note] Anwar Sadat (1918–1981), president of Egypt from October 1970 until his assassination by fundamentalist army officers on October 6, 1981.

22. *Freud and the Non-European* (London: Verso, 2004). A lecture delivered by Edward Said at the Freud Museum of London in December 2001.

23. *The Non-Jewish Jew: And Other Essays* (Oxford: Oxford University Press, 1968) by Isaac Deutscher (1907–1967), a Polish Jewish Marxist writer, journalist, and political activist who moved to the United Kingdom before the outbreak of the Second World War, best known as a biographer of Leon Trotsky and Joseph Stalin and as a commentator on Soviet affairs.

8. NEW YORK: 1939–1945

1. Tisha B'Av, literally the "ninth of Av," is an annual fast day in Judaism on which a number of disasters in Jewish history occurred, primarily the destruction of Solomon's Temple by the Neo-Babylonian Empire and the Second Temple by the Roman Empire in Jerusalem.

2. Starting in 1933 until 1941, the American Jewish Congress spearheaded a consumer boycott of German-made goods in America. See Rona Sheramy, "'There are Times When Silence is a Sin': The Women's Division of the American Jewish Congress and the Anti-Nazi Boycott Movement," *American Jewish History* 89, no. 1 (March 2001): 105–21. Since this meeting was held in March 1933, Yerushalmi may well have heard about it from others.

3. Léon Poliakov, *Bréviaire de la haine: Le IIIe Reich et les Juifs* (Paris: Calmann-Lévy, 1951), translated in 1956 as *Harvest of Hate: The Nazi Program for the Destruction of Jews in Europe* (New York: Syracuse University Press and The American Jewish Committee, 1954).

4. [Tr. note] *Untimely Meditations* [Unzeitgemässe Betrachtungen], also translated as *Unfashionable Observations* and *Thoughts Out of Season*, consists of four works by the German philosopher Friedrich Nietzsche, started in 1873 and completed in 1876.

5. [Tr. note] Royaumont Abbey is a former Cistercian abbey, located near Asnières-sur-Oise in Val-d'Oise, approximately thirty kilometers north of Paris. In the early twentieth century, the abbey was bought by the Goüin family, who in 1964 created the Royaumont Foundation, the first private French cultural foundation.

6. Yosef Hayim Yerushalmi, Nicole Loraux, Hans Mommsen, Jean-Claude Milner, and Gianni Vattimo, *Usages de L'oubli: Colloque de Royaumont* (Paris: Éditions du Seuil, 1988).

9. WHO MAKES HISTORY? QUESTIONS OF INTERPRETATION

1. Nadia Zeldes, *The Former Jews of this Kingdom: Sicilian Converts after the Expulsion, 1492–1516* (Leiden: Brill, 2003).

2. *Assimilation and Racial Anti-Semitism: The Iberian and the German Models* (New York: Leo Baeck Institute, 1982).

3. The *Maskilim* (people of wisdom) were supporters of the Haskalah, the Jewish Enlightenment.

4. Legal correspondence between rabbinical authorities.

5. Joseph Mali, *Mythistory: The Making of a Modern Historiography* (Chicago: University of Chicago Press, 2003).

6. [Tr. note] See Paul Ricoeur, *Freud and Philosophy: An Essay on Interpretation*, trans. Denis Savage (New Haven, CT: Yale University Press, 1970).

10. A JEWISH KID FROM THE BRONX AT HARVARD AND COLUMBIA

1. Isadore Twersky (1930–1997) was an Orthodox rabbi and university professor who held the position of the Nathan Littauer Professor of Hebrew Literature and Philosophy at Harvard University, a chair previously held by Harry Austryn Wolfson. Author of, among other studies, *Introduction to the Code of Maimonides (Mishneh Torah)* (New Haven, CT, and London: Yale University Press, 1980); *Rabad*

of Posquière: A Twelfth-Century Talmudist (Cambridge. MA: Harvard University Press, 1962).

2. [Tr. note] A leader of the Tolna Hasidic dynasty.

3. [Tr. note] The École pratique des hautes études (Practical School of Advanced Studies), founded in 1868, is one of France's most prestigious research and higher education institutions.

4. [Tr. note] The American Jewish conductor and composer Leonard Bernstein attended Harvard from 1935 to 1939. See Claudia Swan, ed., *Leonard Bernstein: The Harvard Years, 1935–1939* (New York: The Eos Orchestra, 1999).

5. [Tr. note] Al-Quds is the Arabic name for the city of Jerusalem, literally meaning "the Holy One." Detroit-born George Abraham Makdisi (1920–2002) was author of *The Rise of Humanism in Classical Islam and the Christian West: With Special Reference to Scholasticism* (Edinburgh: Edinburgh University Press, 1990), and *Ibn 'Aqil: Religion and Culture in Classical Islam* (Edinburgh: Edinburgh University Press, 1997). Spelling the name Makdisi as Maqdisi with the Arabic QDS, rather than the anglicized KDS, highlights the erudite wordplay. For biographical and linguistic elucidations, special thanks to a former colleague of Makdisi and Yerushalmi, Professor William A. Graham, Murray A. Albertson Research Professor of Middle Eastern Studies, and University Distinguished Service Professor, Emeritus at Harvard University.

6. [Tr. note] of or relating to the city of Hierosolyma (Jerusalem).

7. In Harvard's house system, student residences serve as administrative units.

11. PROFESSOR YERUSHALMI

1. Gershom Scholem, *Reshit ha-Kabbalah*, original Hebrew edition (Jerusalem/Tel Aviv: Schocken, 1948); German edition (Berlin: Walter de Gruyter & Co., 1968); trans. by Allan Arkush as *Origins of the Kabbalah* (Princeton, NJ: Princeton University Press, 1987).

2. *Bahir* or *Sefer HaBahir* [Book of the bright] is an anonymous mystical work about Jewish tradition attributed to first-century rabbinic sage Nehunya ben HaKanah (a contemporary of Yochanan ben Zakai) because it begins with the words, "R. Nehunya ben HaKanah said." It is also known as *Midrash of Rabbi Nehunya ben HaKanah*, as one of the main sources of the Provençal kabbalists like R. Isaac the Blind. Scholem wrote his thesis on *Bahir* (*Das Buch Bahir*, 1921) and devoted a good part of the *Origins of the Kabbalah* to it.

3. See the same assertion in Yosef Hayim Yerushalmi, "Toward a History of Jewish Hope," in *The Faith of Fallen Jews: Yosef Hayim Yerushalmi and the Writing of*

Jewish History, edited by David N. Myers and Alexander Kaye (Waltham, MA: Brandeis University Press, 2013), 311.

4. See Marina Rustow, *Heresy and the Politics of Community: The Jews of the Fatimid Caliphate* (Ithaca, NY: Cornell University Press, 2008).

5. Jacob Katz (1904–1998) was a Jewish historian and educator. See his "Zur jüdischen Sozialgeschichte: epochale und über-epochale Geschichtesschreibung," *Tel Aviv Jahrbuch für deutsche Geschichte* 10 (1991): 429–36. "On Jewish Social History: Epochal and Supra-Epochal Historiography," *Jewish History* 7, no. 1 (March 1993): 89–97.

6. See Yosef Hayim Yerushalmi, "Servants of Kings and Not Servants of Servants: Some Aspects of the Political History of the Jews," in *The Faith of the Fallen Jews: Yosef Hayim Yerushalmi and the Writing of Jewish History*, eds. David N. Myers and Alexander Kaye (Waltham, MA: Brandeis University Press, 2013; first published in German (Munich: Siemens Stiftung, 1995), then in French in *Raisons politiques* 7 (August–October 2002): 19–52.

7. Michael Walzer, Menachem Lorberbaum, Noam J. Zohar, and Yair Loberbaum, eds. *The Jewish Political Tradition* (New Haven, CT: Yale University Press, 2000–2018); three of a projected four volumes have appeared with the subtitles, Volume 1: *Authority*; Volume 2: *Membership*; and Volume 3: *Community*.

8. [Tr. note] On *shtadlanut*, Hebrew for intercession or advocacy, see Mirjam Thulin and Björn Siegel, "Transformations and Intersections of *Shtadlanut* and *Tzedakah* in the Early Modern and Modern Period," *Jewish Culture and History* 19, no. 1 (2018): 1–7. See also Eli Lederhendler, *The Road to Modern Jewish Politics: Political Tradition and Political Reconstruction in the Jewish Community of Tsarist Russia* (New York: Oxford University Press, 1989), 19–21.

12. QUESTIONS OF HISTORY AND HISTORIOGRAPHY

1. Shelomo Dov Goitein (1900–1985) was a German Jewish ethnographer, historian, and Arabist known for his research on Jewish life in the Islamic Middle Ages, particularly on the Cairo Geniza. Author of *A Mediterranean Society*, 6 vols. (Berkeley: University of California Press, 1967–1993); an abridged one-volume edition was published by the University of California Press in 1999.

2. The Cairo Geniza, alternatively spelled Genizah, is a collection of some 400,000 Jewish manuscript fragments and Fatimid administrative documents that were found in the *genizah* or storeroom of the Ben Ezra Synagogue in Fustat or Old Cairo, Egypt. These manuscripts, dated from 870 CE to the nineteenth century, comprise the largest and most diverse collection of medieval manuscripts in the world.

3. S. D. Goiten, *Jewish Education in Muslim Countries. Based on records from the Cairo Geniza* (Hebr.) (Jerusalem: The Ben-Zvi Institute the Hebrew University, 1962).

4. [Tr. note] Haim Hillel Ben-Sasson (1914–1977) was professor of medieval Jewish history at the Hebrew University of Jerusalem and the editor of *A History of the Jewish People* (Cambridge, MA: Harvard University Press, 1976).

5. Haim Hillel Ben-Sasson, *The Reformation in Contemporary Jewish Eyes* (Jerusalem: Ahva Press, 1970).

6. [Tr. note] See Ivan G. Marcus, "Israeli Medieval Jewish Historiography: From Nationalist Positivism to New Cultural and Social Histories," *Jewish Studies Quarterly* 17, no. 3 (2010): 244–85.

7. Ahimaaz ben Paltiel (1017–1060) was a Greco-Italian liturgical poet and author of a family chronicle compiled in 1054, intended to glorify his ancestors, but also providing useful information about the history of the early Jewish settlements in Oria, Bari, Otranto, Gaeta, Benevento, Capua, and Amalfi in southern Italy, as well as Pavia in northern Italy. See Robert Bonfil, *History and Folklore in a Medieval Jewish Chronicle: The Family Chronicle of Aḥima'az Ben Paltiel* (Leiden: Brill, 2009). *Sefer Yosippon* is a chronicle of Jewish history from Adam to the age of Titus, named after its supposed author, Josephus Flavius, although it was actually composed in the tenth century in south Italy. See Shulamit Sela, *Sefer Yosef ben Guryon ha-'Arvi*, 2 vols. (Jerusalem: Mekhon Ben-Zvi le-heker kehilot Yiśra'el ba-Mizrah, Yad Yitshak Ben-Tsevi veha-Universitah ha-'Ivrit bi-Yerushalayim, 2009). See also *The Josippon (Josephus Gorionides)*, ed. David Flusser, 2 vols. (Jerusalem: Bialik Institute, 1978, 1980).

8. Shelomo Eidelberg, *The Jews and the Crusaders: The Hebrew Chronicles of the First and Second Crusade* (New York: Ktav, 1996); Eva Haverkamp, *Hebräische Berichte über die Judenverfolgungen während des ersten Kreuzzugs* (Hanover: Hahnsche Buchhandlung, 2005).

9. *Pirkei Avot* begins: "Moses received Torah from God at Sinai. He transmitted it to Joshua, Joshua to the elders, the elders to the prophets, the prophets to the members of the Great Assembly" (1:1).

10. Judah Loew ben Bezalel or Rabbi Loew (between 1512 and 1526?–1609), widely known to scholars of Judaism as the Maharal of Prague, or simply The Maharal, the Hebrew acronym of "Moreinu Ha-Rav Loew" (Our teacher, Rabbi Loew), was an important Talmudic scholar, Jewish mystic, and philosopher who served as rabbi in the cities of Mikulov in Moravia and Prague in Bohemia.

13. THE COLLECTOR

1. Philipp Feldheim (1901–1990), a Viennese Jew who escaped Nazi Austria in 1939, opened a small bookshop on the Lower East Side, and witnessing cus-

tomer demand for Jewish literature, decided to go into publishing at 96 East Broadway.

2. Naphtali Herz Wessely (1725–1805) was a Haskalah poet, linguist, and exegete. He was a pioneer in education and an advocate of the Enlightenment. His *Shirei Tiferet* [Poems of glory] is an epic on the life of Moses and the Exodus from Egypt, containing legends from the Talmud and the Midrash. See *Shirei Tiferet*, 5 vols. (vols. 1–4, Berlin, 1782–1802; vol. 5, Prague, 1829).

3. *The Scepter of Judah* [Shevet Yehudah] was a text produced by the Sephardi historian Solomon Ibn Verga that first appeared in Turkey in 1553, a comprehensive analysis of sixty-four different persecutions that the Jewish people had suffered since antiquity. The *Scepter of Judah* has been considered the first significant work of Jewish historiography.

4. [Tr. note] A kippah is worn as a head covering.

5. Samson Raphael Hirsch (1808–1888) was a German Orthodox rabbi best known as the intellectual founder of the *Torah im Derech Eretz* (the way of the land) school of contemporary Orthodox Judaism. Sometimes termed neo-Orthodoxy, his philosophy has had a considerable influence on the development of Orthodox Judaism.

6. Die Soncino-Gesellschaft der Freunde des jüdischen Buches (The Soncino society of the friends of the Jewish book), founded in Berlin in 1924 and aimed at the typographic improvement of Jewish and Hebrew books. It was named in honor of the Soncino family of Hebrew book-printing pioneers based in Northern Italy.

7. Shmuel Yosef Agnon (1888–1970) was a Nobel Prize laureate writer and one of the central figures of modern Hebrew fiction.

8. Gracia Mendes Nasi (1510–1569) was one of the wealthiest Jewish women of Renaissance Europe. She was the aunt and business partner of Joao Micas (Hebrew name Joseph Nasi), who became a prominent figure in the politics of the Ottoman Empire. She also developed an escape network that saved hundreds of Conversos from the Inquisition.

9. [Tr. note] Psalm 2:8, "Ask of Me, and I will give the nations for thine inheritance, And the ends of the earth for thy possession," from the Jewish Publication Society of America version (JPS) of the Tanakh (1917).

10. Edirne, historically known as Adrianople (Latin: Hadrianopolis), founded by the Roman emperor Hadrian, is a city in the northwestern Turkish province of Edirne in the region of East Thrace, close to Turkey's borders with Greece and Bulgaria.

11. Yehuda F. Baer, *Untersuchungen über Quellen und Komposition des Schebet Jehuda*

[Studies on sources and composition of the Shevet Yehuda] (Berlin: C. A. Schwetschke & Sohn, 1923).

14. GERSHOM SCHOLEM

1. [Tr. note] *Zion* is a Hebrew quarterly peer-reviewed academic journal covering all aspects of the history of the Jews, across all the lands in which Jews lived from antiquity to the modern era. It was first published in 1935 by the Historical Society of Israel and the Zalman Shazar Center. *Tarbiz*, a quarterly for Jewish Studies, is devoted to the full range of Jewish studies. It was first published in 1930 at the Hebrew University of Jerusalem's Institute of Jewish Studies.

2. [Tr. note] The Leo Baeck Institute is an international research institute with centers in New York City, London, and Jerusalem that are devoted to the study of the history and culture of German-speaking Jewry.

3. Raphael Judah (R. J.) Zwi Werblowsky (1924–2015) was an Israeli scholar of religion specializing in comparative religion and interfaith dialogue. Werblowsky served as dean of the faculty of humanities at the Hebrew University of Jerusalem between 1965 and 1969. He translated *Scholem's Sabbatai Sevi: The Mystical Messiah, 1626–1676* (Princeton, NJ: Princeton University Press, 1973; repr. 2016).

4. [Tr. note] Original edition: *Von Berlin nach Jerusalem: Jugenderinnerungen*, (Frankfurt: Suhrkamp, 1977); *From Berlin to Jerusalem: Memories of My Youth* by Gershom Scholem, translated from the German by Harry Zohn (New York: Schocken Books, 1988).

5. The Bene Israel (Sons of Israel) are a community of Jews in India. It has been suggested that it is made up of descendants of one of the disputed Lost Tribes and ancestors who settled there centuries ago. Cochin Jews (also known as Malabar Jews or Kochinim) are the oldest group of Jews in India, with roots that are claimed to date back to the time of King Solomon.

6. The mahzor is the prayer book used by Jews on the High Holy Days of Rosh Hashanah and Yom Kippur. *Mogontiacum* was the Latin name for Mainz, the capital and largest city of Rhineland-Palatinate, Germany. See Adri K. Offenberg, "Libri Sefarditi In Spagnolo E In Portoghese Pubblicati Nei Paesi Bassi Settentrionali Anteriormente A Menasseh Ben Israel (1584–1627)," *La Rassegna Mensile di Israel* 58, nos. 1/2 (1992): 147–62; 151.

7. David Shaltiel (1903–1969) was an Israeli military officer, intelligence officer, and diplomat, who served as district commander of the Haganah in Jerusalem during the 1948 Arab-Israeli war. See Erich Lüth, *David Shaltiel: Hamburger, Fremdenlegionär, Diplomat, Verteidiger von Jerusalem* [David Shaltiel: Son of Hamburg, foreign legionnaire, diplomat, defender of Jerusalem] (Hamburg: Christians, 1970).

I take this opportunity to thank Dominique Bourel for providing biographical details.

8. [Tr. note] The Jewish Infantry Brigade Group, more commonly known as the Jewish Brigade, was a military formation of the British Army in the Second World War. It was formed in late 1944 and commanded by Anglo-Jewish officers. After the war, some members of the Brigade assisted Holocaust survivors to emigrate to Mandatory Palestine as part of Aliyah Bet, or illegal immigration by Jewish refugees from Nazi Germany and other Holocaust survivors to Mandatory Palestine between 1934 and 1948, in violation of restrictions stated in the British White Paper of 1939.

9. Gershom Scholem, ed., *Be-'Iqvot Mashiyah* (Jerusalem: Tarshish Books, 1944).

10. [Tr. note] Nathan of Gaza (1643–1680) was a theologian and author born in Jerusalem. After his marriage in 1663 he moved to Gaza, where he became famous as a prophet for Sabbatai Zevi.

11. [Tr. note] Rechov Abarbanel is a street in Rechavia neighborhood, adjacent to Jerusalem's city center.

12. See above, pages 5, 79.

13. Jacob Katz, "The Possible Relationship between Sabbateanism, Haskalah, and Reform Judaism" (original in Hebrew) in *Studies in Jewish Religious and Intellectual History Presented to Alexander Altmann*, Siegfried Stein and Raphael Loewe, eds. (Tuscaloosa: Alabama: University of Alabama Press, 1979), 83–100; repr., *Divine Law in Human Hands: Case Studies in Halakhic Flexibility* (Jerusalem: Magnes Press, 1998), 504–30.

14. "Tradition and New Creation in the Rituals of the Kabbalists," *On the Kabbalah and its Symbolism* (New York: Schocken Books, 1965), 118–57: "The ritual of Rabbinical Judaism makes nothing happen and transforms nothing," as quoted in Yosef Hayim Yerushalmi, *Zakhor: Jewish History and Jewish Memory* (Seattle: University of Washington Press, 1982), 129.

15. [Tr. note] See chapter 2, note 11, on page 153, on Wissenschaft des Judentums.

16. [Tr. note] See chapter 1, note 11, on page 150, on Saul Lieberman.

17. Rabbi Louis Ginzberg (1873–1953) was a Talmudist and leading figure in the Conservative Movement of Judaism of the twentieth century. Ginzberg began teaching Talmud at the Jewish Theological Seminary from its reorganization in 1902 until his death. He is especially remembered for his *Legends of the Jews* 7 vols. (Philadelphia: Jewish Publication Society, 1909–1938).

Jacob Nahum Epstein (1878–1952) was a scholar of Talmud and rabbinics. In 1925 he became professor of Talmudic philology at the Hebrew University of

Jerusalem. His major work was devoted to rabbinical literature, particularly the Mishnah, his edition of which is still authoritative. See his *Mavo le-Nusaḥ ha-Mishnah*, 2 vols. (Jerusalem: Magnes Press, Hebrew University, 2001; first edition, 1948).

18. Joseph Ber Soloveitchik (1903–1993) was a major American Orthodox rabbi, Talmudist, and modern Jewish philosopher. He was a scion of the Lithuanian Jewish Soloveitchik rabbinic dynasty. As a rosh yeshiva of Rabbi Isaac Elchanan Theological Seminary at Yeshiva University in New York City, he ordained almost 2,000 rabbis during nearly half a century.

15. THE RITUAL EXPERIENCE

1. [Tr. note] There is no movie entitled *From the Halls of Montezuma*. Yerushalmi appears to have confused two titles of films about the United States Marine Corps, following the lyrics of *The Marine's Hymn*: "From the Halls of Montezuma / To the shores of Tripoli." The film he likely saw at this time was *To the Shores of Tripoli* (1942), directed by H. Bruce Humberstone and starring John Payne, Maureen O'Hara, and Randolph Scott, no longer new at the time of the events described. A different film, *Halls of Montezuma* (1951), directed by Lewis Milestone and starring Richard Widmark, Jack Palance, and Reginald Gardiner, was released too late for Yerushalmi to have seen it at the time of this anecdote. In all likelihood he was too upset at the moment to pay much attention to the film or its title.

2. Rosh Hashanah, literally meaning "head of the year," is the Jewish New Year. It is the first of the Jewish High Holy Days. Tashlikh is a customary Jewish atonement ritual performed during the High Holy Days at a large, natural body of flowing water on the afternoon of Rosh Hashanah. The name Tashlikh and the practice itself are derived from an allusion mentioned in the Biblical passage (Micah 7:18–20) recited at the ceremony: "You will cast all their sins into the depths of the sea."

3. [Tr. note] Yehuda Amichai (1924–2000), born Ludwig Pfeuffer in Würzburg, Germany, to an Orthodox Jewish family, grew up to be a celebrated Israeli poet. See *A Life of Poetry, 1948–1994*, selected and translated by Benjamin and Barbara Harshav (New York: HarperCollins, 1994).

16. TRUTH IN HISTORY AND ITS AVATARS

1. [Tr. note] See chapter 2, note 11, on page 153.

2. Moritz Güdemann (1835–1918) was an Austrian rabbi and historian who served as chief rabbi of Vienna. See his *Geschichte des Erziehungswesens und der Kultur der abendländischen Juden während des Mittelalters und der neueren Zeit* [History of the

education and culture of Western Jews during the Middle Ages and more recently] 3 vols. (Vienna: Hölder, 1880–1888).

3. Israel Abrahams (1858–1925), a British academic, wrote *Jewish Life in the Middle Ages* (London: Macmillan and Co., 1896; repr., Philadelphia: Jewish Publication Society, 1993).

4. Peter Novick, *That Noble Dream: The "Objectivity Question" and the American Historical Profession* (Cambridge: Cambridge University Press, 1988).

5. [Tr. note] When the American Historical Association (AHA) celebrated its fiftieth anniversary in 1934, Theodore Clarke Smith (1870–1960), professor of American history at Williams College, proclaimed that his fellow historians followed a "noble dream" of unbiased works on American history pursuing the "ideal of the effort for objective truth." Others disagreed about the utility of this concept.

6. Nicholas Humphrey, *Seeing Red: A Study in Consciousness* (Cambridge, MA: Belknap Press of Harvard University Press, 2006).

7. Ben-Zion Dinur (born Dinaburg, 1884–1973), born in Lithuania, studied at the University of Bern and at the Hochschule für die Wissenschaft des Judentums in Berlin and in Petrograd. He moved to Palestine in 1921 and started to teach at the Hebrew University in 1936. As a Zionist activist, educator, historian, and Israeli politician, he was one of the architects of Zionist historiography, revisiting the history of the Jewish diaspora through the prism of community unity. See his *Yisrael ba-gola* [Israel in the exile], 3rd ed., 5 vols., (Jerusalem: Bialik Institute, 1961–1966.)

8. Joseph Klausner (1874–1958) was a Jewish historian and professor of Hebrew literature. See his *Jesus of Nazareth: His Life, Times, and Teaching*, trans. Herbert Danby (New York: Macmillan, 1921); *A History of Modern Hebrew Literature (1785–1930)*, trans. Herbert Danby (London: M. L. Cailingold, 1932); *From Jesus To Paul*, trans. William Stinespring (New York: Macmillan, 1942); and *The Messianic Idea in Israel: From Its Beginning to the Completion of the Mishnah*, trans. William Stinespring (New York: Macmillan, 1954).

9. The article in question, "Mitokh Hirhurim 'al Khokhmat Yisrael" (Some reflections on the scientific study of Judaism) was written by Scholem in 1944, later reprinted in Gershom Scholem, *On the Possibility of Jewish Mysticism in Our Time & Other Essays*, ed. Avraham Shapira, trans. Jonathan Chipman (Philadelphia: Jewish Publication Society, 1997).

10. Thomas L. Haskell, *Objectivity Is Not Neutrality: Explanatory Schemes in History* (Baltimore: Johns Hopkins University Press, 1998).

11. [Tr. note] Positivism is a philosophical school developed by the French

sociologist and philosopher Auguste Comte (1798–1857) in the mid-nineteenth century.

12. [Tr. note] For *Zion* and *Tarbiz*, see chapter 14, note 1. *The Jewish Quarterly Review* was established in London in 1889 by Israel Abrahams and Claude G. Montefiore as an English-language counterpart of the French *Revue des études juives*, itself an outgrowth of the Wissenschaft des Judentums movement. It is the oldest English-language journal of Judaic scholarship.

13. [Tr. note] Yerushalmi paraphrases a joke often attributed to Woody Allen: "I took a speed-reading course and read *War and Peace* in twenty minutes. It involves Russia."

14. [Tr. note] For Ignaz Goldziher, see chapter 7, note 19.

15. Maya Jasanoff is Coolidge Professor of History at Harvard University. Her article "The Unknown Women of India" appeared in the December 18, 2008, issue of the *New York Review of Books*, as a review of two publications, *Women of the Raj: The Mothers, Wives, and Daughters of the British Empire in India* by Margaret MacMillan (New York: Random House, 2008) and *Sex and the Family in Colonial India: The Making of Empire* by Durba Ghosh (Cambridge: Cambridge University Press, 2008). See Jasanoff's *Edge of Empire: Lives, Cultures, and Conquest in the East, 1750–1850* (New York: Knopf, 2006).

17. MESSIANISM AND ZIONISM

1. For Yitzhak Baer, see chapter 1, note 7. His book *Galut*, tr. Robert Warshow (New York: Schocken Books, 1947) originated with a publication in German, *Galut* (Berlin: Schocken, 1936). See *Galout: l'imaginaire de l'exil dans le judaïsme* (Paris: Calmann-Lévy, 2000), translated by Marc de Launay, with a preface by Yosef Hayim Yerushalmi that was translated from the English by Éric Vigne, 45.

2. See Yosef Hayim Yerushalmi, "Exile and Expulsion in Jewish History," in *Crisis and Creativity in the Sephardic World, 1391–1648*, ed. Benjamin R. Gampel (New York: Columbia University Press, 1997), 3–22.

3. Daniel al-Ḳumisi (d. 946 in Jerusalem) was one of the most prominent early scholars in Karaite Judaism. He flourished at the end of the ninth or the beginning of the tenth century. See the entry "Daniel ben Moses al-Ḳumisi" by Kaufmann Kohler and Samuel Poznansky in the *Jewish Encyclopedia* (New York: Funk and Wagnalls, 1901–1906).

4. [Tr. note] Mourners of Zion [*Avelei Tziyon*] refers to different Jewish groups: a Karaite subsect founded by Daniel al-Ḳumisi in the late ninth century CE; a later Karaite community living in Constantinople in the late Middle Ages who may have been exiles who left Jerusalem during the Crusades; and a Jewish group liv-

ing in the mountains of Yemen, as described by Benjamin of Tudela. The term also appears in a phrase used in the Jewish mourning ritual.

5. [Tr. note] Rabbanites was a name used to designate the opponents of Karaites in the Jewish religion. Rabbinic Judaism, also called Rabbinism, or Judaism espoused by the Rabbanites, has been the mainstream form of Judaism since the sixth century CE, after the codification of the Babylonian Talmud.

6. [Tr. note] Fatimids, a Shi'ite Muslim dynasty that ruled in Egypt (969–1171 CE), and in other parts of North Africa and the Near East, including Palestine from 969 to 1099 CE. Jews enjoyed a degree of tolerance, security, and prosperity during their reign.

7. [Tr. note] Serene (his name is also given in sources as Sherini, Sheria, Serenus, Severus, et al.) the Syrian, according to the *Zuqnin Chronicle*, an account written in Syriac about events from Creation to c. 775 CE, proclaimed himself Moses "sent again for the salvation of Israel." Serene promised "to lead you into the desert in order to introduce you then to the inheritance of the Promised Land which you shall possess as before," more as a "prophet like Moses" than as a Davidic "anointed one." According to Natronai ben Nehemiah, Gaon of Pumbedita from 719 to 730, Serene was hostile to rabbinic Judaism.

8. [Tr. note] Abu Isa (also known as Ovadiah, Ishaq ibn Ya'qub al-Isfahani, and Isaac ibn Jacob al-Isfahani) was a self-proclaimed Jewish prophet sometime in the eighth century CE in Persia and the leader of a short-lived revolt. Proclaimed by some of his followers to be the Messiah, Abu Isa himself never made such a claim.

9. *The Epistle to Yemen* or *Yemen Letter* was an important communication written by Maimonides in 1173–1174 and sent to the Yemenite Jews. See *Moses Maimonides' Epistle to Yemen: The Arabic Original and the Three Hebrew Versions*, edited from manuscripts with introduction and notes by Abraham S. Halkin; and an English translation by Boaz Cohen, (New York: American Academy for Jewish Research, 1952).

10. [Tr. note] Precursorism is a characteristic of historical writing in which authors seek antecedents of present-day institutions or ideas in earlier historical periods. This kind of anachronism is considered to be a form of Whig history and is a special problem among historians of science.

11. Nahum Sokolow (1859–1936) was a Zionist leader and pioneer of Hebrew-language journalism. See Sokolow, *History of Zionism: 1600–1918* (London: Longmans, Green & Co., 1919).

12. [Tr. note] Written by Baruch Spinoza (1632–1677), a Dutch philosopher of Portuguese Sephardi origin, *Tractatus Theologico-Politicus* or *Theologico-Political Treatise* was one of the most controversial texts of the early modern period. It was a

preemptive defense of Spinoza's later work, *Ethics*, published posthumously in 1677, for which he anticipated harsh criticism.

13. One of the principles established by the first synods of Reform Judaism is the distinction between religious and national elements of Jewish law, the latter becoming null and void when Jews are "citizens of the Israelite faith." This idea leads to abandoning the rules of kashrut, rabbinical courts, religious marriage, and even moving Shabbat to Sunday.

14. [Tr. note] *Yom Ha-Zikaron la-Shoah ve-la-G'vurah*, known colloquially in Israel and abroad as *Yom Ha-Shoah* and in English as Holocaust Remembrance Day or Holocaust Day, is observed as Israel's day of commemoration for the millions of Jews murdered in the Holocaust. It was first commemorated in 1951. *Yom Ha-Zikaron* (Memorial Day) or *Yom Ha-Zikaron Le-Halalei Ma'arakhot Yisrael ul'Nifge'ei Pe'ulot Ha-Eivah* (Memorial Day for the Fallen Soldiers of Israel and Victims of Terrorism) is Israel's official remembrance day, enacted into law in 1963.

18. THE STATE OF ISRAEL AND MESSIANIC SIGNIFICANCE

1. [Tr. note] On May 14, 1948, in Tel Aviv, Jewish Agency Chairman David Ben-Gurion proclaimed the State of Israel, establishing the first Jewish state.

2. [Tr. note] The horah is widespread in the Jewish diaspora and played a foundational role in modern Israeli folk dancing. It became the symbol of the reconstruction of the country by the socialistic-agricultural Zionist movement.

3. [Tr. note] The New York city-based *Morgen Freiheit* [Morning Freedom] was a daily Yiddish-language newspaper affiliated with the Communist Party, USA, founded in 1922. After the end of the Second World War, the paper's pro-Israel views brought it into disfavor with the Communist Party.

4. [Tr. note] The Israel Defense Forces (IDF; Tsva ha-Hagana le-Yisra'el or the Army of Defense for Israel), commonly known in Israel by the Hebrew acronym Tzahal, are the military forces of the State of Israel.

5. [Tr. note] The Six-Day War, also known as the June War, 1967 Arab–Israeli War, or Third Arab–Israeli War, was fought from June 5 to 10, 1967, by Israel and the neighboring states of Egypt, Jordan, and Syria.

6. [Tr. note] The special issue of *Life* magazine was dated June 23, 1967, with headlines on the cover: "Wrap-Up of the Astounding War: Israeli soldier cools off in the Suez Canal."

7. [Tr. note] After the Six-Day War in June 1967, Israel occupied Hebron along with the rest of the West Bank, establishing a military government to rule the area. Following the 1995 Oslo Agreement and subsequent 1997 Hebron Agreement, Palestinian cities were placed under the exclusive jurisdiction of the Pales-

tinian Authority, with the exception of Hebron, which was split into two sectors: H1 is controlled by the Palestinian Authority and H2—which includes the Old City of Hebron—remained under the military control of Israel.

8. In the 1990s, the historiographical trend of "new historians" and post-Zionists has called into question the official history of the beginnings of the State of Israel. See Shlomo Sharan, ed., *Israel and the Post-Zionists: A Nation at Risk* (Brighton: Sussex Academic Press, 2003).

9. [Tr. note] The 1982 Lebanon War, known as Operation Peace for Galilee (*Mivtsa Shlom Ha-Galil* or *Mivtsa Sheleg*) by the Israeli government, later known in Israel as the Lebanon War or the First Lebanon War, began on June 6, 1982, when the IDF invaded southern Lebanon, after repeated attacks and counterattacks between the Palestine Liberation Organization (PLO) operating in southern Lebanon and the IDF that had caused civilian casualties on both sides of the border.

10. [Tr. note] The Yom Kippur War, also known as the 1973 Arab–Israeli War, was fought from October 6 to 25, 1973, by a coalition of Arab states led by Egypt and Syria against Israel.

11. Stanley Hoffmann (1928–2015) was the Paul and Catherine Buttenwieser University Professor, emeritus, at Harvard University. See his *World Disorders: Troubled Peace in the Post-Cold War Era* (Lanham, MD and Oxford: Rowman & Littlefield Publishers, 1998; rev. ed., 2000).

12. [Tr. note] The prayer for the government is read during the Saturday morning service on Shabbat. The concept of praying for the well-being of the government was articulated in 586 BCE by the prophet Jeremiah after the first expulsion from Jerusalem.

13. Archival research by Dr. Yoel Rappel, an Israeli scholar of Jewish history, determined that Rabbi Yitzchak Halevi Herzog (1888–1959), Israel's first chief Ashkenazi rabbi, was the author of the Prayer for Peace in the State of Israel, subsequently edited by his friend, the author S. Y. Agnon.

14. Jacob Katz, "Israel and the Messiah," *Commentary* 73, no. 1 (1982): 34–41.

15. Ze'ev Jabotinsky (1880–1940) was a Russian Jewish Revisionist Zionist leader, author, and founder of the Jewish Self-Defense Organization in Odessa. He also established several Jewish organizations, including Betar, Hatzohar, and the Irgun. The Betar Movement is a Revisionist Zionist youth movement founded in 1923 in Riga, Latvia. Jabotinsky's poem "Two Banks Hath the Jordan" [*Sh'nei g'dot la-yarden*] became a standard Betar song.

16. [Tr. note] On Lenin being unwilling to accept the Bund as sole representative of all Jewish workers in the USSR, see Jack Jacobs, ed., *Jewish Politics in Eastern Europe: The Bund at 100* (Basingstoke: Palgrave, 2001). See also Henry J. Tobias, *The*

Jewish Bund in Russia: From Its Origins to 1905 (Stanford, CA: Stanford University Press, 1972) and Henry J. Tobias, "The Bund and Lenin until 1903," *Russian Review* 20, no. 4 (October 1961).

17. [Tr. note] The War in Darfur, a major armed conflict in the Darfur region of Sudan, began in February 2003 when the Sudan Liberation Movement (SLM) and the Justice and Equality Movement (JEM) rebel groups began fighting the government of Sudan, which they accused of oppressing Darfur's non-Arab population. The government responded to attacks by carrying out a campaign of ethnic cleansing against Darfur's non-Arabs. This resulted in the death of hundreds of thousands of civilians and the indictment of Sudan's president, Omar al-Bashir, for genocide, war crimes, and crimes against humanity by the International Criminal Court.

18. [Tr. note] The Book of Amos 3:2 in the 1917 translation of the *Tanakh* from the Jewish Publication Society.

19. Biblical minimalism, also known as the Copenhagen School because two of its most prominent figures taught at Copenhagen University, is a movement or trend in biblical scholarship that began in the 1990s with two main claims: that the Bible cannot be considered reliable evidence for what had happened in ancient Israel; and that "Israel" itself is a problematic subject for historical study.

20. [Tr. note] The Tower of David, also known as the Jerusalem Citadel, is an ancient citadel located near the Jaffa Gate entrance to the western edge of the Old City of Jerusalem. The citadel that stands today dates to the Mamluk and Ottoman periods. It was built on the site of a series of earlier ancient fortifications of the Hasmonean, Herodian-era, Byzantine, and Early Muslim periods, after being destroyed repeatedly during the last decades of Crusader presence in the Holy Land by Ayyubid and Mamluk rulers.

21. [Tr. note] Al-Aqsa Mosque (the Farthest Mosque), located in the Old City of Jerusalem, is the third holiest site in Islam. The mosque is located on top of the Temple Mount, near the Dome of the Rock, an Islamic shrine also located on the Temple Mount.

22. Yehezkel Kaufmann (1889–1963), born in Ukraine, arrived in Palestine in 1928 and joined the Hebrew University in 1949. His main contribution to the study of biblical religion was his thesis that Israel's monotheism was not a gradual development from paganism, but entirely new. See his *Toledot Ha-Emunah Ha-Yisraelit* (4 vols., Jerusalem, 1937–1956), translated and abridged by Moshe Greenberg as *The Religion of Israel: From its Beginnings to the Babylonian Exile* (Chicago: University of Chicago Press, 1960). Interest in Kaufmann has revived in recent years. See Job Y. Jindo, Benjamin D. Sommer, and Thomas Staubli, eds., *Yehezkel*

Kaufmann and the Reinvention of Jewish Biblical Scholarship (Fribourg, Switzerland/ Göttingen, Germany: Vandenhoeck & Ruprecht, 2017).

23. [Tr. note] Abraham Joshua Heschel (1907–1972) was a Polish-born American rabbi and one of the leading Jewish theologians and philosophers of the twentieth century. A professor of Jewish mysticism at the Jewish Theological Seminary, Heschel authored a number of widely read books on Jewish philosophy and was active in the civil rights movement. See his *God in Search of Man: A Philosophy of Judaism* (New York: Farrar, Straus & Cudahy, 1955).

24. [Tr. note] The Paleo-Hebrew alphabet, also known as Proto-Hebrew, was the script used in the historic kingdoms of Israel and Judah, specifically when recording the Hebrew language.

25. [Tr. note] In traditional Jewish practice, daily *tefillot* or prayers are divided into three separate services: *Shacharit* (morning), *Mincha* (afternoon), and *Maariv* (evening).

26. Heschel's doctoral thesis, *Das prophetische Bewustsein* [Prophetic consciousness] (Cracow: Polish Academy of Arts and Sciences, 1936), was later adapted into his well-known book, *Prophets* (New York: Harper & Row, 1962).

27. [Tr. note] The Cathedral of St. John the Divine is the cathedral of the Episcopal Diocese of New York, located at 1047 Amsterdam Avenue in the Morningside Heights neighborhood of Manhattan in New York City, not far from Columbia University.

28. The conference was held in June 1974. Yerushalmi's paper "Response to Rosemary Ruether" was later published in Eva Fleischer, ed., *Auschwitz: Beginning of a New Era?* (New York: Cathedral Church of St John the Divine, 1977), 97–107.

29. "The Protocols of the Elders of Zion" is a fabricated anti-Semitic text purporting to describe a Jewish plan for global domination. The hoax, which was shown to be plagiarized from several earlier sources, some not anti-Semitic in nature, was first published in Russia in 1903, translated into multiple languages, and spread internationally in the early part of the twentieth century.

19. AN AMERICAN JEW

1. Some Reform, Reconstructionist, and Conservative Jews use the word temple to describe what is otherwise called a synagogue, or Jewish house of worship.

2. Aryeh Neier, "The Attack on Human Rights Watch," *New York Review of Books* 53 (November 2, 2006).

3. [Tr. note] Human Rights Watch (HRW) is an international nongovernmental organization, headquartered in New York City, that conducts research and

advocacy on human rights. It often works on behalf of refugees, children, migrants, and political prisoners.

4. [Tr. note] See Irving Howe, *The American Newness: Culture and Politics in the Age of Emerson* (Cambridge, MA and London: Harvard University Press, 1986).

5. [Tr. note] Yerushalmi is referring to George Herbert Walker Bush (1924–2018), who served as the forty-first president of the United States, and his son George Walker Bush, who served as the forty-third president of the United States.

6. [Tr. note] The Jefferson–Hemings controversy is a historical debate over whether a sexual relationship between U.S. President Thomas Jefferson and his slave Sally Hemings resulted in his fathering some or all of her six recorded children. Today, most American historians agree that Jefferson fathered one or more of Sally Hemings's children.

7. [Tr. note] See Eric Foner, *The Fiery Trial: Abraham Lincoln and American Slavery* (New York and London: W. W. Norton, 2010).

8. Charles Beard, *An Economic Interpretation of the Constitution of the United States* (New York: The Macmillan Company, 1913; repr. 1952).

9. [Tr. note] Saul Bellow first produced a parodic Yiddish rendition of T. S. Eliot's "The Love Song of J. Alfred Prufrock" entitled "Der shir hashirim fun Mendl Pumshtok" with his friend the author Isaac Rosenfeld (1918–1956) during their student years in Chicago in the late 1930s. See Michael Boyden, "Isaac Rosenfeld and Saul Bellow's Yiddish 'Translation' of T. S. Eliot's Modernism," *Journal of World Literature* 3, no. 2 (June 1, 2018). The sociologist Daniel Bell (1919–2011; born Bolotsky) helped circulate the translation.

10. [Tr. note] Saul Bellow, *To Jerusalem and Back: A Personal Account* (New York: Viking Press, 1976).

11. [Tr. note] B'nai B'rith (Children of the Covenant) International is a service organization founded in 1843 to support the security and continuity of the Jewish people.

12. The Yishuv (literally "settlement") is the body of Jewish residents in the land of Israel, corresponding to Ottoman Syria until 1917, OETA (Occupied Enemy Territory Administration) South, 1917–1920, and Mandatory Palestine, 1920–1948, before the establishment of the State of Israel in 1948.

13. [Tr. note] Café Atara was located at 7 Ben Yehuda Street in the Downtown Triangle commercial and entertainment district in Western Jerusalem from 1938 to 1996. It was a European-style coffeehouse frequented by Mandate officers, prestate paramilitary groups, Israeli politicians, journalists, and bohemians.

14. [Tr. note] Haim Hillel Ben-Sasson, see chapter 12, note 4.

15. Shmuel Ettinger (1919–1988), Israeli historian. Born in Kiev, USSR, Et-

tinger immigrated to Israel in 1936 and studied at the Hebrew University of Jerusalem, where he received his doctorate in 1956 for his study, "The Jewish Colonization of the Ukraine, 1569–1648." In 1965, he became professor of modern Jewish history. See his university lectures, *Toledot Am Yisrael mi-Yemei ha-Absolutism ad Le-Hakamat Medinat Yisrael* [History of the Jewish people from the era of absolutism until the establishment of the State of Israel] (Jerusalem: Akademon, 1968), and *Toledot Am Yisrael ba-Zeman he-Ḥadash* [History of the Jewish people in modern times] (Jerusalem: Dvir, 1969), translated into English in *A History of the Jewish People*, edited by Haim Hillel Ben Sasson (Cambridge, MA: Harvard University Press, 1976).

16. In Jewish mythology, a dybbuk is a malicious possessing spirit believed to be the dislocated soul of a dead person.

17. A Sabra (Hebrew: *tzabar*) is any Jew born in Israel. The term came into widespread use in the 1930s to refer to a Jew who had been born in the land of Israel (inclusive of the British Mandate of Palestine and Ottoman Palestine), though it may have appeared earlier. Since the establishment of the State of Israel in 1948, Israelis have used the word to refer to a Jewish person born anywhere in the country (inclusive of the Israeli-occupied territories).

18. Moshe Greenberg (1928–2010) was an American rabbi, Bible scholar, and professor emeritus of the Hebrew University of Jerusalem. See his *Biblical Prose Prayer as a Window to the Popular Religion of Ancient Israel* (Berkeley: University of California Press, 1983).

20. FROM YESTERDAY TO TOMORROW

1. *Halakhah* is the collective body of Jewish religious laws derived from the written and oral Torah. *Halakhah* is based on biblical commandments, subsequent Talmudic and rabbinic law, and the customs and traditions compiled in the many books such as the *Shulhan Arukh*.

2. [Tr. note] Traditional Islamic religious law primarily based on the Quran, covering the totality of religious, political, social, and private life.

3. [Tr. note] In the Israeli–Palestine conflict, the First Intifada, named after the Arabic word for uprising, was a Palestinian revolt against the Israeli occupation of the West Bank and Gaza Strip, from December 1987 to 1993, followed by periods of unrest that were also labelled Intifadas.

4. According to the *Halakhah*, any person born of a Jewish mother or converted under the supervision of a rabbinical court is Jewish.

5. [Tr. note] The Book of Ruth is included in the third division, or the Writings [Ketuvim], of the Hebrew Bible. In it, Ruth the Moabite married a Judahite

and even after his death still regarded herself a member of his family; she then married another Judahite and bore him a son, who became an ancestor of David. Contrary to the message of Ezra–Nehemiah, where marriages between Jewish men and non-Jewish women were dissolved, Ruth teaches that foreigners who convert to Judaism can become good Jews, foreign wives can become exemplary followers of Jewish law, and there is no reason to exclude them or their offspring from the community.

6. [Tr. note] See Deuteronomy 23:3, "An Ammonite or a Moabite shall not enter into the assembly of the Lord; even to the tenth generation shall none of them enter into the assembly of the Lord for ever." Jewish Publication Society *Tanakh*, 1917.

7. [Tr. note] Naomi is Ruth's mother-in-law in the Book of Ruth. Yerushalmi's neologism echoes the Noahic Covenant in the Book of Genesis to refer to the way that Ruth the Moabite joined the family line of Naomi, thereby being integrated into Judaism without going through the conversion process.

8. [Tr. note] The Chief Rabbinate of Israel is recognized by law as the supreme rabbinic authority for Judaism in Israel.

9. [Tr. note] On Yohanan ben Zakkai, see chaper 6, note 22.

10. See Y. H. Yerushalmi, *Israel the Unexpected State: Messianism, Sectarianism, and the Zionist Revolution* (Tübingen: Mohr Siebeck, 2006).

11. Oswald Spengler (1880–1936) was a German historian and philosopher of history whose interests included mathematics, science, and art and their relation to his cyclical theory of history. He is best known for his book, *The Decline of the West* [Der Untergang des Abendlandes], published in 1918 and 1922, covering all of world history. Spengler's model of history postulates that any culture is a superorganism with a limited and predictable lifespan.

12. Arnold Toynbee (1889–1975) was a British historian and philosopher of history, author of the 12-volume *A Study of History* (1934–1961), on the birth and death of civilizations without Spengler's determinism. Toynbee was widely read and discussed in the 1940s and 1950s, but by the 1960s his magnum opus had fallen out of favor among mainstream historians and his readership had faded, possibly in part due to what were seen as tendentious attacks against the Jewish religion and Israel.

13. Isaiah Berlin (1909–1997), of Russian Jewish origin, was a British social and political theorist, philosopher, and historian of ideas. See his *Four Essays on Liberty* (Oxford: Oxford University Press, 1969).

14. Isaiah Berlin, *Historical Inevitability* (London, New York, and Toronto: Oxford University Press, 1955).

15. 1 Corinthians 13:12, King James Bible.

16. [Tr. note] 2 Baruch, also known as the Apocalypse of Baruch or the Syriac Apocalypse of Baruch, is a Jewish pseudepigraphical text thought to have been written in the late 1st century or early 2nd century AD, after the destruction of the Temple in AD 70. It is attributed to the biblical Baruch and so is associated with the Old Testament, but not regarded as scripture by Jews or by most Christian groups.

17. Judah Leib Gordon (1830–1892) was among the most important Hebrew poets of the Jewish Enlightenment.

18. Michael Stanislawski, *For Whom Do I Toil?: Judah Leib Gordon and the Crisis of Russian Jewry* (New York: Oxford University Press, 1988).

CLIO AND THE JEWS (*Notes are Yerushalmi's*)

1. This essay is a lightly expanded version of a Hebrew lecture given by me in June of 1977 to the combined faculties of the Institute of Jewish Studies at the Hebrew University in Jerusalem. While adding some necessary footnotes, I have deliberately eschewed an extensive and cumbersome apparatus, and have thus made no attempt to give a bibliography of existing monographs on sixteenth-century Jewish historiography or on individual historical works.

2. *Sippur David ha-Reubeni*, ed. A. Z. Aescoly (Jerusalem: The Society for History and Ethnography, 1940), v–xii.

3. See Abravanel, *Ma'ayeney ha-yeshu'ah* (Ferrara, 1551), Ma'ayan II, Tomer 3, fol. 21v.

4. Moses Ibn Ezra, *Kitab al-Muhadara wal-Mudhakara*, ed. with Hebrew tr. by A. S. Halkin (Jerusalem: Mekize Nirdamim, 1975), 50f.

5. *Shebet Yehudah*, ed. A. Shohat, introduction by Y. Baer (Jerusalem, 1947), 21.

6. See H. H. Ben-Sasson, "Li-megamot ha-kronografiah ha-Yehudit shel yemey ha-benayim," in *Historionim v'askolot historiot* (Jerusalem, 1963), 30.

7. First printed in *Ozar Tob* (supplement to *Magazin für die Wissenschaft des Judenthums*) (Berlin, 1877–1878), 17ff. Reprinted in *Sefer Yosippon*, ed. H. Hominer (Jerusalem, 1965), 37.

8. Reprinted by Hominer, *Sefer Yosippon*, 41.

9. Hominer, *Sefer Yosippon*, 43.

10. Most of the important apocalyptic texts of this period are assembled in Y. Eben-Shmuel, *Midreshey ge'ulah*, 2nd ed. (Jerusalem, 1954). Cf. also B. Lewis, "An Apocalyptic Vision of Islamic History" (analysis and translation of *Tefilat R. Shimon bar Yohai*), *Bulletin of the School of Oriental and African Studies* 13 (1949–1951): 308–38.

11. Sherira's epistle was first printed with Zacuto's *Yuhasin* (Constantinople, 1566). The other three works were generally printed together in one volume (Mantua, 1513–1514; Venice, 1545; Basel, 1580).

12. Gersonides, *Perush 'al ha-Torah*, on Lev. 26:38.

13. Abravanel, *Perush nebi'im aharonim*, on Is. 43:6.

14. Zacuto, *Sefer Yuhasin*, ed. H. Filipowski, introduction by A. H. Freimann (Frankfurt am Main, 1924), 223.

15. See Hans Baron, *The Crisis of the Early Italian Renaissance*, 2 vols. (Princeton, NJ: Princeton University Press, 1955), especially chs. 1–3.

16. This view derives from Yitzhak Baer. See his introduction to Shohat's edition of *Shebet Yehudah*, 11f, 13f, as well as his "He'arot hadashot le-Sefer Shebet Yehudah," *Tarbiz* 6 (1934–1935): 152–79, and *Galut* (English trans.) (New York, 1947), 77ff.

17. See M. Benayahu, "Makor 'al megorashey Sefarad be-Portugal ve-zetam 'aharey gezerat RaSaV le-Saloniki," *Sefunot*, 11 (1971–1978): 233–65.

18. Joseph b. Joshua ha-Kohen, *Sefer dibrey ha-yamim le-malkhey Zarefat u-malkhey Bet Ottoman ha-Togar* (ed. Amsterdam, 1733), preface.

19. See now the recent edition of both the *Seder Eliyahu Zuta* and the Venetian chronicle by A. Shmuelevitz, S. Simonsohn, and M. Benayahu, 2 vols. (Jerusalem, 1976–1977).

20. Both works are extant in four manuscripts: Paris (Alliance, H8JA); Berlin (160); New York (Columbia University, K82); Moscow (Günzberg, 212). All of these also contain his Hebrew version of Joannes Boemius's historical-geographical work *Omnium gentium mores, leges et ritus*.

21. To these we may also properly add the account of the reign of Suleiman the Magnificent in the Judeo-Spanish *Extremos y grandezas de Constantinople*, written by the sixteenth-century Salonikan rabbi Moses Almosnino.

22. *'Emek ha-bakha*, ed. M. Letteris (Krakow, 1895), 102f; *Sefer dibrey ha-yamim*, Pt. 1, fol. 36v. Cf. also the account of the martyred messianic enthusiast Solomon Molkho in the latter work (Pt. 2, fol. 19v), introduced by the significant phrase: "And a shoot came forth from Portugal (*va-yeze hoter mi-Portugal*), Solomon Molkho was his name."

23. See Yosef Hayim Yerushalmi, *The Lisbon Massacre of 1506 and the Royal Image in the* Shebet Yehudah (Cincinnati: Hebrew Union College Press, 1976), Supplement No. 1, *Hebrew Union College Annual*.

24. *Yuhasin*, author's introduction, 1.

25. *Yosippon*, ed. Hominer, 43. Compare, in the seventeenth century, Joseph Delmedigo's list of recommended readings to the Karaite Zerah ben Menahem.

The historical works, largely those with which we have been dealing, are endorsed "for cheering the soul when one is sad" (*le-ta'anug ha-nefesh bi-she'at ha-'izabon*). For the text, see S. Assaf, *Mekorot le-toledot ha-hinnukh be-Yisrael* (Tel Aviv, 1936), vol. 1, 101.

26. See, for example, Joseph Karo, *Shulhan 'Arukh*, Orah hayyim, no. 307:16, and the gloss of Moses Isserles *ad loc.*

27. *Sefer Me'or 'Einayim*, ed. D. Cassel (Vilna, 1866; rept, Jerusalem, 1970), Pt. 1, 182.

The phrase *mai de-havah* derives from the Talmud (Yoma, fol. 5v), where the question of the manner in which Aaron and his sons were dressed in their priestly garments is temporarily rejected as being of purely antiquarian interest ("what was—was"). On Azariah's methodology as a whole, see Salo Baron, "La méthode historique d'Azaria de' Rossi," *Revue des Etudes Juives*, 86 (1928): 151–75; 87 (1929): 43–78.

28. *Me'or 'Einayim*, Pt. 1, 189.

29. *Me'or 'Einayim*, Pt. 2, 275.

30. See David Kaufmann, "Contributions à l'histoire des luttes d'Azaria de Rossi," *Revue des Etudes Juives* 33 (1896): 77–87; David Kaufmann, "La défense de lire le Meor Enayim d'Azaria de Rossi," *Revue des Etudes Juives* 38 (1899): 280–81. Cf. S. Z. H. Halberstamm, "Sheloshah ketabim 'al debar Sefer Me'or 'Einayim," in *Tehilah le-Mosheh* (Leipzig, 1896), Steinschneider Festschrift; Hebrew Section, 1–8.

31. See the attack of Judah Loew b. Bezalel (Maharal), *Be'er ha-golah* (New York, 1969), 126–41, and the report of a ban issued by Joseph Karo on his deathbed, published by Kaufmann in "La défense de lire le Meor Enayim d'Azaria de Rossi."

32. *Me'or 'Einayim*, Pt. 1, 214–19.

33. A striking instance in the sixteenth century, though perhaps an isolated one, of the most extreme antagonism to nonliteral interpretation of aggadah, is provided by the Safed Mishnaic scholar Joseph Ashkenazi. See Gershom Scholem, "Yediot hadashot 'al R. Yosef Ashkenazi, ha-Tanna mi-Zefat," *Tarbiz* 28 (1959): 59–89, 201–33.

34. The change can be seen within the span of a generation. Compare, for example, the discussion of the uses of history in *Ha-Me'assef* 1 (1784): 7–28, where the function of history is still perceived as ancillary to traditional religious concerns, and Immanuel Wolf's famous manifesto of 1822, "On the Concept of a Science of Judaism" (English trans. by L. Kochan in *Leo Baeck Institute Yearbook*, 2 [1957]: 194–204), in which historical studies are assigned the central role of clar-

ifying "the fundamental idea of Judaism," and "the scientific [i.e. historico-critical] attitude" is hailed as "the characteristic of our time."

35. I refer here only to the absorption by Jews of the historical spirit and method. The specific deficiencies or biases of nineteenth-century *Wissenschaft* are a separate matter, and need not detain us here.

INDEX

ABOUT THE AUTHORS

Yosef Hayim Yerushalmi (1932–2009) was one of the most eminent Jewish historians of the twentieth century. He was Jacob E. Safra Professor of Jewish History and Sephardic Civilization at Harvard University, and from 1980 was Salo W. Baron Professor of Jewish History, Culture and Society at Columbia University. His publications, written in his incomparable literary style, include *From Spanish Court to Italian Ghetto* (1971); *Haggadah and History* (1974); *The Lisbon Massacre of 1506 and the Royal Image in the* Shebet Yehudah (1979); *Zakhor: Jewish History and Jewish Memory* (1982) and *Freud's Moses: Judaism Terminable and Interminable* (1991). Some of his essays appear in *The Faith of Fallen Jews* (2014). Yerushalmi's broad erudition in all areas of Jewish history and European culture attracted students from all over the world, many of whom now hold leading academic positions.

Sylvie Anne Goldberg is a Professor at l'Ecole des hautes études en sciences sociales (Paris) where she heads the Jewish Studies Program. With her numerous publications— *Crossing the Jabbok: Illness and Death in Ashkenazi Judaism in Sixteenth- through Nineteenth-Century Prague* (University of California Press, 1996), and *Clepsydra: On the Plurality of Time in Judaism* (Stanford University Press, 2016; National Jewish Book Council finalist in Scholarship, 2016)—she introduced into the field of Jewish history the major topics of death, illness, and care, and conceptualizations of time and temporality.

Benjamin Ivry is author of biographies of Francis Poulenc, Arthur Rimbaud, and Maurice Ravel, as well as a poetry collection, *Paradise for the Portuguese Queen*. He has translated books from the French by André Gide, Jules Verne, Witold Gombrowicz, and Balthus, among others, and written about the arts and culture for numerous media.

Alexander Kaye is the Karl, Harry, and Helen Stoll Chair of Israel Studies and Assistant Professor in the Department of Near Eastern and Judaic Studies at Brandeis University. He coedited, with David N. Myers, *The Faith of Fallen Jews: Yosef Hayim Yerushalmi and the Writing of Jewish History* (Brandeis University Press, 2013), and is the author most recently of *The Invention of Jewish Theocracy* (Oxford University Press, 2020).